KNIGHT OF THE HOLY SPIRIT

A study of William Lyon Mackenzie King

University of Toronto Press / Toronto Buffalo London

Knight of
the Holy Spirit

A STUDY OF
WILLIAM LYON
MACKENZIE KING

JOY E. ESBEREY

© University of Toronto Press 1980
Toronto Buffalo London
Printed in Canada
ISBN 0-8020-5502-8

Canadian Cataloguing in Publication Data

Esberey, Joy E., 1934–
  Knight of the Holy Spirit
  Includes index.
  ISBN 0-8020-5502-8
  1. King, William Lyon Mackenzie, 1874–1950 – Personality.
  2. Prime ministers – Canada – Biography. I. Title.
  FC581.K5E82   971.063'2'0924   C80-094527-1
  F1033.K5E82

54,418

The *Idylls of the King* are full of the noblest sentiments & thought. A round table of chivalrous men in our day we need greatly. The true knight is the man who would be always courteous, brave & true. I think it a fine ideal of noble manhood which Tennyson has given us, ever to my thoughts comes the desire to be such a knight, to live for purity & right. It was my aim, it will be & it is.

Diary, 22 July 1899

I like to think of you as one of Heine's 'Knights of the Holy Spirit' girt with the sword of justice, truth and purity waging war against all sin & sordidness.

V. Markham to WLMK, 4 June 1909

I think of you as a true knight of the Spirit clad in shining armour.
V. Markham to WLMK, 26 January 1940

Contents

Acknowledgments / ix

Introduction / 3

THE GENESIS OF A NEUROSIS: INSECURE FOUNDATIONS

1 Growing up unsure / 11

In the bosom of the family / 11
Who am I to be? 20
To stand alone / 32

2 The ties that bind / 39

Wrestling with the apron strings / 39
Chasing the phantom of love / 43
What am I to be? 58

3 The crucible / 65

The despondent knight / 65
Friends to count on / 71
Ordeal by fire / 80

NEUROTIC DEFENCES: SHORING UP THE FOUNDATIONS

4 The neurotic self / 95

Internalizing the fantasies / 95
In the steps of the master / 101
The cult of money / 110
Obsessive-compulsive neurosis / 123

POLITICIZING THE NEUROSIS: THE FIRST CANADIAN

5 In the bosom of the party / 135

Dicing for the mantle / 135
Defender of the faith / 139
Gathering the forces of good / 147

6 Knights of the Round Table / 161

The king's man / 163
Squires to the body politic / 172
The search for knightly companions / 184

7 Consensus not compromise / 191

With chart and compass / 192
The peacemaking model / 196
Friend or foe – Britain and Canada / 200
Friend or fiend – King and Hitler / 209

Epilogue / 216

Notes / 223

Chronology / 235

Index / 237

Acknowledgments

I am indebted to the executors of the King papers for access to certain closed sections of this collection and to the staff of the Public Archives of Canada for their help with this and other collections in their custody. Miss Persis Tallents extended to me her hospitality and free access to the papers of Violet Markham in her possession, and the staff of the Queen's University Archives were most helpful in regard to the Buchan papers.

This book has been published with the help of a grant from the Social Science Federation of Canada, using funds provided by the Social Sciences and Humanities Research Council of Canada, and a grant from the Andrew W. Mellon Foundation to the University of Toronto Press. The Canada Council granted me a doctoral fellowship and other financial assistance for the basic research on which this study is based; the Social Science Division of Scarborough College provided help towards the preparation of the original draft of the manuscript. The greatest debt is to Paul Fox without whose enthusiasm and encouragement the original study, daunting in its extent, would never have been finished. His interest, advice, and criticism helped the research through its successive stages, a task subsequently assumed by R.I.K. Davidson and Mary McD. Maude of the University of Toronto Press. The responsibility for any faults that may remain is naturally mine.

KNIGHT OF THE HOLY SPIRIT

A study of William Lyon Mackenzie King

Introduction

William Lyon Mackenzie King is one of the best known and least understood of all Canadian prime ministers. He was 'to his own great satisfaction ... prime minister longer than any man in British history.'[1] But it is not longevity alone that matters. It has recently been suggested that Mackenzie King's approach to politics 'took such deep roots that people mistook it for politics itself.'[2] This lonely bachelor, apparently devoted to the memory of his mother and obsessed by life beyond the veil, has been described as an enigma, yet has been explained in simple one-dimensional terms. A direct consequence has been the tendency to separate Mackenzie King's private life from his public career, an approach which makes much of his behaviour inexplicable except in the crude terms of hypocrisy or political expediency. This misleading and dysfunctional 'double vision' of King is challenged in this study, which provides a comprehensive analysis of King's personal development and a consideration of selected examples of his political behaviour to demonstrate that the separation of the private and public King is invalid.

Because the impact of his personality is considered to be an essential dimension of King's political actions, it is not enough to rely on selected incidents in King's life or on the obvious Freudian explanations of some of his reactions. Instead I have attempted to trace the development of the main lines of the personality from its roots in the family to its flowering in the adult political leader. To do so the accepted picture of the King family has had to be redrawn to show a more balanced view of King's relationship with his parents, especially his mother, and of his interaction with his siblings. His patterns of behaviour are traced from this source through the search for appropriate sexual and occupational roles to the crisis of identity and its eventual partial resolution in political self. At the same time I give some

attention to the development of his attitudes, especially the importance of religion and the cult of money, and to the general perceptual
framework, dominated by the idea of the enemy, through which King
viewed the world.

The analysis of King's personality is to a considerable extent a
study of neurotic tendencies. Most of his apparently bizarre behaviour
is explicable in these terms, as are many of the apparent paradoxes in
his career. To suggest that King's behaviour reflected neurotic trends is
neither to judge nor to condemn. The clinical label is useful only in so
far as it is a key to identifying a complex and interrelated set of
interactions and defences, which had political as well as personal
repercussions. It should be noted that these tendencies, while pronounced, were debilitating rather than incapacitating. To the extent
that the defences could be related to the constructive facets of his
personality, King was able to maintain contact with reality and to
function relatively effectively in the uncertain world of politics. To the
extent that King failed to achieve his objectives, these time- and ener-
gy-consuming defences cannot be dismissed as marginal to understanding his political career.

Selecting an approach for the analysis of personality involved choosing a framework for the study, a level of analysis, and a method of
presenting conclusions. For the basic study of King's personality the
concept of the life cycle developed by Erik Erikson seemed the most
useful.[3] It covers the whole life span of the subject without neglecting
the formative years. It gives due attention to the impact of socialization
and to environmental factors without losing sight of the epigenetic
dimension of the personality. Erikson views the life cycle as a sequence
of developmental stages within which conflicts between opposing
forces must be resolved. It is a dynamic concept which gives due
regard to the place of set-backs and regressions in the total growth
pattern termed personality. Perhaps the most important virtue is that
the life cycle offers a systematic way of organizing ideas about the
growth of personality and it presents specific things to look for, giving
a description of the external and internal factors that will indicate a
successful or unsucessful solution to the crisis of each stage. Thus this
approach enables one to examine the idiosyncrasies of the personality
with some objectivity.

Having selected the framework I then considered the level at which
the analysis should be developed. Greenstein suggests 'three overlap-
ping but analytically separable operations: the characterization of phenomenology, the dynamics, and the genesis of personality.'[4] Of these

the emphasis was placed on the first two. The phenomenology constituted the basis on which the deeper layers of the analysis are identified
and consists of the identification of recurring patterns of behaviour.
The dynamics then relate to the circumstances under which these
patterns of behaviour become dominant and how the various patterns
interact with each other. Although it may be interesting to speculate on
the causes of various patterns of response, evidence is lacking on the
early years of most political leaders, and as causal answers are not
essential to an understanding of personality in action they need be
developed no further.

The problem of presenting the personality and relating it to political
behaviour was less easily resolved. King's political activity could not be
fully covered without having the analysis of the life cycle swamped by
a vast sea of detail.[5] I therefore decided to concentrate on presenting
those aspects of personality which had important political consequences and to incorporate where necessary additional explanatory
material drawn from both Freudian and neo-Freudian sources.[6] As
Erikson's work constitutes a bridge between these two schools this
compromise did not involve any theoretical incongruity. Although the
analysis of King's life and career is arranged in a generally chronologi-
cal pattern, this study is in no sense a biography. The story of King's
life and times has already been told by the historians. This work
retreads old ground only when it presents a challenge to existing
views.

The application of the insight gained from an understanding of
King's personality to his political career also raised methodological
problems. Any study of a career as long as King's must be selective.
Each incident in his political life is in itself the product of a multi-
faceted and complex process and is interrelated to every other incident. Some of these incidents are important enough to the overall
pattern of personality development to require detailed analysis; others
are not. The criteria for importance are the contribution each incident
makes to the general patterns of behaviour which constitute the adult
personality and the amount of time and energy the subject expended
on each response.

Some of the examples were obvious. The importance of party and
party leadership in a parliamentary system of government is such that
it can be neglected only by the foolhardy. The fusion of personal and
political identity in King's case, however, made it evident that this was
one area which could not be ignored. The focus of King's relations with
governors general and with his support staff, on the other hand, is

important because it was idiosyncratic of King to devote so much personal concern to these matters. The relationship with Buchan is also important as a link in the search for supportive others so characteristic of King's interpersonal relations.

The selection of illustrative material from the field of policy making was more difficult. It was tempting to consider the dramatic developments of the 1940s when the war, the conscription crisis, and the social-welfare policy proposals of the post-war period dominate the field. But these events climaxed rather than characterized his career, and since they are already well documented in existing literature an interested reader would have little difficulty applying the insight of the psycho-analytical study to these examples. I therefore restricted my choice to those areas where the type of explanation that personality studies offer would be most helpful. One of the subjects that conventional explanations have not explained satisfactorily is why King persisted in emphasizing the tariff issue long after it had ceased to be of popular concern. This study offers an explanation along with a consideration of the apparent ambiguities in King's relation with the British government. The visit to Hitler and King's attitude to personal diplomacy were selected to illustrate the consistency of behavioural patterns in King's career and the way in which such well-entrenched actions were not always politically efficacious.

The discussion of these events must of necessity be limited, and the structural and environmental components of the interaction are given less attention than the psychological necessities. This emphasis is not reductionist but a logical progression from the original objective. In attempting to demonstrate the connection between personality and political behaviour emphasis must be given to psychological elements. Nowhere in this study do I suggest that only psychological explanations are needed to understand King's political behaviour. I do maintain, however, that the personality variable is crucial to this understanding. I suggest that the inner psychology of the leader ensured that particular sets of circumstances produced specific results and that another leader given the same set of circumstances might have chosen another course. The settlement of the dispute over the relative importance of personal and environmental factors must await detailed studies of specific incidents in which both variables are adequately examined. This study aims only to provide the basis for the personality dimension of such works. Similarly, within the limits of this study, it was not possible to offer any conclusions about the contribution King's personality made to his success. Discussion of this problem would involve an examination of the whole Canadian political process, the electoral system, and the historical climate of the times. My aim is to illuminate the psyche in action in the political field, not to rewrite the history of the 1920s and 1930s, although to the extent that King and the Liberal party dominated these decades the two cannot be completely separated. The study makes heavy demands on the reader because it assumes some knowledge of the incidents and individuals mentioned. The focus at all times is on King and the complexities of his personality.

Obviously, King's diary constitutes an essential source for any study of his personality, but it should not be the only source. An equal amount of attention must be given to the family and personal letters in the King papers. King was an enthusiastic and diligent correspondent throughout his life and often devoted dozens of pages in his letters to incidents that only merited a few lines in the diary. Much that is obscure in the diary can be explained in the light of letters written at the time and subsequently returned to King.[7]

It is equally clear that neither source can be taken at face value. They constitute a complex integration of King as he was and King as he wished to be. It is the analyst's task to sift the 'real' self from the 'idealized' self, and the defence mechanisms from the factual descriptions. This is a complex process and one can do little more now than identify the signals of inner conflict – fatigue, inconsistent reactions, repetition – hidden under the surface narration of feelings and events.

It is possible that King's diary represented a substitute 'wife-confidante' but it is not clear that it was intended to be a secret.[8] The first entry in the first volume (6 September 1893) expressed the hope that 'the reader may be able to trace how the author has sought to improve his time.' And the sentiment is repeated the following January and at various places throughout the volumes. Even when King went so far as to declare, 'this journal is strictly private,' as he did on the fly leaf in 1902, he continued to write 'and none should look upon its pages save with reverent eyes.' Obviously, strictly private in King's view did not mean for his eyes only.

Nevertheless, a diary is a personal rather than a public work, and the author is less concerned with communicating with others than with a personal record and self-evaluation; consequently, large sections of the entries are ambiguous or even obscure. In reading a diary, it is essential to seek the author's meanings rather than impose standard or preconceived ideas on the material. Thus a certain circularity is inevitable: without the diary, it is impossible to present an accurate picture of King's personality, but without a clear view of King's personality it is impossible to understand the diary. A simple phrase – 'tonight was practically wasted' – means little in itself without some understanding of what the individual considers a waste of time, an understanding that might be obtained, for example, by comparing his intentions with his actions.

In interpreting the diary it is helpful to keep in mind that King was essentially Victorian in his outlook and responses. Anyone familiar with the writings of nineteenth-century evangelical Christians will have little difficulty with the style of the King diaries. They show the same emotionalism, the same extensive use of Christian symbolism, the same 'conscious record of sins,' the compulsive self-examination, and concern for mental and spiritual well-being that dominated the private papers of such people.[9] This piety is as much a part of King's personality as his pragmatism in later years. These were not two different faces of the same man; they were an integrated whole. But the integration was often imperfect and it required a great deal of psychic energy to maintain. The diary was one of the avenues wherein this endeavour could be sustained: 'I am taking up this diary again as a means of keeping me true to my true purpose ... it has helped to clear me in my thoughts and convictions ... I shall seek to be true in what I record in its pages ... revealing a desire to work ... to make the will of God prevail among men, to achieve personal righteousness, truth in thought & word, purity in heart, constancy and courage in action.'[10] It was the earnest Christian rather than the scholar or the politician who set the tone of the diary.

The genesis of a neurosis: Insecure foundations

1 ✢ Growing up unsure

IN THE BOSOM OF THE FAMILY

In 1886 John King, one of the leading lawyers in Berlin, Ontario, leased the property of 'Woodside' and moved his wife Isabel and their growing family from a house in town to this impressive country estate. The eleven acres of parkland offered ample opportunity for healthy exercise and youthful enjoyment, and the large rambling house became the setting for the reading sessions, the discussions, and the communal hymn singing which played such a large part in the children's development. Although the family stayed only a few years, Woodside provided the ideal location for the development of a romantic fantasy of family life which became a substitute for reality and a shelter from the harsher facts of life.

To understand the King family and the influence it exerted on the character and subsequent political career of the elder son, one must examine the myth as well as the reality and explore both the dimensions of the group and the character of the individuals. Although King maintained throughout his life that they were all equally loving and loved, and meticulously included them all in his eulogies – 'my dear dear father, mother, sisters and brother' – the record reveals a classical pattern of oedipal conflict with its associated idealization of the mother and rejection of the rival male. The whole scene must also be seen in two contrasting foci: the family as idealized by King and the reality discernible to the observer. In both, the mother was the pivot around which the family revolved, and it is with her that one must seek the origins of subsequent developments.

Isabel Grace Mackenzie had had no ordinary childhood. The youngest of thirteen children, she had been born in the United States during her father's exile following his leadership of the ill-fated 1837 rebellion. The physical hardship of her early years is recorded in the early death of several of her siblings, and the family's genteel poverty after their return to Toronto did little to remove the psychological scars. Her personality and ambitions were marked by the insecurity and disappointment that dogged her father's footsteps and by the frustrations and humiliations of their hand-to-mouth existence. Above all else Isabel Mackenzie craved social acceptance and financial security, and in her thirtieth year marriage to a young professional man might well have appeared a way out of the dependency and social stigma associated with being a Mackenzie. The law was a respectable calling and one which provided the opportunity for social advancement and prosperity. Although her husband lacked distinguished forbears, the pedestrian conventionality of the King family might appeal to a woman who had suffered from the taint of radicalism and the consequences of extremism.

The conventional picture of the Kings at Woodside is a reassuring one. With temporary financial security and an assured position within the upper circle of a small town society, the parents were able to offer themselves as models of the type of men and women they wished their children to be. From this perspective one can see Isabel King as a poised and mature woman, sensitive and affectionate, a loving wife, and devoted mother. Under her guidance the children acquired such social graces as piano playing and dancing, and their polished manners enabled them to mingle freely with the people who counted. John King represented the scholarly and gentlemanly virtues; he was a pillar of the church, active in town affairs, the stern but kindly father, and the devoted husband. He developed the children's interest in learning and service to others as well as in outdoor pursuits. The children were encouraged to bring suitable friends home and to mix in the social life of the church and town. In so far as the models were partially founded in reality, they provided the basis for moderate personal growth for the offspring. But it was not the whole story, and as John King failed to prosper the underlying tensions became more dominant and the consequences for the children more serious.

In practice Isabel King's quiet husband proved no more successful than her spectacular father in meeting her needs, and part of the responsibility must be laid at her door. She was a bitter, sometimes malicious woman, self-centred and possessive; in many respects she was an immature woman likely to feel anxious and apprehensive about her domestic responsibilities. In particular she failed to give her husband the type of support necessary to achieve her aims. John King's early connections with the Liberal party could have been used to ensure financial and professional success but Isabel King was reluctant to see her husband following a path she associated with her father's downfall. Holding him back virtually ensured stagnation, for her husband was not of the type to make his mark on the world without aid.

John King was a gentle, rather ineffectual man, with a preference for a dignified and scholarly life. He despised the rough-and-tumble competitiveness of an ordinary law practice and lacked the drive necessary to succeed. He continued to hope for political preferment, but without direct political participation this was not forthcoming. Family responsibilities forced him to show a greater concern for material things and he strove diligently, but not particularly adeptly, to acquire financial substance and a patron who would ensure social status.

These anxieties and uncertainties reinforced the general tensions of child rearing to encourage the development of number of dysfunctional elements in the King family. With both parents generally dissatisfied with their station in life, and possibly unconsciously holding the other partner responsible, it is not surprising that they turned to their children as vehicles through which a more desirable situation could be achieved. In the early years such an attitude might mean no more than great plans for each child and the rewarding of industry in school work, development of social graces, or cultivation of good manners. Later the parents' desire for security and upward mobility would produce an active attempt to control the children's lives to ensure the desired end. However, their endeavours were continually thwarted by the exigencies of their financial insecurity. For the girls, fulfilment meant little more than a gentle upbringing and the idea of marrying well. They were only able to send the older girl, Bella, to a private school for a short time but could console themselves with the belief that she was making connections with the daughters of influential people. In the same way they could oppose Bella's wish to train as a nurse while allowing the younger daughter Jennie to go as a paid companion to the influential Mulock family.

For the boys nothing less than a brilliant educational and professional career would suffice. What would be more natural than for the elder son to follow his father into law while the younger (Max) turned to medicine – both respectable and well-paid careers. By making the best of the opportunities for useful contacts that the university would provide, both boys could become well established and successful and could help to provide for their sisters and parents the type of life the family felt was its due. But such a future depended on the development of self-control and on dedication to a common purpose.

To this end Isabel and John King provided a rather intense, oversolicitous pattern of child rearing dominated by a concern for their children's future status and by the need to keep them firmly on the path. Theirs was a love characterized by form rather than substance, by demanding rather than giving; it was a control exercised indirectly in the guise of love and covertly by playing on their children's affections and manipulating their feelings. The family became a close-knit social group dominated by the essentially self-centred figure of Isabel King. Parental rewards, especially maternal rewards, became linked to conformity, and the emphasis on achievement was distorted so that appearance became the prime criterion. Church going was more important than Christian service to others; people who could be helpful should be assiduously cultivated and companions selected from among their offspring; attainments should be pursued for financial rewards and enhanced status rather than for their own sake.

As John King's inadequacies became more obvious, his wife did little to conceal her frustration from her children. His devotion to her strengthened the egotistical and single-minded elements in her character, and she turned increasingly to her elder son as the potential saviour of them all, reducing her husband to a subordinate position in their lives. Such an emotional devouring of her son at an earlier stage could well have encouraged sibling rivalry, but generally Willie was accepted as beloved brother as well as a much loved son.

Both girls were expected to concern themselves with the welfare of their brothers as well as that of their parents. Bella, throughout her life, showed little resentment of the privileged position of her brothers and seems to have personified the ideal of Christian service and concern for others that her parents verbally espoused. (The parents did not feel a need to discourage such feelings and actions on the part of the girls as they did with their elder son.) As the eldest, Bella had experienced the family at its best and seems to have drawn strength from it. Jennie experienced more of the hardship, and in material terms she got least out of the family resources. Lacking Bella's more spiritual outlook on life, she saw the family with clearer eyes; she also had to assume more of its burdens. Only Jennie was prepared to express resentment of the attention given to Willie – 'it seems to me you have had more love and understanding than the rest of us here,' she wrote on 6 April 1898. Her tendency to see her brother as he was, rather than as he wanted to be, was to create difficulties between them in later years.

Max, the youngest of the family, became the object of his brother's exploration of a paternal role. King was particularly concerned to give direction to his brother and in doing so revealed a great deal about himself. It is easy to detect the paternal note in a comment such as the following from a letter to Jennie (15 February 1898): 'As for Max, I have such hopes for him. I would have him a physician and a writer as well, and in both the top of his profession. This he can be, this he must be and this he will be.' On 8 August 1899, King recorded in his diary further endeavours along this line: 'Tonight after getting into bed, I had a long talk with Max pointing out to him the importance of the "know thyself," spoke to him of life & his place in it, of Religion, of the life of Christ ... & the need of being a good man.' Max does not appear to have resented this rather ponderous interest even though it reflected more self-concern than genuine interest on the part of his brother.

The components of the King family are incomplete without discussion of the maternal grandparent, William Lyon Mackenzie. The conventional view is that Willie learned of his grandfather's deeds and beliefs at his mother's knee and that his mother was proud of her father. But Isabel's relationship with her father was too complex to be explained so simplistically. The extent to which she blamed him for her early suffering is not known, but it is unlikely that she held him up to her young family as a positive model. Certainly she seemed determined to crush in her children any signs of the impetuous, emotional behaviour characteristic of his life. At the same time, in naming the boy William Lyon Mackenzie, she was not encouraging him to overlook this side of his heritage. As long as admiration for grandfather was restricted to verbalizing or the rehabilitation of his memory and name, it was acceptable. But any action seen as modelled on grandfather could not be tolerated. It must be suggested that the role of Mackenzie in his grandson's life has been consistently overrated. None of the children appears to have shown any great knowledge of, interest in, or concern for the exploits of grandfather in the early years.

The other three children appear to have been able to work out satisfactory solutions to the problems created by the discrepancies and tensions in the family relationship. Only Willie seems to have been strongly marked by the burdens of parental affection and expectations, although all carried signs of their upbringing. There seems good evidence for concluding that despite assertions to the contrary Willie was indeed treated in a different manner than the others and that this had important consequences for the development of the neurotic trends in his personality. Our concern with the nature of the King family is based on the belief that the family exerted a dominant influence on King's personal development; it is the general form of this influence as it appeared during Willie King's adolescent years that must now be outlined.

An obvious weakness in the family relationship was the failure of Isabel and John King to maintain a strictly parental relationship with their son. Each made demands on him for companionship and attempted to enlist him as an ally. In revealing a dependence on him they abdicated their parental role, and their obvious weakness in the face of external forces underlined their inability to protect him and fostered his insecurity and lack of trust in himself and others. In their anxiety, they also revealed much of the self-seeking and veniality which characterized the less pleasant side of their natures. To avoid recognizing these discrepancies King was forced into defensive rationalizations which increased the distance between the myth of the family relationship and the reality.

The blurring of the generational boundaries was further complicated by the difficulties associated with the establishment of sex-linked roles. In the King family one can observe a fairly positive role reversal. Isabel King was the instrumental leader as far as general family behaviour was concerned, and John King a failure as protector and provider. His self-denigration in later years and Willie's thinly disguised contempt for his father's financial mismanagement suggest a fairly consistent pattern of denigration by the wife in earlier years. Though basically kind and well-intended John King must be seen in this respect as an inadequate and ineffectual father.[a]

This distorted parental coalition impinged directly on the oedipal issue in King's life. Although King was always lavish in his praise for both parents, it is possible to discern a clear pattern of differentiation in his responses: a pattern which makes it clear that he was acting out the

[a] Psycho-analytical psychology suggests that such a distortion of the family structure may create a serious problem for the son who is presented with this ambiguous model to follow into maturity. The child needs to identify with the father as the first step away from his initial dependence upon the mother. The masculine identity requires identification with the instrumental leader of the family, but in the King family this was the mother's position. John King's dependency on his wife and subordination to her thus undermined his son's gender identity.

oedipal fantasy characteristic of an early age.[b] Compare, for example, the simple statement of his father's character: 'I question if in Toronto there is a man of purer moral character or more loving regard for his family,' with the exaggerated comparisons in a description of his mother's face: 'It is the face of only the greatest, the noblest, the strongest, the best. Had it been the face of a Luther, a Savonarola, an Elisha or other great prophet of God, it could not have been more beautiful.' A walk with mother made him feel proud, but he accompanied his father much more reluctantly – 'I hesitate to refuse him.' Compare the gentle tone of his feelings – 'I could not help crying as I thought of mother. dear little mother How I love her' – with the repeated criticism of his father: 'I fear I spoke too impatiently [to him],' 'I tried not to become impatient with him,' 'I perhaps said too much, losing my patience a little.'[1]

Father was tolerated more as a necessary part of the family image than as an individual to be admired for his own sake. Not so Isabel King. Mother was not only the preferred companion but also the model on which other companions would be judged. Descriptions of his mother are easily interchanged with descriptions of his ideal woman and future wife: 'If I can only win such a wife as I have such a mother, how infinitely happy [I will be].' 'She [mother] is so beautiful of soul, so pure and wonderful, so lovely and lovable and full of love.' 'I have met no woman, so true & lovely a woman in every way as my mother.'[2]

The self-absorption of the immature King is reflected in the wish to find someone 'who truly loved him' rather than someone 'to truly love.' But the search was not urgent for he believed he already had such a love from the mother whose image he carried with him at all times. It was a photo showing the 'character, love and beauty' of the ethereal being which made up the false ideal, rather than one that showed her as a human being. Of the latter he wrote, 'some of the photos were in low neck. I did not care for them at all … did not want that sort of photo of mother.'[3]

[b] Psycho-analytical theory suggests that successful post-oedipal growth requires the child to abandon his wish to divide the parents and possess one. Such a development involves a deliberate but gradual severing of the child's close attachment and intimacy with the mother. A stern father figure, a bigger, stronger man, will by his presence compel the child to relinquish hopes of continuing the earlier relationship. At the same time the mother by her actions indicates to the child an acceptable alternative model – usually shown through her admiration of her husband. None of these elements occurred in King's life, at least not in any continuous and unambiguous form.

The idealized mother was also portrayed as a woman of sensitivity and culture, attuned to the beauty and the truth of great literature. In practice the response of Isabel King to their joint literary endeavours was less sympathetic: 'this afternoon I read aloud to mother ... [she] went to sleep.' This was not an isolated incident. Two days earlier King had recorded an even more revealing session. 'Mother broke down a little & said not to read anything about "thinking" ... But we went on & the descriptive account ... we found beautiful & interesting, or rather I did for mother soon went to sleep.'[4] King's illusion of the identity of interest and response between himself and his mother was so strong that her active participation was not necessary; it was considered a common endeavour, whether or not it was.

Maintaining this idealized mother image involved a considerable expenditure of psychic energy. The following extracts from Isabel King's letters to her son are not untypical of her actual behaviour.

Please tear up this note as soon as you read it for I do not like the idea of you leaving your letters open as you do in your room ... Eliza Mackintosh is quite ill in fact I think it is quite serious. I sometimes wonder what she cares to live for. I wish grandma would die for she is getting more trouble to me everyday.

Yesterday when we were a few steps from Fosters studio ... who should we see but that little sneak Charles Lindsey ... I said to your father he is not going to put me off ... as he stepped into the elevator which was pretty full I pushed my way in. The man said there were too many in but I held my post with my back turned deliberately on that piece of humanity and several men stepped out.[5]

King could not allow his mother any human failing and any distaste that her behaviour might have aroused was ruthlessly suppressed. To admit that his mother was less than perfect would threaten the whole basis of his fantasy. It would debase the quest to win her, the love itself, and ultimately himself as the object of her love. Maintaining the charade required him to be ruthless in ignoring the discrepancies and to be verbally oversolicitous of his parents' needs and wishes.

Displacing the father in the mother's affection is a victory not without its costs in terms of personal integration. King could not ensure the love and affection of his mother by modelling himself on his father. The unsatisfactory status of John King also meant that the love and support he showered on his son would be less satisfying than it might have been. John King's lack of overt resentment of his wife's dominant position in the family and his encouragment of the children's devotion to their mother would have reduced any conflict or guilt associated with residual oedipal feelings and so further retarded the transference of affection.

It is possible that Isabel King did begin in the early period to place greater distance between herself and her elder son if only because of the needs of the younger children. If so, it was a pattern she had reversed by King's adolescent years. Here she can be seen clearly encouraging a continued attachment, possibly even increased intimacy. An important element in King's later extreme egocentricity may be the fact that he was not forced to recognize that he was not the centre of his mother's world – for he was.

In considering the dysfunctional aspects of the King family it is important to remember that the elements of conflict and tension are clearer to the observer than to the participants. They make up the real world of the King family but are masked by the fantasy world which hid most of the darker patches of the relationships. In internalizing parental patterns of behaviour the individual is selective, but the process is more unconscious than conscious. Willie King consciously rejected much of the reality but nevertheless imcorporated it into his inner self.

Throughout his political life King was to demonstrate that he had incorporated the value of belonging to a mutually protective unit modelled on the family fantasy, and it met a definite need in his life. In particular, the idea of a close and loving family made an essential contribution to his security needs. King expressed just such a response when he wrote on his return from Chicago in 1896: 'once again [I] was safe in the midst of loving family and dearest friends on earth.'[6] He had great expectations of his family. Home was a haven, a place where he sought shelter from the pressures and uncertainties of an independent existence. In the outside world he risked criticism and rejection, his self-image was constantly challenged, support was limited, and companionship was something to be cultivated rather than merely enjoyed. But in the family fantasy King was cast as the cherished heir in a mutually protective unit, and he could expect acceptance, help, support, and admiration to be automatically and unstintingly bestowed on him irrespective of his actual behaviour. He believed love was his due simply because he was, rather than because of what he was; and he thought he got it from the family. Thus a sojourn with the family could be therapeutic. Describing a visit in 1898 King said, 'my visit home cost me about $30, but it was the best investment I have made in years.'[7] The mantle of the beloved son was a comfortable and well-worn garment. However limited his own responses, he believed he could count on his family's enthusiastic welcome and continued praise, and King always had an unlimited capacity to absorb praise.

The family fantasy provided the springboard from which Willie could safely be launched into the outside world to seek his fame and fortune. Family support could contribute positively by minimizing the risks and the consequences of failure. Any rebuffs experienced in the widening circle of interaction could be offset by family reassurance. The tightly-knit group gave love and praise unstintingly and demanded nothing directly; the resulting self-confidence helped King to find a self acceptable to all. In his behaviour and responses we can observe an interesting mixture of the real and the mythological elements of the family model.

WHO AM I TO BE?

September 1891 had been an important milestone in the life of young Willie King for it marked his first real experience of life outside the shelter of the family. His years as a student, first at University College, Toronto, and later at the University of Chicago and Harvard, offered King an opportunity to try his wings away from direct parental supervision. The new world of the university was to provide the environment within which King would attempt, in a typical adolescent rebellion, to establish both his individuality and his masculinity. The endeavour was doomed to failure, however, as the possessiveness, the indirect pressures, and hidden demands of the family put narrow limits on his bid for autonomy. At the core of the problem was King's inability to accept as natural his desire to break out of the smothering embrace of parental care. To maintain the illusion he was forced to develop an idealized self as much at variance with the real self as the family relationship was from the family fantasy.

The search for identity became a process of differentiation rather than growth, a covert struggle for control between Willie and his parents.[c] And the struggle created tensions because neither side gave expression to the hostility that the restraint and rebellion produced.

---

[c] One of the prerequisites for healthy growth is parental encouragement of attempts at individual development and autonomy. Insecure or possessive parents may find it impossible to give their children this freedom to grow. By making affection and support conditional on subordination of self-interest they may undermine the individual's attempt to explore the dimensions of the self. Such parents thwart initiative, overemphasize the threatening nature of the world, and draw their offspring back into the sheltered parental care.

The failure of Isabel King to provide the ideal maternal support for growth drove King to concentrate on 'strengthening himself through controlling [his] own body and mind.'[8] The need for self-control supported by the tenets of his religious beliefs was a dominant theme of this troubled adolescent period.

In many respects the university was a strange new world to King. The King family environment must be characterized as essentially feminine. The male role fell mainly to the thrusting, aggressive Isabel King rather than to the mild, supportive John King, but even the former was masked by the image of the 'childlike,' 'girlish' mother. A close relationship with two loving sisters, the extensive religious overtones of their life, and affection for quiet activities such as hymn singing and reading aloud emphasized the non-aggressive, soft tones of the idealized family.

From this background King was thrust into the dominantly masculine world of University College and boardinghouse life. A revolt against the underlying feminine traits which took the form of an 'exaggerated, loud, masculinity' would not be unexpected.[9] But just as the family situation was ambiguous so was King's revolt against it. The world not only offered a challenge and an opportunity for self-development but also an insidious threat. Away from the family for the first time, Willie was faced with the problem of aloneness and all that this involved.

King was in no sense a loner, and one way of easing the anxieties aloneness provoked was to cultivate a wide circle of acquaintances. The superficial picture of King's early years as a student is one of a typical varsity student active in student affairs at all levels. The days of his diary are filled with an endless round of interaction with fellow students, but this continual activity lacked spontaneity. King socialized not merely because he wanted to but because he had to. It is possible that the small-town boy from a less-than-affluent background experienced feelings of inferiority and inadequacy when mixing with his peers. There seems to have been an element of compulsiveness about his actions, a tendency to show off and to seek to impress others. One obvious defence against anxiety is to 'narcotize it,' to plunge into social activity because of the fear of being alone.

For a time Rex King seemed to strive very hard to be one of the gang – the élite of campus life.[d] Although more studious and earnest than

---

[d] The nickname 'Rex' seems to have been acquired fairly early in his student days and represented a more masculine mature self-image that the diminutives Willie or Billy used by family and childhood friends. In later years his close friends continued to call him Rex.

most of his contemporaries he did not hold back from rowdy episodes involving the student body. But although he joined in the activities, his experiences were more often followed by feelings of shame than of enjoyment. Following some group clowning during a visit to a Methodist church, he wrote, 'nor did I like our conduct in church. I must reform.' After the fraternity initiation ceremony in 1893, he wrote, 'of todays doings nothing much here can be said,' and his response to an evening spent at the fraternity room was the note, I 'will need to guard myself very closely.'[10]

King had in his late childhood shown signs of a precocious conscience, and one of the functions that diary-keeping served was the meticulous searching and evaluating of his daily round. In general he found much cause for concern and he was forced to record a great deal of wasted and worse-than-wasted time. An afternoon and evening spent working for the student handbook and newspaper were described as 'practically wasted' and 'wasted,' as was a morning without lectures and a morning devoted only to lectures. In contrast, time spent at the Sick Children's Hospital was part of the resolve 'to live a better life' and 'to serve Christ.' Clearly the diary records a young Christian striving to serve his master and castigating himself for sins which others might have dismissed as trivial. After a day spent only partly at his desk owing to visits home and to the fraternity house he resolved, 'I must be a better boy and make better use of my time.[11]

Almost any activity could become a source of self-censure. After a morning spent at church and an afternoon skating with friends and family he had written: 'I have done much wrong today & feel how very weak I am without my Saviour to continually help me. I will strive to do somewhat better.' King's problem was his inability to reconcile his conscious 'longing to become more earnest & zealous,' his desire to 'show by my work & activity that I belong to him [Christ],' and the wish to 'purify and educate my mind as much as possible,' with an unconscious need for social contact and for limelight.[12] His basic anxiety and insecurity drove him to divert a great deal of his energies away from the earnest paths he wished to follow into the more frivolous activities which could remove feelings of loneliness. Throughout his life King was to long to have some space around him, yet find it difficult to cope with solitude once he had achieved it.

He also longed for close intimate relations with others. The university environment seemed to provide a suitable locale for exploring the pleasures of mateship in the company of a few close male friends, and King took advantage of the opportunities offered:

After dinner Burb, Dick, Dunk, Carl & myself all had a happy reunion in my room ... we all talked & laughed, & after drinking a little Raspberry vinegar we all went downstairs and had a long talk.

We had a long talk the three of us [Charlie, Curly, and King] after which Curly & I went down to parlor where we sang a few songs.

After fooling around the town [with Billy Douglas] we walked out 2 miles to a peach farm ... went to K.A. [fraternity] rooms ... had a pleasant hours chat, then Courtney Kingston & I walked up Yonge ... then I came home ... [13]

One of the most obvious advantages of this interaction was the opportunity of talking over the problems of growing up with 'men' who were experiencing the same problems: 'I committed a sin today which reminded me of my weakness & so aroused me that I went over & had a long talk with Murray tonight. We had a short prayer which I hope will be answered.'[14]

Although these relationships partially met King's need for affection, they invariably fell short of the ideal. It is a characteristic of neurotic anxiety that the individual makes an 'intolerable demand for perfection' on those with whom he associates. King approached each new social encounter with such absurdly high expectations that he was inevitably disappointed with the reality, and his disappointment easily turned to disgust. The situation was exacerbated by King's unacknowledged need to excel – to turn each interaction into a competitive struggle which he must win. His concern for grades, class standings, and class office reflected this need to measure himself against others. Less obvious was the process by which he unconsciously transformed friends into rivals and shown in his compulsive need to disparage them. 'I had a long talk with Boulton, a talk on higher things. He is going to try and lead a better life ... Met Duncan, Burb & Doc coming from the theatre was sorry for them.'[15]

This inability to sustain spontaneous relations with his peers over any length of time led King to emphasize the more juvenile associations characterized as 'special chums': friends who would reflect his own ideal self, the significant others who would share his deepest feelings and longings.[e] At the same time such friends had to pander to his greed for affection, his unlimited need for praise and admiration.

[e] King's comments regarding student friendships are typically couched in terms of future intimacy: 'I have reflected on what we might have done while opportunity presented itself had we learned the hidden secrets & longings of the other's heart while at college.' King to H.A. Harper, 28 June 1895, Harper Papers, PAC.

This affection could best be demonstrated through relieving him of unwanted responsibilities, by making sacrifices on his behalf, or conversely by refraining from making demands on him. The key dimension of friendship was an absence of any rivalry with him in his chosen sphere. It is not surprising that he failed to locate the splendid set of like-minded fellows on which he had set his heart.

At a time when King was grappling with the problems of physical maturation, the fiery rebel, grandfather Mackenzie, offered a more blatantly masculine model with which he could identify than John King, and for a time he appeared to be moving along this line when he took an active role in the abortive student strike and boycott of lectures at the University of Toronto in 1895. William Lyon Mackenzie was in many respects an appealing model showing great strength of character and dedication to principle at the expense of self-interest – all moral qualities which King sought to develop in himself and which John King apparently lacked. In January 1894 King had read his father's pamphlet, which defended Mackenzie and began the transformation of the outspoken journalist into a constitutional reformer, with avid interest following a class debate on the 1837 rebellion.[16] Even after the fiasco of the strike King continued to show interest in his grandfather, pressing his family to secure for him a copy of Charles Lindsey's biography and a family portrait of Mackenzie. King's reaction to reading the former was typically excessive: 'I read over parts of it with what intenseness! Cry! how could I help it feeling his every thought on my own breast. His mantle has fallen upon me, and it shall be taken up and worn ... His voice, his words shall be heard in Canada again & the cause he so nobly fought shall be carried on.'[17] One must be careful in reading extracts from King's diary not to confuse rhetoric with deeds.[f] The fact that King never knew his grandfather allowed him to construct a grandfather image which was even more satisfactory than the idealized mother, for in the latter case there was always the ever-present reality to undermine the edifice.

In this way King could adapt his grandfather to serve his own

---

[f] It is true that throughout his life King made frequent references to Mackenzie, to his devotion to the memory, and his determination to follow the lead. But his actions do not support a literal interpretation of this commitment, and it is a particularly emaciated version of grandfather which appears in the pages of the King diary. It is difficult to find examples in King's career in which it is clear that he is following in the path of Mackenzie. As with King's relationship to Sir Wilfrid Laurier, one must consider the possibility that King projected his own beliefs and objectives onto Mackenzie rather than accepting any influence from his grandfather's beliefs.

purpose. The mantle that he adopted was the mantle of Mackenzie's achievements. King's own tardiness and his rather conservative actions could be masked beneath the impetuous radicalism of grandfather. At the same time the grandson could avoid the trauma of failure by learning from the grandfather's mistakes. It is as a negative model that Mackenzie exerted the greatest influence. The one occasion during which King came closest to acting in the manner of his grandfather – the student strike at the University of Toronto in 1895 – was an ignominious failure, which brought only ridicule from his fellow students.

It is clear that his parents were ambiguous in their attitude to the Mackenzie heritage, fearing any sign that their son might have inherited grandfather's recklessness. Their defence of Mackenzie was to a considerable extent motivated by self-interest. To be the descendants of an unsuccessful rebel was a social stigma difficult to bear. The transformation of Mackenzie into a hero could only lead to an improvement in their own social standing. The Kings were fortunate that Mackenzie's activities mellowed with time. Ideals and actions that were traitorous in the 1830s were merely far-sighted in the 1900s. The King who was afraid to stand alone could be submerged into a Mackenzie King comforted by an affinity which was largely of his own creation. King's love for his grandfather was of a similar nature to his love for his parents – a sustaining illusion rather than practical reality.

But adolescence is more than a set of postures, and manhood involves more than overtly aggressive behaviour and idealization of masculine models. It is a period of physical maturation when a young boy experiences the first stirrings of love and sexuality. King's attempts to form satisfactory relations with young women were bedevilled by the neurotic paradox – the drive towards detachment from people and the craving for affection. Further, social and cultural pressures encouraged the repression of physical needs until material security was achieved. In the meantime the young man was encouraged to develop an interest in girls as social companions rather than as prospective brides. In Victorian times a sister or cousin was acceptable in this role, and after the King family moved to Toronto in 1892 King's diary frequently carried entries saying: 'Bella & I went to Mrs Mason's where we spent a very pleasant little evening, talking, playing cards'; 'went with Bella to an at-home & social evening at Y.M.C.A.'[18]

King also joined enthusiastically in the less conventional activities directed towards catching the attention of young ladies of the better families: 'we had a great parade ... up to Bishop Strachan's School, the

Presbyterian Ladies College & Moulton College at each we had a good reception.' These group contacts were followed up by individual encounters – 'I called on Miss Cascadden at the P.L'sC ... I then called on Miss Hunter,' 'strolled around [with Doc] met two young ladies, connected with the Bishop Strachan school, walked to Rosedale with them.'[19] Although King actively sought social encounters and listed regularly the young ladies with whom he had danced or talked he was never completely happy with this behaviour. Frequently, entries describing social events would on reflection be followed by assertions such as 'I would rather have been thinking on more real and great problems of life and eternity.'[20]

One way of reconciling these divergent needs was to couple his socializing with his service activities. Thus he could take the opportunity of his visits to the Sick Children's Hospital to hold religious services, to befriend the nurses, and to find in their company the combination of feminine companionship and earnest purpose that he sought. With Nurse Cooper he could talk 'about things that are real and eternal' and feel that such activity was part of his religious endeavour, directed as he believed it was to recruiting her to 'do what she could for Christ during the coming year.' We should note here the recurrent theme of talk – 'I had a long talk,' 'I had a long and beautiful talk', ' we had a long talk together,' – and his repeated concern that the girls should be good Christians and dedicated to Christian work.[21]

Later, in his graduate student days, King was to find the same satisfaction through social contact with the young ladies involved in the settlement work at Hull House (Chicago) and Passmore Edwards (London). These young ladies were treated no differently than the young men of his acquaintance and this activity reflected his efforts to surround himself with significant others who reflected his longing to be a worthier person. It is in this context of social concern and a dedication to a life of service that King's contact with prostitutes during his student days should be considered.

The rural life of Berlin, Ontario, had done little to prepare the young Willie King for life in the city. Toronto was a new experience, fascinating and repelling at the same time. During the fall of 1893 King's diary recorded an increased awareness of how the other half lived. After his excursions around town he noted: 'a little seen of the wickedness of the world,' 'saw a little of the darker side of the world,' and 'learned more of the great evils to be conquered in the city.' Drunkenness was the most frequently observed vice but he also recorded examples of ordinary human difficulties: 'on my way home I saw a girl who had just been run over ... She had her leg badly hurt.'[22] King was already devoting much of his free time to Christian work in his visits to the Sick Children's Hospital and kindred activities, but he resolved to do more.

Early in the new year he had written: '[I] must become more earnest in my work for the Master, it will not do to be half hearted. I hope I can do more & more every day to lift up the fallen, & hope that my life may be a pure and holy one devoted to Christ alone.'[23] His endeavours in this direction occupied a great deal of his time in the year that followed. It should be emphasized, however, that this was not part of any secret or double life. It was an open act of Christian service, an act which he shared with others and which fitted clearly into the city mission activity of the YMCA. This desire to uplift the fallen had its roots in the prevailing concerns of the day – drunkenness and prostitution – the two great social evils of the times. Whether it was wise for a young man struggling to come to grips with his own physical maturity to concern himself with the latter is another question, but for an emotional Christian like King the illustrious precedent set by the Saviour himself was undeniable.

The first object of King's reforming zeal was a working-class Toronto family, the Camerons, and on 6 January 1894 he had had a long talk with them in an attempt to 'be able to draw them all nearer to the Saviour.' His efforts were partially rewarded when he had Mrs Cameron's assurance that they were going to attend church. His main effort was directed towards Mina Cameron, then living in a house on King St. His endeavours seemed to have followed a fairly standard pattern – 'we had a long talk together, and I did all in my power to stop her wicked life and to turn to Christ.' Two days later he sought her out again: 'we had a long and beautiful talk together. Poor girl she cried a great deal and promised to leave the life she was leading.' The reformation did not last long. A week later Mina had to be rescued again and returned to her family. He lost contact with her for some time but in June he wrote: 'Went over to my own little "mission field" called to see Mr Cameron ... I was momentarily shocked on hearing there that poor Mina Cameron was in the Mercer's Reformatory for stealing.' When four months later he met her on the street she did not respond to his show in interest. 'Tonight I tried to find Mina but found she gave me the wrong number. I have felt very bad about this all night.'[24]

By chance his meeting with Mina coincided with his second reforming venture. He had that evening met two King St girls, and he and his friend Duncan had been down to their rooms till 2:00 A.M. C.P. Stacey has concluded that a mixture of two young students and two girls in a room at night could mean only one thing.[25] But there is nothing in the record to substantiate the assumption. King said, 'I got pretty well the history of the girls lives,'[26] and this explanation of the activity seems to be supported by the subsequent developments. The following day was spent in student festivities in which he played a major role. He noted in his diary that 2 October 1894 had been a red-letter day:

But tonight far outshone any other part. Sinos & I went to see the 2 girls on King Street. I had a long talk with Jennie ... A beautiful talk she told me her story ... After Sinos left, Etta, the one who was nurse at Mimico Ayslum, joined us, these girls told very sad stories of their lives. I tried to point out the love of the Saviour to them. I must have spoken for nearly 4 hours. Poor girls, my heart nearly broke as I talked with them. They do feel an awful consciousness of their sin & yet feel it holds them very fast. We all three kneeled down & had a little prayer together ... They said they loved to hear any one speak thus to them and that they hated to see me go away. I know they did poor girls, they kissed me as tho' I had done them a great kindness.

It is difficult to believe that the person who wrote this entry had the previous evening contributed to their degradation in the company of a fellow student as C.P. Stacey has suggested. Could King have felt so unconcerned for his own soul? Two days later he saw Jennie again – 'we talked and cried ... when I spoke to her of heaven & of death.'[27]

It would be tedious to repeat the details of each subsequent encounter for they all conformed to the pattern described above: 'long, earnest, & extremely interesting talk,' 'we talked earnestly for 2 hours, sang hymns, had prayers etc.'[28] The activities were all aimed at persuading the young girls to change their ways and come to Christ. A month later he met yet another girl in the street and arranged to see her later. 'We had a wonderful talk walking about until 2 o'clock ... I found out from her her whole story.' It was a harrowing tale of a nine-year-old stolen from home and led into a life of ill fame but now raised up to a good life; 'she is more over trying to help fallen girls.' Several other young women became the object of this reforming zeal in the months that followed but he was losing heart. 'I feel discouraged I cannot spare any more time,' he wrote. 'I believe firmly this girl would reform & had I been here all would have been well.' He believed that 'God has certainly given me a talent I must use aright.'[29] He had yet to learn that powerful persuasion was useless when no other workable alternative to a life of sin was forthcoming.

Discouraged in his own personal efforts he turned his concern to a more abstract level of endeavour: 'I am going to make a careful study of the poorer classes and the worst social evil with a view to remedying to some degree the latter, and bettering the conditions of the former.'[30] And so he did. It became a lifelong concern, but it did not mean the neglect of individual contact. During a train journey to Chicago he met a young girl in company with a drunken woman. 'I pleaded with her to consider the downward path she was taking,' he wrote. Whether his words were heeded or not we are not told. It should be noted that on several occasions the girls who were prepared to talk and listen to him were rewarded with small gifts – 'got a box of candies for Maud,' 'I met the girls & got candies at McConkie's.'[31] It is quite possible that other records of money spent while in the company of young women might have been devoted to a similar end.

It is likely that in the course of such activity King had to face the fact that there was more to physical development than social contact and talk. It meant coping with changes in the body and with new demands and feelings which accompanied maturation. It is natural for a young man to show a strong interest in the opposite sex, especially given the predominately male atmosphere of university life. It is also natural for these feelings to be associated with a desire for physical contact. It is all part of the mating game – the ritual of search, approach, and withdrawal. Such feelings were not always satisfied by the formal social contacts with girls of his own social class, but prostitutes are not the only alternative. In the company of his college friends King could indulge in more casual association with girls of a different social strata: 'Billy Douglas & I wandered down town then met some girls.' 'Went out and met my friend Miss Worthy we had a long walk then I met Miss White & had a little talk.' 'Went to the residence got Doc we went to Spadina Ave. where we met Miss Worthy. We had a long talk & a little walk with her she was very nice ... '[32]

The boat trip to Niagara appeared to be a popular venue for 'pick ups' of the more casual kind: 'On boat we had great fun. Met Misses Edith & Florence Macdonald of Lindsey, after a great deal of engineering. We sat and talked with them on the side of the boat, and will see them at the train tomorrow.' Occasionally these friendships progressed as far as fondling as in the excursion with Billy Douglas in June 1894. 'We saw two young ladies who we fell very much in love with.' Later they walked with the girls to the park where, although it was raining they walked, talked, and loved.[8] After which they crossed into

[8] There is no reason to assume, given the circumstances (a public place in broad daylight in the rain) that this term described anything more than a little embracing and/or kissing, if this.

New York State to meet the girls' mother. King's declaration, 'I love Blanche very much she is a dear girl,' should not be taken too seriously; he was not frugal in his use of the term. In fact the ease with which he verbally dispensed his love was his one major extravagance. He was only put out if the recipients took his declarations at face value and struggled to understand why a girl should feel so hurt when he later revealed that though he said love he meant no more than friendship. He was often to record his sorrow that 'my words were so strongly construed,' but fault was always with the girl and not with his lavish misuse of the term.[33]

It is not suggested that King was immune to the temptations of the flesh. He was if anything only too conscious of the problem. As a devout and practising Christian, King was justifiably concerned with eradicating error in word, thought, and deed. One of the prime motivations for keeping a diary was the practice of continous self-examination directed at rooting out sinfulness and encouraging the practice of a pure Christian life. In this context, it should be remembered that Christian law identifies seven deadly or capital sins – pride, avarice, lust, anger, gluttony, envy, and sloth. Thus it is probable that when King used the term sin in his diary he could have been referring to any of these.[h] For the specific meaning of each reference it is necessary to consider its context. The end-of-the-year observation 'truly it [the diary] is almost black with sins' must be interpreted in terms of the objective expressed in September that he would be ashamed 'to let even one day have nothing worthy of its showing ... [of] how the author has sought to improve his time.'[34] It thus seems feasible that the sins were sins of omission – particularly sloth – and comparable to the activities described above as time wasted.

It is also possible, given the nature of physical development, that some of his concern was directed towards sins of the flesh. The religious and moral ideals which pervaded the Victorian society in which he lived made this aspect of life particularly difficult for the young adolescent. Establishing a satisfactory sexual identity is one of the tasks that faces every young man. Although Victorian society saw sex as a problem, their attitude to it was highly ambiguous.[i] What was the

---

h C.P. Stacey's assumption that the term is synonymous with lust and its physical manifestation, sexual intercourse, is not in this author's view tenable on the evidence available.

i Steven Marcus in his study of Victorian pornography, *The other Victorians* (London 1970), 18, notes: 'although sexual desire in youth is a "natural instinct," and has its own "beneficial purpose ... mature and lawful love," the young man is warned against fulfilling that desire. Indeed, "such indulgence is *fatal*".'

worst sin that could befall the adolescent male at this time? According to Steven Marcus, the Victorian answer was that 'incontinence in all forms is harmful, but the "most vicious" form it can take is that of masturbation.'[35] This was the route not merely to stunted growth but also to insanity, and there was much more guilt over masturbation among young men in this period than over sexuality generally. The remedy that society proposed to the young was the 'complete control over the passions.'[36] King's diary reveals a persistent concern with this problem. 'There has been a fierce war of flesh & spiritual all day,' he wrote. 'When will I subdue the evil in me?'[37] Exercising control appeared to be particularly difficult when King was occupied in sedentary pursuits such as studying and when he was in his room alone. Thus on 1 February 1894 he wrote: 'I was left alone to work ... it was very hard for me to stay in. I felt I must go out & stroll around. Alas I have much to conquer as yet. Oh I wish I could overcome sin in some of its terrible forms, tonight has proven to me that I am very weak ...'

After a day spent alone at home rearranging his room King had written, 'I committed a sin today which reminded me of my weakness ... ' The danger was particularly great at night – 'I cried after coming home tonight. I felt very sorry for something I did last night.' Two weeks later he wrote, 'tonight again I sinned,' this after an evening spent at the theatre. Clearly King recognized that the individual must control his thoughts as well as his actions.[j] Entries following social engagements expressed the resolve 'I must seek to guard myself more & more,' 'have tried to guard myself today but I find I have still many battles to fight.' At the same time he seemed almost to go out of his way to make this control difficult. Visits to saloons and dives, where 'we must have looked at or met over 500 prostitutes,' could hardly have contributed to control over thoughts, even though King believed he 'came thro' untouched.' Were similar visits origins of such statements as 'got into another trap cost me $1' and 'I wandered about street of Boston ... went completely to the devil with my passions, wasted money & came home sad'? It is possible that these expressions of remorse followed visits to prostitutes. It is also possible that these visits could have been to gambling saloons, liquor parlors, pornographic bookstores, a burlesque show, or any activity of a frivolous though non-sexual nature.[38]

---

[j] Was it significant that, at the time King was most concerned with sinning, one of his student friends (Dave Bowman) was in an asylum in Guelph? King's comments include the statements 'it is inconceivable how one vice drags in its chain hundreds of others,' 'his sad misfortune ought to be a grave lesson to many,' and 'oh the hold that sin gets on people is something terrible.' Diary, 19 Jan. 1894.

Clearly King was very concerned about his own sexuality and its effect on his desire 'to be a better man, to work always, to live purely, & humbly, to aim at perfection of character ... ' He recognized that self-control was 'the first element of greatness.' He was aware that lapses were habit-forming and that once the first false step was taken doom could follow swiftly. Yet the self-disgust that he expressed following his frequent falls from grace is extremely mild. After an evening during which it has been suggested that he had intercourse with a prostitute while earnestly trying to persuade her to give up her wicked life and turn to Christ, he merely states, 'we both felt rather badly.' On other occasions he recorded the fact 'I spent $1.25,' and feelings such as 'went to bed tired & sorry at the mistake I had made,' and 'how I do wish I had more strength.' Only in Chicago in November 1896 is the record consistent with extreme remorse. Here there is a record of five days of disappointment and depression, but even this prolonged concern ended in the expression of a feeling that perhaps he should go into the ministry.[39] Does a young man turn to the service of God only out of self-disgust and sinfulness? Is it not just as likely that an individual who finds himself unable to restrain from sin might consider himself unfit for the service of God? In the face of the lack of evidence this author prefers to leave the question of King's alleged patronizing of prostitutes as unproven.

TO STAND ALONE

In the search for autonomy usually 'one primary group (a voluntary one) [peers] helps to break the emotional hold of the other primary group (an involuntary one) [the family].'[40] King's difficulties in estab-lishing satisfactory relations with his peer group increased after his family followed him to Toronto in 1892.[k] His behaviour had on several occasions run directly contrary to parental advice to make friends and influence people – influential people. They apparently felt that unless they could keep his feet on the path they might lose all. In a confronta-tion between family need and personal development the latter must give way and King appeared to accept the situation with no outward rebellion.

The twenty-one-year-old King went walking in Toronto, not with

---

k The precise reason for the move is not known. Possibly the parents felt that the other children would profit from the greater opportunities in the city. Or it may be that the parents worried by letters concerning Willie's social-work activities and boisterous behaviour, felt he needed their steadying influence.

young men and women of his own age, but with his mother. He had always emphasized her youthfulness – 'she is like a little girl' – and to the child-like mother was added the dependent father. As early as 1895 John King's inadequacies as a provider were being underlined. Willie was in that year recalled from a holiday at Barrie with the Micawber-like cry 'all hands are needed at home to fight the battle of surrounding difficulties.'[41]

While King's sentiments of filial love and duty led him to accede to these demands he began to show signs that he consciously resented the frustration that the responsibilities and parental demands produced. The possessive nature of the family tie had been highlighted on his graduation in 1895 when he decided to pursue graduate studies at the University of Chicago rather than follow his father into the legal profession. The dispute involved more than the mere choice of a career. On Willie's side it was a choice between self-determination and subordination; for Isabel King it was stark necessity. She feared his impetuousness and his tendency to get side-tracked by social work, and she depended on him to complete his professional training as quickly as possible so he could contribute to their future security.

King was not strong enough to resolve the conflict by a positive act; instead he repressed his feelings of frustration and apparently subordinated his own wishes to the common good and joined his father to study law. He justified his decision in terms of filial duty and a desire for 'a closer relationship with my own father & a greater desire to make his cares & pleasures my cares & pleasures.'[42] In fact the experience made him less tolerant of his father's weaknesses and less friendly towards his father than he had been earlier.

Obviously at one level King could recognize the nature of the demand that was family affection, and he resented it as a restriction on his autonomy. On another level, he lacked the capacity to publicly renounce the pressure by rejecting his parents and following his own course. He may have unconsciously recognized that the continuance of their affection was dependent upon such subordination of self. Any resentment or hostility towards them must be repressed for the same reason. But just as his parents could clothe their demands in a coat of affection, so Mackenzie King could cloak his resentment and resistance in the garments of compliance. If the decision could not be avoided or postponed then King usually complied outwardly. The real nature of his response can be gauged by his comments on the legal profession made to his friend Harper: 'I have been undergoing a peculiar strain of late trying to make up my mind what profession to follow ... I want to stay with it [the law] till I become so thoroughly sickened of the business that I may never regret the day I have gone against my father's desires and abandoned a profession which ... I have tried to steer clear of ... '[43] King was giving no more than lip-service to his parents' wishes. It was a token, a time-wasting gesture, which maintained the facade of unity and common purpose even as it denied the ultimate objective.

The compliance was no more than a postponing of his own intentions, for the next year he again sought and this time accepted a fellowship at the University of Chicago. His parents, unwilling to risk losing all by provoking open conflict, gave their unwilling support, at least superficially. King noted, 'father congratulated me, Mother cried at times, and yet was pleased.'[44] One thing all the Kings shared was the capacity to maintain the fantasy of co-operation and unity with words even when their behaviour denied it. John King followed his words of congratulations with efforts to persuade his son to reapply to the University of Toronto, even though King had failed to gain a fellowship there the previous year. King was fully aware of his parents' preference: 'father feels he needs me as a companion and he longs for me to be with him. Mother certainly hates the thought of my leaving home.'[45] But now it was his turn and he resisted their demands in his own modest way – 'all the while I worked against the idea and gave him little encouragement, was it easy to go against a love like that?'[46] Whether he would have actually made the break if the choice had been left to him there is no way of knowing. The failure of the University of Toronto to offer a fellowship meant that King was able to avoid any confrontation and maintain his belief in the mutual interests of himself and his parents.

The incident was a minor skirmish in a lifelong battle for autonomy. The next occasion arose when King decided to leave his comfortable lodgings in Chicago and move to the working-class settlement project at Hull House. Isabel King's response reflects the indirect approach of the family embrace. It appears to say nothing of the change yet subtly conveys a sense of things not being right, of questionable behaviour on Willie's part:

I have missed you very much and this last week ... [felt] particularly lonely without you. I miss your morning kiss and the loving little talks we used to have ... What a great advantage it must be to be among such a lot of fine men. How much environment has to do with our lives.

Please God the months will soon roll past and we will be together again perhaps wiser and better for the little separation ... Father and I have been

talking about how he could manage about getting you into the varsity here ...
We will have you here this year. Home for a time is the best place for all of us
'united we stand divided we fall' ... Oh! how much there is before you and
such a wealth of love and hope all the inmates of this house have for you.[47]

King was once again faced with trying to find the path of selflessness
and duty without sacrificing autonomy and self-development, but
each postponement made the choice more difficult, for it was a thorny
path along which he risked losing parental affection.

The tenacity of the embrace is seen clearly in 1897 when the twenty-
three-year-old King informed his family of his attachment for a Chicago nurse. The family response was characterized by panic and subtle
pressure from all angles to stop Willie doing anything foolish. Isabel
King's letters were the most devastating. As was customary in her
approach, she denied any desire to influence him but applied the
utmost pressure: 'For hours I have been lying awake thinking of you. I
have never crossed your life and I do not intend to do so now but I
think there are many things to think about.'[48] An indirect approach is
always the hardest to combat. Outright opposition to the liaison or
direct advice against it might have driven King to rebel – to seize the
autonomy which was being denied him. But an appeal to his love and
affection, disguised as an appeal to his reason and betraying a maudlin
and almost hysterical selfishness, hit him where he was most vulnerable. He could not fail to detect the nuances of such statements as:

The struggles have been long and hard at home and I hope you will not think
me selfish when I say I had counted on you to help to lift the cloud.

I am getting old now Willie and disappointment wearies and the heart grows
sick ... charity begins at home and as you do so shall it be done unto you ... I
trust an answer will come that will relieve my mind.

I am very wearied but that is nothing new for mother it is only one more lesson
not to put your trust in anything under the sun.[49]

To the suggestion that he was lonely the family offered another
negative solution – an intimate and intellectually stimulating companionship with his father: 'your father was longing to have you with
him,' and 'father had hoped to have you as a companion and he knows
that all that must now vanish for ... your whole thought will be of ...
the girl you are to marry.' To complete the confusion King was accused
of being too young and too inexperienced to think of love, yet was
reminded of the adult responsibilities he must assume. His father
wrote, 'I had confidently counted on you giving very valuable assist-

ance' in seeing those that were dependent settled. All the clues to behaviour point back to earlier stages and offer regressive solutions to King's personal needs. On the eve of adulthood King was told: 'Your first duty is to those at home; it is a duty that should outweigh every other consideration, and the performance of it in a loyal and manly spirit will do more to give you lasting satisfaction and happiness than any other course you can lay out for yourself.'[50]

There could be no individual autonomy in the King family. Even intensely personal matters such as love and marriage must be settled at a family council. The method that the family chose to deal with King's waywardness was a repetition of that used successfully a few months before when he was persuaded to leave Hull House.

Come home and let us talk it all over dear boy and feel that wiser old heads than yours may teach you what in the future you will thank them for.

And now in this step before you go *too* far come home and with hearts only prompted by love we may discuss what may change this tenor of your life.

We will leave any further comment on the love making until we can talk together ... It is with greatest thankfulness that we look to having you home before any decided step is taken.[51]

King was not an individual in his own right with a life of his own to live as he chose; he was the family hostage, their avenue to a more prosperous future, and he was not to be allowed to neglect this responsibility.

King came home as requested. He listened to the voice of the family and outwardly accepted the path they had chosen. For the rest of his life he was loud in praise of his family, especially his mother, to such an extent that the liturgy must have denoted a deep unconscious antagonism and resentment that he could not permit himself to express consciously. Although there was no overt rebellion, there were small signs that the decision to accept the family's advice had not been wholeheartedly taken. He continued to see the girl and to correspond with her even though his father had advised against both courses.

In the months that followed King began to show increased concern for his mother. He had her copy out for him the words of two hymns, one of the love of God and the other of the love of mother. In the copy of the words of the second hymn, Isabel King underlines the phrase 'no love like mother love'[52] but her son already had the message. She also began to write long letters to him; previously she had only added brief notes to the letters sent by the rest of the family. She dreamed that he was dead and the family rushed into plans for her to visit him. King responded with enthusiasm – he would have her over to Chicago and they would have a holiday together – but the plans came to nothing. King continued to reply in words full of submission and agreement, but ambiguity continued to dominate his behaviour since he could neither accept parental guidance or act independently He withdrew his application for a fellowship at the University of Pennsylvania, which would have met his financial needs adequately, even though, or perhaps because, his father advised him to secure this option. When he failed to secure a fellowship at Toronto and had to settle for a needy students' scholarship at Harvard, he expected his father to come to his aid financially although fully aware of the latter's straitened financial state and showed no remorse about a demand that would send his father into debt.[1] King appeared to have turned the parental weapon of indirect pressure on them. His request for financial help was made in the same letter as the statement 'I am thinking of leaving college for a year and taking a place as a factory inspector in Boston,'[53] a suggestion which would obviously cause panic at home.

His behaviour had become increasingly capricious, and the gap between the myth and reality wider, as his stay away from Toronto lengthened. The idealized son, through frugal management and meticulous balancing of income and expenditure, could believe that he was making no demands on the family resources and was therefore under no obligation to them. However, it would not have been unrealistic to expect such a 'loving' son to finish his academic training in the shortest time so as to be in a position to help the others. An older son and brother who was not a wage earner was forcing sacrifices on the family by failing to contribute to the common purse. In the next stage in his vacillation, with the Harvard doctorate seemingly within his grasp, King decided to spend a year abroad.

This behaviour illustrates a consistent pattern of procrastination and selfishness clothed in a complex mesh of self-justification in which his self-interest was presented as beneficial to all, as something the family would want him to do. He did not risk disillusionment by actually consulting them; he felt sure that 'on the whole they [would] ... welcome this change.' He decided to spend some time at Oxford and Cambridge since 'this will please him [father] greatly.'[54] He ignored the fact that the one thing that would really please them all would be to have him through his training and earning money.

---

[1] By 1898 John King was regularly discussing his financial difficulties with his son and a year later King had moved into the role of financial auditor. He noted the occurrence in his diary: 'Tonight father and I ... had a good talk. Father reviewed his income of the last year ... He paid off many debts – all contracted while in Berlin.'

King occasionally recognized the gap between his intentions and his actions but banished guilt through identifying his actions not as signs of rebellion or lack of concern but as sins of omission. 'I fear I was too selfish. Only now as I reflect do I see what I might have done.' 'If I had been more thoughtful in the past my heart might not so reproach me.' This self-deception involved a belief that he felt deeply his prolonged absences from the family: 'my only regret is leaving mother & the others at home for a period of almost a year.' And this belief was supported by a resolve to 'go home for the summer, [and] be with all there,' but his actions belied his words. Not only did he go ahead with plans for the year abroad but he also made commitments which involved his staying in the United States for most of the summer. But he was able to justify the latter to himself as a sacrifice of wishes to need: 'I would much rather be home, but the money is needed & it helps to get the education, the competition & stress of the times demands this sort of thing. Yet my heart aches as I think of so long a separat'n. I long for home & all there, & long to be doing something to make their lot easier. But go abroad one must to be abreast of times here & for academic work & the sooner the better ... ' Consciously King appeared to recognize the self-centredness in his nature: 'Despite my efforts to be otherwise I find I am terribly selfish ... I am thinking only of myself and not of my father or mother or sisters. A selfishness tells me I must look after my own interest first, it is a false voice. I must seek to do for them, seek to feel they deserve this and infinitely more of me.' But his behaviour continued along the path indicated by the false voice rather than the voice of conscience.[55]

When he was away, King craved the 'romance,' the apparently undemanding affection and attention, the corporate feeling of belonging and support, that was the family. Yet when he was home, he found the demands and expectations of the family restrictive of his autonomy, and he rationalized that he could best help the family by leaving it and making his mark elsewhere. There was no simple answer to this problem which continued to bedevil him throughout his adult life.

2 ❖ The ties that bind

The beginning of a new century could have marked a new phase in Mackenzie King's life. He had ceased to be a dependant and had become a wage earner for the first time. It would now be possible for him to think seriously about establishing a family of his own. Throughout his life King was to show a neurotic need for affection – an 'excessive dependence on the approval or affection of others,' 'an indiscriminate hunger for appreciation or affection,'[1] – in marked contrast to his capacity to give affection. There seems little doubt that King was incapable of love in any real sense of the word, but he had learned to camouflage his lack of genuine feeling of warmth and affection by excessive verbalizing. Throughout his adolescence and early adulthood he made a word game out of love ; he romanticized and fantasized it, and in common with many other young men he fell in love with love itself.

The struggle between self and family continued throughout the first decade of the century. The conflict remained unresolved, the frustration and the resulting aggressive feelings were less well disguised, and the ambiguity and the neurotic components of personality increasingly pronounced. As we explore the next stage of King's struggle to achieve a mature adult identity while maintaining family support, we see that his inability to break the ties with the family in a satisfactory way precluded any satisfactory conclusion to his search for love and resulted in regression to a work identity.

WRESTLING WITH THE APRON STRINGS

From the moment that King returned from abroad in 1900 Isabel King moved to keep him on a tight rein of love and responsibility. She seemed to have associated his impetuous conduct while in Chicago and at Harvard with his loneliness, or rather his aloneness, and took steps to avoid any repetition of this situation. As she wrote him:

Now about coming down to Ottawa. If you feel lonely and have any way of putting me up I will come at once. ... If you could strike on the spot in the meantime where you and I could stay temporarily we could go around and find a more permanent abode ... I think two heads would be better than one ... If you and I were together we could take long walks and talk over things in general ... Now remember when ever you wish me to come Barkis is willing.[2]

Within the context of the unresolved oedipal issue it should be remembered that in the original Dickens 'Barkis is willing' referred to a proposal of marriage, and it was certainly as an alternative to marriage that Isabel King was offering her company.

King was left in no doubt that his first responsibility was to continue to be his mother and her family. They only asked that he postpone selfish thoughts of a home of his own until they were more secure and the future less hazardous. King showed no conscious reaction to this frustration of his own desires and needs, though it is possible to detect signs of disquiet and anxiety and an undercurrent of petulance and rebelliousness. His protestations of affection in his letters and his diary became louder, the descriptions more exaggerated, and the rhetoric further divorced from action. These reactions were part of a defence mechanism designed to keep from himself the knowledge that he resented, possibly even hated, his mother and resented the ties of his family. Isabel King had been the voice of the siren – a loving but compelling voice, calling him back from the paths of scholarship and service, which he believed he wished to follow, into a more petty, worldly environment, which he believed he detested.

The basis of Isabel and John King's possessiveness was predominantly financial. With their son secure in a good government job the future looked more promising and it was not unrealistic of them to expect that their son now repay earlier family sacrifices by assuming responsibility for the financial welfare of the family unit. Consciously, King reiterated his intention to devote himself to this end, but the gap between his intentions and the reality began to widen. He had justified his decision to accept the position in Ottawa in terms of family need – 'this should allow me to be of some real assistance to you'[3] – and there is no doubt that this was his intention. His ability to carry it out however, was severely limited. For years his parents had counselled restraint, advising him not to take on responsibilities until he was settled. The lesson of caution was one that he learned too well. King's capriciousness in this early period in Ottawa, during which he frequently wrote of his intention of throwing up the appointment and of returning to Harvard, drove his family to accept his limited help without reproach. But faced with a worsening financial situation at home, Isabel King had no qualms about encouraging her son to supplant his father as the family provider. This development involved Willie's seeing his father as a negative figure, embodying all that his son feared in terms of imprudence, inefficiency, lack of foresight, and extravangance. Only thus could the loving son of the family fantasy reject the father he unconsciously devalued and was in the process of supplanting. This unconscious rivalry made it necessary that any assistance King gave should be limited to that which would not in any way endanger his security – his ability to prove himself superior to his grandfather and his father, both in caring for their daughter/wife and for himself.

John King had not been ashamed to reveal his need to his son in a letter of 20 November 1900. 'I do wish my mind were relieved as to some future permanent position ... I have always thought you being where you are might have given me a pull with Mulock and the government ... I really must find something before long so as to give the girls a chance in life and also to give your mother some more comfort and pleasure.' But while his son was prepared to advance small sums of money for the financial support of his mother and sisters, he was prepared to do little to help his father re-establish himself. Letters written on his father's behalf were models of diffidence and self-effacement and concerned more with his own embarrassment at having to approach the recipient than with his father's future.

The dominant role in maintaining the family illusion had now passed to the son. The King family's self-image was of a group motivated and sustained by reciprocal love. In fact the terms in which this relationship was activated were the sterner notes of sacrifice and duty. The whole family had made and continued to make sacrifices; the recipient of these sacrifices – Willie – accumulated duties. The sacrifice must not go unrewarded and the measure of reward, the indicator that their behaviour was motivated only by the highest, noblest intentions was Willie's advancement. This process would in turn ensure the distribution of rewards to all the family.

Such a situation is high in psychic costs. Enmeshed in the love offering of the family King struggled to find an autonomy which would not forfeit his virtue. The problem was complicated by the fact that much the family said and did was openly self-seeking and opportunistic. Mrs King made little attempt to disguise from her family her burning ambition, her need to be secure and comfortable, and her willingness to follow the paths that this situation dictated. Such naked self-seeking was repugnant to her son, and any sign of it in himself must be ruthlessly suppressed, as was any conscious recognition that these were the actual characteristics of his mother. One defence open to King was to take unto himself all the virtues that he sought to identify in his family and totally repress all evidence that he was behaving to the contrary. Their sacrifices had become his sacrifices, and his duties their duties. At the cost of his autonomy he would embody the stated virtues of his family and use them in his own defence. Part of this defence required him to withhold actual financial aid from them. The whole family must bear the burden as he had, economizing and postponing the dispersal of the funds accumulated. The first demand on his savings was the future not the past. Only when his future, their future, was secure could the needs of the present be met and the debts of the past redeemed. In fact, owing to the intensity of the crisis and its effect on certain neurotic tendencies in King's attitude towards money, the right time need never arrive.

Stern rectitude in the face of the family's immediate need carried with it a heavy load of guilt, which was difficult to deal with when constantly faced with the objective reality. His residence in Ottawa and later his summer property at Kingsmere, Quebec, were the first steps in a process of distantiation and autonomy. At the same time King sought and found in a new circle of acquaintances substitute relationships, which would partially meet his needs. Long letters continued to pass between the two units of the family, but on Willie's part they lacked the candour and spontaneous self-revelation of earlier years. They focused more and more on his achievements and met with the same enthusiastic response from his parents as had the recitation of achievements in his youth. Nothing seemed impossible for her son in Isabel King's eyes, as her letter of 15 January 1908 shows. 'So you are going to Washington I think that is fine. To think of Roosevelt wanting to talk over labour matters with you. The next thing we will hear the King of England will be wanting to have a private interview with you.' King's deeper spiritual searching and longings for higher causes are confined more and more to his diary and letters to friends. The family are no longer party to these feelings. He continued to put great emphasis on the role of dutiful son and on the public display of the closeness of the relationship, but such actions were usually limited to public occasions and more concerned with show than with real feelings. Beneath the surface picture of a loving and devoted son, glimmers appear of a son vexed with the difficulties that a possessive mother and an inadequate father can provide. Such views are reflected in diary entries like that of 2 October 1909:

I had a talk with father about mother and him coming down for the opening of prlmt. He is most anxious and mother also desires it. I cannot but be annoyed at somethings in father, he wants all the pleasure but is unwilling to work for it. He could write articles to pay expenses to come down, but will not do it, Mother suffers in consequence ... However, I feel ... I should do all I can to promote happiness of father & mother & I have decided in the matter of their coming down to the opening to arrange for it. It will be a pleasure to me as well, the only feeling it can have is that the situation should be reversed & father by his own efforts meet the means of his own pleasure.

King in fact saw comparatively little of his parents during the time he served in the Laurier government, but he could justify this neglect in terms of the demands of his official responsibilities. The visits that did occur very often took the form described in the following: 'arrived at Toronto at 7.30 went home for breakfast had a talk with mother, father and the girls.' (King was on his way from Ottawa to Port Burwell on Department of Labour business.) The diary entry of 21 February two years later reinforces this impression of limited contact: 'I am too neglectful of home, & its love.' Even in the period when they were together King would write, 'I feel some regret at the thought that I was not as constantly with her as I might have been ... Still I have comfort in the thought that I made some sacrifices, and in the knowledge that others were kind to her.' At the same time as King was struggling with family ties he was continuing to search for a woman with whom he could establish a family of his own.[4]

CHASING THE PHANTOM OF LOVE

At this point it is necessary to go back to the 1890s and pick up the story of King's search for a masculine identity and an adult sexual role. The discussion of the physical aspects of King's development, however, must not distract us from the fact that he was essentially a romantic and it was this facet of his personality which dominated his approach to women and marriage. An infinite variety of names and faces fill the pages of King's diary, but it is not variety which characterized these relationships. A reader of the diary is immediately struck by the similarity of his responses, even to the use of the same phrases and expressions. Because of this patterned nature of King's courting it is not necessary to examine in detail every relationship.

King's early romantic overtures can be seen in the friendship with Kitty Riordan in 1896. On meeting the seventeen-year-old Kitty while holidaying in Muskoka, King wrote: 'I admired her every action word and thought ... I could see only purity and goodness in her character, a beautiful innocence of heart and mind and yet ... a very intellectual girl.'[5] Just such extravagant expectations and unrealistic images characterized the early stages of all his relationships with individuals of either sex and are not uncharacteristic of adolescents generally. But King was now twenty-one and his reactions lacked any kind of maturity.

He fell into blissful daydreams – 'I must confess that despite myself I could [not] help ... falling insensibly in love with Kitty.' This new experience did not fill him with joy, however; rather the possibility of greater intimacy filled him with foreboding, and he hastened to tell her that his feelings could lead to 'a life's friendship and nothing more.' When Kitty failed to appreciate this decision, King began to revise his estimate of her nature. He declared, 'I found that she is not the sincere and beautiful character I thought but one who will ever be purse proud.' He regretted the time spent with her and turned back to long letters to the family, solitary walks, and talks with male friends instead. In the retreat from intimacy one notes the recurrence of words. Kitty offended King when she did not turn up to be read to; this had been the dominant activity of their relationship. He stressed the utility of the verbal alternative – 'such talks are good ... they really influence a man's life more than anything else in a way.'[6]

The main difficulty in the way of entering into close relationships was that he feared the openness of such intimacy. While he longed for confidence in mutual understanding he lacked the capacity to give and feared the vulnerability that such encounters involved. King was still in the process of exploring the dimensions of self, in particular the question 'who am I to be?' He had recorded his approval of his friend Bert Harper's observation that he was 'a sort of compound one that could be a saint or a devil, a doctor Jekyll and Mr. Hyde.'[7] He was aware of the possibilities and he felt that it was the responsibility of the loved one to bring out the best in him. He sought in the loved one the type of overall concern for his welfare and the self-sacrifice to his needs that characterized a parent-child relationship. His reaction to an explicitly demanding relationship was a repression of sexual needs in favour of the search for an illusional ideal of love.

This feature can be seen clearly in the friendship formed in Chicago with Mathilde Grossert. King had been hospitalized for an attack of typhoid fever and had begun to weave into his romantic fantasies the various nurses with whom he had contact.[a] King was strongly attracted to the idea of being in love and he enjoyed undemanding feminine company.[b] By May 1897 King appeared to be showing a more active personal interest in one of the nurses, to the extent of calling at the hospital and taking her for short walks and talks. The visits ended with a promise to correspond and a shared vow from each to do all they could in Christian service. His feelings for her were not such that he was prepared to prolong his studies in Chicago. She did reflect his ideal, however, and he observed that she was very 'much the type of woman I long to know well and be associated with.' The next month he was back in Ontario repeating with yet another young woman the exploratory behaviour of the previous summers – paddling on the lake, talking earnestly about life, and reading aloud. Now another woman seemed to have all the virtue he sought: 'I have been thinking a good deal of Helen all day. I could not help admiring her more & more ... In truth I cannot help loving her. She has such a pure Christian heart I often wonder if I will ever marry her. She would be a good pure wife, an earnest helper in Christian work.'[8]

By now King was physically a fully mature adult, and he found it extremely difficult to reconcile the demands of the flesh with his romantic image of personal relations. In part, the ambiguity was a consequence of a conscious desire to live a good Christian life and his knowledge that he was not in a position to assume the additional financial burden of a wife. At least as significant, however, was the less conscious ambiguity derived from his habit of associating his ideal of womanhood with his mother and sisters. The women he admired were frequently compared with the women of his family. Of Josie Downie he had written, 'I like her better than any girl I know except of course

---

[a] His expressions of admiration at this time were not restricted to any one individual. 'It would be hard indeed to express the unbounded admiration which one has for these nurses,' he wrote. 'I have seen here what is noblest and best in women.' Diary, 9 Mar. 1897.

[b] If the woman began to make demands on him, however, King began to retreat. When one of the nurses became too demanding he developed a painful shoulder during the walk and resolved 'to get a fresh start in life in earnest.' Diary, 30 Mar. 1897.

my sisters.' To Miss Grossert he wrote: 'I find in your words and thoughts and actions a truer expression of those graces and virtues which constitute the ideal woman that I have found in the world over my mother and sisters alone excepted.'[9] As a consequence any stronger feelings associated with love could arouse great anxiety.[c]

The physical aspects of sexual maturity still had no acceptable part in King's identity. For King, being male meant trying to be virtuous: a spiritual and courtly identity; however, he remained excessively concerned with his inability to control the physical side of his nature.[d] This battle with self intensified during the prolonged verbal courtship with Miss Grossert in the spring of 1898. In his diary entry for 24 March 1898, King records the course of his struggle:[e]

This has been a sad and gloomy day for me. I have felt ashamed for myself all the time for having allowed my thoughts to have wandered so far away from the centre of purity ... the old story fighting ever fighting ... This clay will sink its spark immortal. Yet I have not fallen. This year presents a clean sheet in that respect and it will be clean to the end, but, that I could bring every thought into subjection. Why should I wander in thought now that I have conquered in act, but I will win yet and be as pure in thought, word and act as the newly driven snow.

The emphasis on purity runs through the whole relationship with Miss

---

[c] He could only love a woman who combined in her person all the high moral qualities and sense of purpose that he believed characterized his mother and sisters. Because of this, however, the love he felt for them must be as pure as that he felt for the members of the family. More profane feelings about the one he loved might lead to profane feelings about the other, especially his mother.

[d] His record of his reaction to a minor incident which occurred on his journey back to Harvard in 1898 revealed the basic features of this unresolved conflict. 'It was after eight when I awoke this morning. Owing to the ill constructed berth I was able to see the lady in the berth below making her toilet. What man could have resisted the temptation to look? I should have, & might have but did not. However, I fought hard against possible temptations last night & won completely. I am determined that this year shall not witness some of the stains of the old. This resolve I have made above every other, to aim ever at becoming pure in thought & word & act.' The very next night he repeated the determination to succeed: 'I have resolved that this book shall not have to record some of the sins of the old ones "Chastity is the gate of the censors."' I feel a strong spirit within me, more of a love of Christ.' Diary, 4 Jan., 5 Jan. 1898.

[e] It is clear that King is still at this time troubled by physical responses to his uncontrolled thoughts. Marcus noted how concerned Victorians were that 'impure thoughts could lead to "emissions or pollutions which were considered as undesirable as masturbation".' Marcus, *Other Victorians*, 24.

Grossert.[f] King inevitably felt guilty if his thoughts regarding her strayed beyond spiritual bounds. When writing to declare his love on 29 March 1898, he included the words: 'believe me if I ever get you in these arms you will never break from them in this world or the next.' But he could not bring himself to post it because, as he noted in his diary entry of the same day, 'there are references in it to [sic] earthy in their nature and the truest love is far above all of these.'

One of his devices to reduce nervous anxiety regarding impure thoughts and acts was through words.[g] Verbalizing his feelings and expectations, his hopes and desires, his fears and failings brought great relief. In a way it became a substitute for living, a means of vicariously experiencing joy and sorrow without exerting too much of a demand on the immature self. In this sense the whole of his romance with Miss Grossert was an exercise in creative fantasy.[h] Words could also be used to mask anxiety. To declare his love openly was to risk the possibility of rejection, to expose the vulnerable self. A difficult enough process for any individual, this was almost impossible for one of King's complex background.[i]

Every letter to Miss Grossert was followed by a period in which he agonized over her response while exhibiting all the signs of his ner-

[f] Although King used some twenty-five different phrases to describe Miss Grossert at various times, the words pure and purity are used more than any other, both in reference to her character and to their future association. Enthusiastically he declared, 'we will make the world purer and better for our being together in it.' The purity also carried with it religious overtones as in the statements 'when my thoughts are most sacred I think most of her' and 'her letter was like holy incense.' Diary, 1 Apr., 20 Mar., 3 Apr. 1898.

[g] Not just plain words were used but 'long, earnest & inspiring talk,' which bared the soul and revealed the highest and purest in his nature and in the nature of those with whom he was associated. Diary, 7 Jan. 1898.

[h] In a world of his own creating King was to a certain extent master of his fate and could exert the kind of control on responses that he desired. Although he wrote in his diary of his great emotions, his letters were phrased in a mode which left him less exposed to the judgment and criticisms of others. He noted, '[I] used the world "friendship" a good deal but hated it – it is love not friendship deep deep love and has been all along.' Diary, 25 Feb. 1898.

[i] His diary abounds with doubt: 'does the girl love me?', 'The thought that she may not love me freezes the words I would write.' He also prepared a defence just in case his fears proved justified: 'It seemed to me as if good & evil were both fighting the one to gain [her] for me the other to keep her away.' If all else failed he could always fall back on the consolation of God's will. As he awaited her verdict he wrote, 'I prayed before reading her note that only God's will be done & I believe it is His mighty plan to have us both carrying on a noble work for Him.' Diary, 6 Jan., 2 Mar., 4 Mar., 5 Mar. 1898.

vous reaction to vulnerability. 'My body pains me & my heart & head aches,' he wrote. The physical symptoms disappeared as soon as the mental uncertainty passed.[j] 'I received a note from Miss Grossert tonight & with it care & pain all pass away.'[10] It is clear that King was seeking an alternative supporting and protective figure rather than a companion for life.[k] His stress on her bringing out the best in him seems to involve a subconscious rejection of his mother and the side of his character which she emphasized in his upbringing. It could also involve an unconscious rejection of Isabel King herself for her vanity and lack of ideals. It is important to note that King believed he would feel safe in Miss Grossert's hands, that he could trust himself to this woman so different in outlook to his mother.[l]

King had kept the knowledge of the developing relationship from the family, which suggests that although he hoped for their approval he did not expect it. In fact the news unleashed a torrent of family disapproval and pressure which he was not strong enough to with-

[j] Part of the cause of his anxiety was his increased lack of control over the situation. He believed that for the first time in his life he loved deeply, but it is doubtful that he intended more than the pleasures of romantic fantasy. What he needed was a partner with the moral strength, the unswerving sense of purpose, that he lacked. In January he had written, 'I believe that if I felt someone really loved me that I would work to better effect.' By March he had no doubts about who this someone was to be: 'Is there anyone in the world who could influence me more and better than Miss Grossert I feel in her power already and feel she is stronger and better than I am and will make a truly noble man of me.' Diary, 31 Jan., 11 Mar., 26 Feb., 14 Mar. 1898.

[k] Such a woman could also help him cope with the troublesome physical needs. The standard Victorian view is presented by Marcus: 'Sex is a curse and a torture, and ... the only salvation for man lies in marriage to a woman who has no sexual desires and who will therefore make no sexual demands on her husband ... she being required to save man from himself.' Marcus, *Other Victorians*, 32.

[l] In the concept of the ideal woman one sees reflected the ideal self with overtones of the idealized mother. Of Miss Grossert King had written, 'she comes so near my ideal in her love for others, in her life of devot'n to the helpless, her constant aim, her purity and noble mind.' At the same time this idealized woman can be seen as a mirror image of the ideal self: 'we look upon the world with the same thoughts & feelings we look upon each other with the same thought and I almost feel that we look to each other for the same trust and fidelity. It is the thought that if together our lives might each be doubly blessed and a double blessing to those around ... Unless the deepest thoughts & feelings are akin it would be idle to attempt to bind our lives by other threads.' Further evidence to support a speculation that King was seeking a refurbished mother rather than a wife is suggested by the fact that he dreamt about Miss Grossert at Woodside and noted that he felt 'a most intense love for her,' the woman whom he had previously described as loving him as a child. Even her letters to him were addressed 'My Dear Child.' Diary, 5 Jan., 18 Mar., 22 Jan., 5 Jan. 1898.

stand.[m] He determined to stand firm even as he began to beat a retreat. He returned from Boston to Toronto via Montreal rather than via Chicago as he had intended. His heart was sick. He was haunted with doubts concerning the one that he longed to love but no longer did: 'I longed to love Miss Grossert and some how it seems as tho' I cannot.'[11]

His sense of honour would not allow him to retract his overtures to Miss Grossert. His need for support would not allow him to defy his parents. Was there a third alternative? King found one: 'my prayer is that Miss Grossert may not love me.' He compromised by agreeing not to 'become engaged but I would not promise not to love the girl or not to engage myself at a later time to her.' Miss Grossert would be required to show herself worthy by acceding to this extended time span. But it is clear from King's reaction that the decision had been made. He travelled to Chicago to see Miss Grossert but his behaviour was not that of an ardent swain:

Went for a walk after getting something to eat and writing Miss Grossert a line telling her I was in the city. I could not but walk to the hospital walked all round it, taking care I was not seen. My poor heart was being so crushed I have been told so much of my folly and worthlessness that I am like a hunted stag, that fears everything. I came back and went to bed where I slept for about two hours – not sleep but semi-unconscious. I have been wondering how I could break off this love. After all I have heard and all my doubts and fears I had a moments determine [sic] to do so. To tell Miss Grossert that it could not be, that I was young, that I did not know my own strength etc. but all of this has now passed away and for ever I hope and pray. I recognize this morning the forces at work within me. It is only the evil forces that have drawn me from her and would make me lose her all the good that is in me has made me love her and made me cling to her.[12]

[m] 'I told them of my love for Miss Grossert. God grant that my words may bring gladness and saddness [sic] to their hearts.' He declared his intention to 'stand by her though the whole world is against us,' but ends the entry with the words 'my heart is so dull & heavy.' The next day all of his worry was justified. The family did not approve. Further letters from home included 'one from mother that makes me sick at heart.' He could not cope: 'I am quite undone ... tired, anxious, exhausted.' 'These words from home make my heart sick, they craze my brain they distract [me],' he wrote. He prayed to God for 'help in this struggle with all who are at home ... But in the end he agreed with his parents' statement that he had been too hasty and was suddenly aware that Miss Grossert was older than he. But he was equally ambiguous about his feelings for the family, seeing them as strangers and talking of 'feeling no emotion, all indifference cold and hard' on his return to Toronto. Diary, 3 Apr., 5 Apr., 6 Apr., 7 Apr., 9 Apr. 1898.

The next day he was face to face with reality, meeting Miss Grossert after an absence of nearly a year, and his fears were fully realized:

Oh life does not become changed in a day. I have had [her] … in my arms I have kissed her lips. I have seen she loves me and I am still the same. Oh God, oh God, where! where! where! what! oh what! where is the love that was so beautiful and strong in me, what are these feelings of pain and anguish that now fill my breast. The little one rushed to my arms, she said nothing for many minutes, she only clung to me, she looked at me, she kissed me, she would not let me leave her. I could not speak. I did not have the thoughts I longed to have nor was I carried as I had hoped I might to other worlds. I was more of the earthy, earthy. Oh miserable man that I am what sort of man am I. We talked together, we had dinner together. I felt more like crying than eating. We walked together to the lakeshore drive and stood on the bridge together. She was only mine. The waves rolled by our side, we were alone. She was not altogether happy, nor was I. There was not enough reality in it all, or perhaps to [sic] much. I left her at midnight.[13]

He decided to stay over another day but declared, 'my heart becomes sadder & sadder. I was almost sick this is killing me … My heart is breaking.' When they met he read to her the back pages of his diary as evidence of his love. Even then he expected the earnestness of his original intent rather than the tardiness of his actions to be the criteria on which he would be judged. He persuaded Miss Grossert that they were not ready for an engagement, and when she agreed he believed that the conflict had been ended without compromise. Now once again she was the woman of his ideal: 'I love her more than ever, and I somehow feel that she will some day be my wife. I have kept faith with those at home, with [her] … and myself and I am happy now.'[14]

Once again his subsequent reactions belie his words. He began to write about Miss Grossert deceiving him, to declare that 'she is not the girl she was a year ago,' and that she 'never loved' him. He decided that 'her whole manner to me was not that of a woman in love … I was worshipping an ideal but Miss Grossert was not the ideal.' He was even prepared to accept a limited amount of the blame himself, declaring 'I have been like Peter, I denied my Lord for a girl's sake.' He again showed signs of nervous tension whenever he thought or dreamed of her: 'my temple espec. left burn. Burn very hard at times and my brain feels as it were contracted. In moments I have a fear as if I had been hunted down.' The latter was a rationalization that transferred the responsibility of the initiative outside himself. He cannot leave the matter alone. He continued to think about Mis Grossert, to write to her, even to tell her he loved her; but it was to come to nothing. Back at Harvard he began again the whole process of romantic fantasizing. He was unwilling to admit that a decision had been made or to renounce the option of loving her. He assured himself that time alone would tell if they were to be together. The news that his mother was ill climaxed two months of intense emotionalism, and he cried: 'I am sad tonight & tired. I long for rest ... I long for rest. I am tired out, weary & tonight am sad. I expected a letter from Miss Grossert & none has come. I wonder if it would not be well for us to break off correspondence & yet I cannot. I love the little girl & she is such a woman.'[15]

With great unconscious insight King recorded his thought of writing the whole incident up 'as a romance, ending by making it an incident in the present war, making myself go to Cuba ...'[16] A more accurate summing up of the nature of the whole relationship it would be difficult to find.[n] He continued to cling to the idea of being friends with Miss Grossert but the correspondence faltered and writing caused him much pain because it involved feelings of guilt about his behaviour towards the girl.

The experience served to make King more cautious in his interaction with women. After taking one young lady for a drive he noted, 'I took care to let her know, it was only a holiday lark & as such she must take it.' He continued to strive to be pure in word, thought, and deed and wrote of his disgust after attending a student party where whisky was drunk and 'filthy stories told most of the time.' He withdrew further and farther into himself, observing 'I have become an old hermit & feel it so ... My nerves are giving me much trouble.' His reluctance to face further entanglements with women drove him back to seeking intimate relations with his own sex. He resolved to meet more men and wished that he 'could find one congenial fellow to walk with.'[17]

King's romance with Miss Grossert has been considered in detail because it set the style for all subsequent attempts at intimacy. King's lifelong bachelor state was not of his own conscious choosing. He

[n] No matter how unimaginative and cautious King was in his later behaviour, in his mind's eye he was a great romantic. The fantasy world also served as a useful psychological mechanism. Without some such expulsion of feelings he remained anxious. The original feelings of inadequacy, of loneliness, of drive towards intimate relationships, persisted and cried out for a solution. Almost every entry of the diary from March through June 1898 made some reference to this love affair in terms which vacillated from blank despair to optimistic declarations that they would be together. But the script had changed from the Arthurian legend to Greek tragedy: 'I am a miserable wretched sinner, one who has been playing at life, deceiving the world, deceiving his friends, deceiving himself.' Diary, 5 June 1898.

yearned for a wife and family, a home of his own, but he could not bring himself to select a partner and accept the demands and self-exposure that such a relationship involved. In the wake of his withdrawal he became more concerned with self-control, and it drove him to greater rigidity and artificiality in his life: 'I must keep quiet for the next few years, study hard, watch each day, be careful of the steps I take. I am apt to rush too quickly into action of one sort or another. It is well to see the advantage of being too conservative. I need hardly fear that I will become too conservative, I am radical by nature & belief to an extent.'[18] There was little chance that King would keep this resolve. His need for reassurance would drive him again and again to the impetuous, uncontrolled emotionalism that he renounced.

As early as 1901 King declared, 'I love her [mother] with all my heart and I will never feel a longing for the love of another if she were always with me ...'[19] It is too simplistic to conclude, however, that King was seeking a wife formed in the image of his mother. On one level King sought a wife who would be a doting mother-substitute, a woman who would always think he was wonderful and would accept him as he wanted to be. In such a non-critical supportive relationship he could go on dreaming and planning and doing little. He could find happiness in loving himself, provided someone else could prove that he was lovable by loving him absolutely. He was also looking for a helpmate who would reflect his concern for social work and Christian purpose. A woman whose virtue would keep him on the right road as they worked together in God's service. At the same time he could not tolerate a woman who would want him to prove himself, or who made demands on him, or who expressed any criticism of him. More symptoms of this neurotic craving for affection can be seen throughout King's pursuit of matrimony.

One element of his pursuit of a galaxy of eligibles (young ladies of good background) was a need for reassurance. In early years King, a rather impecunious young civil servant from an undistinguished professional background, needed the reassurance that the attention of virtuous, yet wealthy, beautiful, and socially eligible young ladies could bring him. Even after his brief ministerial career and his service with the Rockefeller Foundation, he needed the security that such associations could bring him. These women provided him with a mirror in which he could see himself clothed in their attributes. This reflective quality led him to stress worthiness as the most desirable quality. He needed assurance that his spiritual side was triumphing over temporal concerns, and this state of affairs could best be assured through the love of a good woman. Thus eligibles must be true Christians and as virtuous as King himself. King could never consciously marry for money or even seek wealth for its own sake. But there was no barrier to 'marrying where the money was,' for marriage without adequate financial resources would be intolerable.

King's relations with the various candidates for the role of Mrs King Jr were always volatile. His impetuousness led him to blow the most casual of social contacts into courtship, and his exaggerated expectations made for early difficulties. He was hurt and bewildered if these ladies were tardy in answering his letters, acknowledging receipt of his gifts, or failing to read the mind-improving volumes he recommended. When Lady Ruby Elliot failed to respond enthusiastically to his suggestion that they might correspond, he noted, 'from that moment my feelings towards her seemed to undergo a change.' Miss Fowler made a similar *faux pas*, and King admitted to 'a wounded feeling when I spoke of Harper's letters, and she mentioned not having had time to read since her return.'[20]

King's refusal to marry for wealth and his inability to marry without it meant that matrimony could only be a long-term intention. Young single girls with whom he had contact often found it difficult to accept this extended time scale and showed less than acceptable sensitivity to his problem. At the same time King craved love and affection and the company of close, responsive companions. A solution to this apparent impasse was found in the ineligibles – often women already committed to another who could make no direct demands on him, women who by their unattainableness most closely resembled his mother. It is in these affectionate relationships with married women that King came closest to finding the perfect mother substitute. It is interesting to note that many of these women became lifelong friends of King, prepared to continue to contribute to his need for affection and reassurance in letters, gifts, and short visits.

It is probable that Mathilde Grossert (who could not be a true eligible because of her age and background) was the first example of this type of relationship, the second was that with Marjorie Herridge, established after his move to Ottawa. In both cases he was in the early stages of a period away from the family. Both women were older than King and associated with desirable characteristics lacking in the family; Miss Grossert was a nurse and Mrs Herridge the wife of a clergyman. It is likely that the second relationship was also mainly a romantic fantasy. It shares the fluctuations of advance and retreat characteristic of the earlier romance. King loved her for the maternal comfort she could give him: 'At 10 went over to Dr Herridge's & spent the morning there talking with Mrs Herridge. We sat up in the library I read her first some of the report ... then I felt my head aching and a fresh sickness of the stomach [he had woken up feeling ill] so I laid [sic] down, & she read aloud.'[21] She gave strong support to his earnestness. After a long talk with her, he wrote in his diary for 25 January 1902: 'I am convinced of one thing more & more & that is that man can do no greater thing than to [be] purely noble. If he is this in all his relations with men and women, its influence will be deeper & far reaching.'

He also appreciated the opportunity she provided for him to be the comforter in situations where only a limited demand would be made on him. 'Spent an hour or more talking with Mrs Herridge. Poor soul, she has more to bear than any woman's heart deserves. One joy I feel is that I seem to be some comfort to Mrs Herridge.'[22] In this dimension King saw himself as more of a marriage counsellor than a potential lover: 'The truth is she loves me, and my problem is here. I am determined to do nothing that will cause any estrangement of feeling between her and the doctor ... The love I have for her, and it is a real love, is not to win her to myself. That is impossible – is not desired, but knowing her to help her ... to be a blessing to their home.'[23] This early idyllic phase came to an end when the innocent nature of their relationship was misunderstood by King's associates and then by Dr Herridge. King was incensed by the criticism. He knew that 'there could be no objection to a closer friendship – where it was as ours has been, on intellectual and spiritual lines, – only of the purest & of the best ... .'[24] His actions, however, do not support his words, but his retreat was motivated more by Mrs Herridge's intenseness and the increasingly demanding quality of her feelings:

Mrs Herridge rang me up this morning to say she wanted a long talk with me. I found it hard to be other than formal in reply, cold and bitter.

I seemed to feel it impossible to be myself with Mrs H. ... I must draw aloof from her.

I did tell her I feared that I was going too much to the manse ... that I was seeking to stop.

I told her I wd. cease to come if I felt I were in any way robbing another ...

I must be the strong one for she is the woman.

I am determined to stay away for some time.[25]

It is hard to follow the ramifications of this relationship as the diary was kept very spasmodically during this year. When the diary was resumed in June 1902 the relationship seems to have returned to being a close friendship, which was pure and which in no way detracted from Mrs Herridge's marital responsibilities. He saw it as a friendship which was above reproach and which would bring peace and happiness to the Herridge family.°

It was not long before King began to retreat once more. In July he decided to spend his time in Toronto working on his doctoral thesis. Mrs Herridge was expected to demonstrate the depth of her affection by joyfully accepting this course and by continuing her support through regular letters. It seems that she was not completely reconciled to this role for he noted on 8 July 1902: 'There was also a promised letter from Mrs. H. which made me feel some little contrition of heart, for it seemed to have a note of sadness running through it, as though I had purposely come away at this time.' And so he may well have done. King operated best when he could put a little distance between himself and the objects of his affection. But he needed to feel that his capricious behaviour in no way endangered his security. The love that others had for him must be all encompassing and in no way dependent on his acting in a lovable way. Thus, although he chose to put space between them, he needed her letters to reassure him.

I had hoped by chance for a note from there [Kingsmere] today, and when none came ... my heart pained me so.

I have thought a great deal ... all day, and somehow hoped I might get a line from her. I feel lonely and miss her greatly. Am a little sick at heart that in any way she could feel resentment or misunderstanding towards me for being away at this time ... I trust she is well, and happy, tho' with some longing thought of me.[26]

° Once again the reader is reminded of the danger of reading too much into King's extravagant and emotional descriptions: 'I never saw Mrs H. so command her best self, and reveal it in its sweetest ... light. We had an earnest night, and parted almost passion pale with the desire to live out life to its highest and best, to strive after the purpose of God in our lives and its realization in His Universe.' To suggest that their relationship is anything but innocent at this stage is to believe that as earnest a Christian as King could ask for God's aid to commit adultery: the entry concluded with the prayer 'God bless her, and help me to be to her more than I could ever hope to be.' There is no sign of an appeal for forgiveness in this record of their solemn feelings on Communion Sunday. Diary, 3 June 1902.

King had no difficulty working himself up into quite a state about it despite his resolve that this period should be devoted entirely to work: 'Why no letter then to me I cannot understand, my heart is sick, sick, and I am suffering genuine pain.' 'Could there be any intentional unkindness in this ... a feeling of resentment expressing itself in this way.'[27] He was sensitive to any possibility of rejection with its implied humiliation but could not freely express any resulting animosity against a mother substitute. Instead he took refuge in disbelief, but symptoms of ill health suggest that even he was not entirely convinced. 'I could not believe – would not let me suffer so, and she must know what suffering is. It has been the loneliest day for months, and my head as I write aches with pain, while my heart is sick.'[28]

Both King and Mrs Herridge spent part of the summer at Kingsmere. Just how much is not clear since there is a gap in the diary from 11 July to 21 September 1902, but there is no reason to believe that their relationship was any less innocent in this period than at any earlier stage.[P] Although Dr Herridge did not accompany his wife, their children did, and it is unlikely that King and Mrs Herridge were alone for much of the time. Stacey's assertion that King and Mrs Herridge had become lovers during the summer is based on the diary entry of 21 September 1902 when King stated: 'Our summer has been lived together, lived to ourselves and now we are to live apart, and the duties of life rather than its pleasures are to receive their emphasis. What is to be the outcome of this love ... I have reason to love her as I never had reason to before. I tremble at moments when I think of what our lives are to each other.' There is little difference between this emotional fantasy and those related to Mathilde Grossert. Again there is no sign of guilt. The words are not those in which a sincere Christian would contemplate his adultery as he turned to work out a solution in the 'fuller presence of God.' Could this Christian say of an adulterous relationship: 'God has never drawn us so together unless for a purpose of His own'[29] It seems more likely that the intimacy had been verbal for this was the activity that followed their return: 'The child came over to my room ... we sat and talked quietly together.' 'She came to my room and we talked till after nine.' 'I spent the evening with the child. We talked.' 'After ten went over to Manse and had a last hours talk with

P C.P. Stacey puts a great deal of significance on the fact that when the diary is begun again King has a new name for Mrs H. – child. It must be pointed out that this is inaccurate. As early as 1 March 1902 King had written of Mrs Herridge as 'poor child.' We should also remember King's tendency to call his mother 'child' or at least to describe her as a child.

the child.'[30] There is no definitive answer to be given to questions about the nature of this relationship. It must be suggested however that King's feelings as expressed in the diary are open to interpretation in terms of paternal and supportive dimensions rather than the physical dimensions of romance.[q]

As he became more involved with his work in Ottawa and less unsettled about his future, the relationship died a natural death. King returned to the pursuit of eligibles and the other dimension of his romantic fantasy. In fact fifteen years later the pattern was unchanged. Anyone reading the pages of King's diary for July 1917 could be forgiven for thinking that they had picked up the volume for the summer of 1897 by mistake. Here was the young Willie King taking young ladies out in his canoe, spending evening after evening on the lake and in hymn singing, and reading the *Idylls of the King* aloud. But now the hero is the forty-two-year-old King and the heroines are Florence Lynch and her sisters. This time, however, King was more cautious and any misinterpretation of his intentions was quickly nipped in the bud. 'It is evident that Florence is doing "some thinking",' King wrote, 'so I made plain to her that I had no intentions beyond friendship.'[31] Miss Lynch can be forgiven for feeling confused; King continued to dance attendance on her with daily visits and moonlight walks and paddles. In case she had failed to get the message King took time to explain to the family that his intentions were not matrimonial and was surprised that 'Florence felt a little hurt at my having told B.B. [her father?] some of the things we spoke of together.'[32] When the family continued to mistake his frequent visits for courting activity King found it necessary to put down his own interpretation of their obtuseness:

Mrs Lynch shewed me an old copy of Thomas a Kempis 'Following after Christ' which she has & loaned me. Just what her motive was I don't know, but I did not altogether like it, as it seemed to have some reference to my being with Florence. I have made it plain to all that while I like Florence very much it is as a friend only. Were she & her family not Roman Catholics I would feel that she might be the right one to share the rest of life with me, but this is a real barrier,

[q] King's neglect of his diary during the summer of 1902 was not a unique event brought about by the clandestine nature of his activities. In October 1903 King began his entry after a lapse of time with the words, 'I am taking up this diary as a means of personal betterment.' Note the echo of the early year when he had begun his entry, 'after a lapse of several months I take up this little volume again. It is a return to self and conscience ... ' The relationship with Mrs Herridge continued into 1903 along lines similar to the previous year. Diary, 5 Oct. 1903, 21 Sept. 1902.

having regard to the whole of life & my work in it, & her nature as well as my own ... in this [religion] the deepest of all things there must be a line of cleavage which might prove serious with time.[33]

One more pleasant interlude was to come to an end without any declaration being made. While his mother remained alive there was little chance that King would take a positive step towards marriage. With the problem of sexual identity unsolved, King poured most of his energy into a work identity.

WHAT AM I TO BE?

At the core of the interpersonal problem which King had experienced were the twin issues of self-image and identity. Both involved a simple question: who am I? In this respect King can be seen in terms of Reik's comment: 'it is not easy to follow the advice, "to thine own self be true," when this self has itself become uncertain.'[34] In the five years before the turn of the century, King had displayed all the characteristics of identity confusion, including role experimentation, withdrawal, and avoidance of opportunity. The offer of the editorship of the *Labour Gazette* in 1900 provided King with an opportunity to overcome the problem through the regressive solution of a work identity.

During the period 1900–11 King served as an editor, a deputy minister, an industrial relations conciliator, a royal commissioner, an international negotiator, a member of parliament, and a cabinet minister, but the impression of variety is deceptive. In terms of patterns of behaviour and self-image this was a period of consolidation and regularity rather than one of movement. Once he had committed himself to editing the *Labour Gazette* King believed that this was the purpose he had been seeking and preparing for during his student days – a cause to which he was prepared to devote his life. It was also a commitment to the identity of a man of action, one who influenced the solutions to problems troubling the people and the honest working men. These general concepts represented King's ego-ideal, the self-image that he needed to have recognized and accepted by those he respected. It was the self he would defend above all else, and appeals to his self never fell on deaf ears, although his response might be no more than sympathetic understanding.

Changes in occupation became means by which he could deal with the challenges of this identity.[r] Naturally the greater his position in the

---

[r] King's work identity was comparatively unconsolidated since he had only postponed the need to find a progressive solution to the identity crisis, and he was in no sense

national hierarchy the better opportunity he would have to serve the poor and needy. Opportunism for himself was not an acceptable motive to King, but opportunism that gained better access to avenues through which he could help others was a duty he would not shirk. If such promotions led to incidental improvements for himself and his family, it was merely another sign that God rewarded those who were prepared to sacrifice themselves for others.

King's need for a 'sense of belonging,' for assurances of his status as an 'insider,' was prominent during this period. The need to be accepted as an integral part of the group meant that his desire to effect social reform had to be reconciled with the moves of the group within which he lived and worked. Here was the root of a great deal of King's ambiguity as a reformer. Much of King's behaviour during this period can be explained in terms of the difficulty of reconciling these two needs. His interest in social reform had always been an element of his self-image.[5]

Acceptance of the *Gazette* post at Ottawa involved King in two other regressive tendencies: one involving his reaction to powerful father surrogates like William Mulock, and the other involving his solution to the need for a significant other in adolescent mateship – Henry Albert Harper. As editor of the *Gazette*, King came within the political responsibilities of Postmaster General Mulock. Of this relationship Dawson had said, 'no man can expect to be a hero to one who has stood "in loco

---

ready to handle the issues of the adult period. Work identities are highly unstable, and tensions re-emerge and become dominant when the individual has to make decisions or during periods of physical and mental indisposition. The individual feels vulnerable, and a great deal of time and energy has to be expended to cope with the tensions in a way that can be reconciled with the self-image. Because the work identity is basically a regression to the solution of a pre-genital period, it naturally is characterized by many of the features of this earlier stage. One distinctive element of such a regressive solution is a continuation of the preference for relationships with members of the same sex. Another feature is a continued preoccupation with games, as seen in compulsive striving to excel in competition. Both of these elements were particularly strong in King's personality; he behaved as if he were surrounded by rivals rather than associates and as if he faced contests rather than problems. Many of the conventional 'game' images of politics would serve to reinforce this tendency in King's personal development.

[5] It had been present in his university years as was demonstrated by his interest in settlement work in Chicago and in London. But the strongest impetus was derived from his interest in the work of the young English reformer, Arnold Toynbee: 'I was simply enraptured by his writings & believe I have at last found a model for my future work in life.' The closeness with which King came to identify with this truly religious and humanitarian model is revealed in his response to public praise of Toynbee: 'the reference brought all the blood to my face in a rush. I felt it almost as a personal reference.' Diary, 5 Apr. 1898.

parentis".'[35] Mulock had been an associate of John King and the focus of much of the latter's attempt to obtain preferment through political patronage. Mulock had encouraged the son and followed his early endeavours in the field of labour research with interest. He had been instrumental in King's getting the post in Ottawa and was now King's immediate superior.

The situation offered King the possibility to displace part of the struggle for autonomy from his parents to his departmental minister. He was unusually capricious and demanding with Mulock. A simple example of his behaviour can be seen in the letter to Mulock of 11 August 1904: 'I wish also to ask if you would kindly grant me a longer leave of absence ... than the three weeks which is customary to members of the service ... I have for some time felt that unless relieved of some of the pressure of work and given opportunity of a rest I would be unable to discharge the duties of my office with the efficiency they demand, or endure the strain without permanent injury to my health.' Mulock had to show that he was worthy of King's affection by giving him trust and special status, thus acknowledging that he was not just another civil servant. A similar motive made King obstructive and resentful when Mulock exercised his powers as a minister to call King to account. In resisting the demands that Mulock made on him, King was working out the aggressive feelings he had been unable to show to his parents. When Mulock returned from abroad and sent for his deputy minister, King resented it. Dawson noted that 'King was furious with this attempted infringement of his rights. On Saturday morning he developed a severe headache ... '[36] The resistance was only moderate, however, for the wealthy, powerful Mulock was in a much better position to help his protégé than John King had been. When Mulock allowed King to take the lead in the relationship they worked together fairly smoothly, but King would not be patronized in any obvious way. His appreciation of Mulock's support fluctuated according to whether Mulock criticized or deferred to the younger man.

An alternative partial solution to doubts about his identity could be found in intense relationships with significant others. Although he was by no means the earliest of King's university companions, Bert Harper was probably the most significant, because of the relationship established on the *Labour Gazette* and the impact of Harper's early death. They had known each other at University College but at this time King regarded Harper as just a fellow student. After a social evening King noted, 'walked over with Harper to his room we had a rambling talk for an hour or two but profitable I believe. I really enjoy a good chat with a fellow.' In the summer of 1894 King was able to visit Harper's home in Barrie and to attempt to put the relationship on a closer footing.[37] What was developing was a typical adolescent friendship, but it continued as such long after both men were in their late twenties.

The fact that Harper shared King's interests and idealism was an important feature of their association. It strengthened King's faith in the validity of his beliefs and the worthiness of his objectives. This need was particularly strong in King's case, for although he had great talks with his parents, his idealism echoed from hollow walls. Any feedback was limited to areas of opportunity for advancement, making contacts with important people, and getting on in the world. It was to his parents that King wrote of all the important people that he met; to his friend he wrote of his longing for a life of service and his deep religious feelings. With Harper he could feel that he was not alone; they would do great things together.[38]

Harper's friendship could satisfy King's need for support from a kindred spirit, but at the same time King had to establish his superiority in a way that did not threaten the relationship. The pattern began to develop in 1896. King's activities enabled him to see himself as the man on the move, the partner who was establishing significant achievements. His letters to Harper recounted in detail his successes and growing stature, as well as his hopes, plans, and dreams for the future. Harper's letters are full of congratulations, praise, support, and self-effacement. While Harper was continuing the routine life of a country journalist, King was holidaying in millionaire society, touring Europe, and meeting leading figures in the world of letters and social work. By 9 May 1900, in a letter to Harper, King has become the comforter, the one who can explain the mystery of life to a friend saddened by the death of his parents. 'He wants you to know first the depths of your own soul, He wants you to probe the mystery of your own immortality, and He wants you to reveal His purpose to the world ... We have heard His voice together before this, and now ... ' A development characteristic of King's friendships, as of his romances, was the fact that it was an intimacy based on distance. Except for short visits during the summer holidays, their relationship was through letters – a situation less demanding of inner awareness than a friendship dependent on face-to-face contact. Harper was a friend of King's imagination as much as of his experience. A belief in their harmony of minds was not too difficult to maintain under these circumstances.

The real test came when they met again in Ottawa in 1900. As there was no longer any semblance of equality between the newly appointed editor and his journalist friend, there was no rivalry and therefore no barrier to increased intimacy. By October King was able to have Harper appointed to his staff, and the common bond of work was strengthened by the sharing of living quarters and leisure time. For King it was an ideal relationship, and it foreshadowed the pattern of many of his later civil service appointments, for example, O.D. Skelton and A.P. Heeney. First he selected a man who he felt shared his outlook and particular views, and then he appointed him to a position in which he could remove a number of crucial burdens from King's shoulders and provide an unlimited source of encouragement, support, and loyalty. The result was a man to whom he could safely turn for advice: the advice would be in accord with his own views and thus could be depended upon. The men selected were given sufficient independence, within this framework, that they were not made to feel mere cyphers. There was however a limit to the extent to which they could disagree with King or suggest that he might be wrong, especially if such a disagreement reflected on his motives or the high moral quality of his efforts.

To Harper the role did not appear to be unacceptable. Although he was not blind to the weaknesses and faults of his friend, he could see, as many others did, that King shared his ideals and objectives and was in an advantageous position to do something positive about them. Whether he began to tire of this relationship, to diverge from King on method and principle before his death, is not clear. His letters continue to be as full of praise and support as ever and King's replies were equally cordial.

Your strength lies in the fact that what you seek is fairness, truth and justice, as well as the promotion of industrial peace and the country's welfare ... It is not the strong arm of a commission, nor yet the power of public opinion, that is your strongest weapon ... but the commending influence of a high minded manhood moved by noble impulses, and unalloyed by selfish motives.

You are my great help and comfort to me and my life, and I would feel my work but partly done if you were not there to share it with me. May these moments of clearer faith and purer vision be often with us that God's love may work out through us His purpose in our lives.[39]

The suggestion that the mining dispute in Rossland, B.C., 'precipitated a conflict ... between King and his friend Harper'[40] is based on rather limited evidence, but although not probable it is not outside the bounds of possibility. Given King's strong lack of trust, his sense of doubt, his fragile identity, it is not inconceivable that an intimate relationship would have moments of tension, particularly if the man at the office did not accept that King, the man on the spot, knew the true facts of the situation. Harper's accidental death by drowning in December 1901 put an end to any cloud that might have been on the horizon. King's diary is silent for the period following Harper's death, a response characteristic of all the important partings in his life. But later he was able to merge his concern for his brother and his mourning for Bert. When Max went to South Africa during the Boer War, his brother wrote, 'the thought of his going away, after Bert's loss makes me a little ill.' A few days later he wrote: 'Yesterday I dreamt of Bert for the first time since his death, I dreamt that he was at Halifax & was going to S.A. ... When I woke to find it was not a year, – never more, here, old Bert, but over there – yes.'[41] In his book, *The secret of heroism*, King could portray his friend as he believed him to be – a man formed in King's own image by similar forces, a loyal colleague, and a true and faithful friend. In death, even more than in life, they were one in King's eyes.

Although King was unable to find a solution to his need for love and intimacy in marriage, he did find satisfaction in mateship-type friendships with members of either sex. This solution contained many regressive elements, but it would be inaccurate to see these compromises as dysfunctional. His work identify is analogous.

A young man full of mental and physical vigour, King had a way to make and the energy and drive to pursue it. For a time, his canvassing of alternative ways of life was reduced to a minimum and he exerted considerable effort to succeed where he must serve. There were numerous signs of unrest during this period but as long as he was successful, in a manner which he could interpret as fulfilling his ideal, his defences could cope with any disquiet. At times King was anxious and resorted to importuning in an attempt to further his cause. At times he was impetuous, throwing caution aside in his drive towards an objective. But in general King was able to handle the demands of the environment in a socially acceptable manner. This was probably the most creative period in his life and personally the most trouble-free. He had pursued the field of labour relations in a number of different occupations but had not made a commitment to any of them as a long-time occupation. It is possible that by 1911 he had come to see himself as a professional politician: a man devoted to full-time public duties, who was sustained only by a parliamentary indemnity.

As he kept his annual vigil on the eve of 1911, King felt a strong sense of accomplishment; he reviewed another year of duty well done and the prospect of wider opportunity for service in the immediate future. The cabinet was full of ageing, tired men; only one other Ontario minister – George Graham – appeared to stand at his shoulder, a possible obstacle in the path to his destiny. King's work identity had continued to prove a satisfactory solution to his personal needs. However, the intense activity and productiveness of the past decade had strengthened the regressive elements of his personality in which work, involving recognition and acclaim, had become his sole criterion of personal worth. Thus, the apparent harmony of King's personal needs and public identity could be sustained only by continued progress in his career. Any check in this development would undermine the foundations of his identity and bring to the surface the tensions and unsolved problems that were being kept in abeyance. The need for wider service drove him to seek recognition as heir apparent to Prime Minister Sir Wilfrid Laurier. The defeat of the Liberal government in the election of 1911 and King's failure to retain his own seat brought this dream tumbling down around his ears. King faced another crisis just when his work identity was under its greatest strain. Thus, the period 1911–14 saw the re-emergence of identity confusion in a more intense and less rational form and the onset of a pronounced pattern of neurosis.

3 ❖ The crucible

By mid-1912 King's optimism about his future had given way to recurring feelings of gloom and depression. In a statement made three years later, he described what he had felt: 'I was in the government that was defeated and it seemed to me like a revolution.'[1] In terms of his personal development this is what it came close to being. All the problems that had dogged his adolescent and early years remained unsolved. The family remained a support and a burden, a tie he could not break, although he came to resent the demands more and more. His sexuality remained a source of anxiety, associated as it was with his inability to select a life partner and establish a family of his own. His lack of financial security intensified the whole problem of his political failure and increased his need for a source of direction outside himself – a significant powerful other who would protect him and show him the way.

The King who emerged at the end of the prolonged mid-life crisis was in many important aspects a less mature personality than the earlier King. Although the new identity contained the same strengths and weaknesses as the earlier identity, the balance had changed, and the neurotic defences necessary to support the concept of self became more pronounced. During the period March 1912 to June 1914 King made only five entries in his diary. This failure to keep the record could be an indication of his bewilderment and reflect the fact that it was for him a period of intense anxiety.

With his work identity undermined by his failure to find suitable labour work, and his political career endangered by his electoral defeat, King found it increasingly difficult to maintain a sense of self at all during this period. His letters became less concerned with plans for future projects and more directed towards self-examination and doubt:

'You will see by all these rambling thoughts that I am very unsettled in mind, but I am making them known to you because I value your superior judgment and would be glad to have it.'[2] The problem was not one of lack of opportunity; it was rather the lack of opportunity to continue to maintain the work identity and the associated sense of destiny. He had been offered both a position on the Toronto *Star* and the leadership of the Ontario Liberal party. Both offers had been made through the efforts of the *Star*'s owner and publisher, J.E. Atkinson. Although Atkinson was one of King's personal friends the opportunities proffered lacked any real support of King's ego defences. It was impossible to interpret the former in terms of opportunity of service, and Ontario politics provided too small a stage for King while opportunity for advancement at the federal level still existed. His reaction to the idea of a business career was even more hostile. He told Violet Markham in a letter on 17 December 1911 that he would rather starve than be involved in mere money making. The capriciousness of his behaviour is underlined by the fact that, having turned down the opportunity of the Ontario Liberals, King accepted the position of president of the Ontario Reform Association without salary (although this deficiency was later remedied).

The pattern of behaviour during this period is particularly interesting because it demonstrates the difficulties faced by an insecure personality in politics. As long as the individual is successful, he can keep his insecurity under control. King was not only insecure but handicapped by a rigid, regressive self-image. He had begun to see himself as nothing less than a national statesman, and to accept anything else – journalism, business, teaching, even provincial politics – was a betrayal of his destiny. Thus, offers that would appear to others as opportunities were to King traps tempting him from the true path.

His customary solution to anxiety, throwing himself into intense activity or movement, was restricted by the family and his need to juggle self-interest and family responsibility in a way which allowed him to neglect the latter while maintaining the 'image' of a dutiful son. In 1912 he was anxious to travel to England to see if there might be opportunity for service there but was restrained by the increased frailness and illness of his parents. He described his problem to Violet Markham, his prospective hostess:

She [mother] was not well part of the time and we were obliged to delay our return a little.

I have been brought face to face with the fact that my father is failing somewhat in health, both he and my mother are in their 70th year, I can not hope to have them spared to me much longer. I must recognize what their passing may mean. I would like to have them come down for a few weeks to this cottage [Kingsmere] and then I would go abroad if that were to suit you or I could cross over almost immediately and have them come later, but a month in the woods first would, I think make me a better companion.

It has been a shock to us all [John King's eye operation] and I can only pray that this operation may save him what sight he has, he has lost much of the sight of one eye.[3]

Beyond prayers and statements of good intent, however, the awareness of his parents' health made little difference to his plans. He went to England and so produced unconscious tensions which could not be completely repressed. These tensions were revealed in the fact that he found himself 'strangely weary' and in need of the recuperative power of nature and silence. This recurrent wish for 'a little space around my life,' a longing to 'be with nature, chopping trees, digging in the earth,' and for 'a life for a while ... away from people,'[4] like his bouts of psychosomatic ill health, coincides with periods in which demands were made on him. And these demands were ones he could neither consent to nor refuse, ones he could ignore but which he unconsciously resented. It is possible that his state of mind was also a response to repressed aggressive feelings towards his parents which arose when his father's operation seemed likely to frustrate his summer plans. King's aggressive resentfulness, manifested in an 'agitated mind,' was directed towards his father, and therefore involved less inner conflict than later manifestations directed towards his mother. Denial of these feelings was further masked by the ritualistic exchange of token care – birthday letters full of extravagant praise, brief contacts on sacred occasions, limited and carefully secured financial assistance – gestures that gave a semblance of reality to the belief that he was deeply concerned and responsive to his parents' needs. His belief in the need for rigid control of his emotions served King in good stead in this matter. Although concerned about his father, he felt no compunction about spending two and a half months abroad on what was in fact little more than a prolonged holiday.

Because of his parents' obvious ill health and need, King had to develop more extensive self-justifications to account for his refusal to take any of the opportunities that would ensure the financial resources necessary for him to provide adequately for their welfare. He turned down several positions with quite adequate salaries preferring to make do on a small amount of money until the opportunity to return to politics presented itself. The unsatisfactory nature of this explanation can be seen in the anxiety and restlessness that he demonstrated in the period 1911–4.

As the months went by his letters to close personal friends became more despondent and his self-evaluation more defeatist. Following his visit to England, Miss Markham wrote a letter which provides important insight into the extent of King's personal crisis and into two increasingly prominent aspects of his political behaviour.

When you talk of being robbed of your life's work and of being unconnected with other men in the work of the world it proves to me that for the moment your sense of proportion is dislocated. Poor tired Rex – you are like a weary child hardly knowing its own mind for a few lines on you say that your whole nature is craving for peace!

Dear friend am I not right in thinking that you have not yet made that act of absolute submission [of your will to the will of God] ... That extraordinary power of emotion you possess unless you guard it carefully may prove your peril and undoing ... I know that particular gift is the most double edged weapon in a man's hands. During the last fortnight I realised its existence in you to a degree I had never previously suspected.

Had your party returned with a secure majority, had you gone on from success to success how would it have been with you my friend? ... the finest and the best in you might have been blunted and blunted – that you might have been swept to the brink of the abyss ... had there been a better way than that of pain and renunciation Christ would have taken it.[5]

This visit was the first time Miss Markham had seen King when he was neither on the way to success nor wielding power. The confusion she noted was characteristic of the identity crisis, and it remained a lasting feature of King's personality.

King's longing for peace, for removal from strain and the burdens of public life, always coincided with strong bursts of activity directed towards maintaining himself in public life. The latter had always to dominate, for without a public identity there was no King. He had written at the height of his success: 'The way of the cross is a hard way, but it is the path of progress and of life, sacrifice is the law of growth, immortality is born of travail and of pain ... its truth and reality is borne in upon our deepest consciousness, and we share the companionship of that Life which trod the path we are called upon to share at times.'[6] But he found it difficult to practise what he preached. Although he consciously acknowledged the likelihood of God's purpose in his removal from public life, he could not tolerate the situation for long.

He wrote without much conviction: 'I am beginning to realize as I have not for many years past how kind God has been to me, not merely in what he has given but in what he has withheld. I seek to keep my mind fixed on the things that are eternal and live by faith in the purpose of God in this world and in my own life.'[7] As far as was consciously possible, this was his standard. In practice, however, his behaviour reflected a not completely inarticulate commitment to the maxim that God helps those who help themselves. He continued his frantic effort for a seat, for signs of preferment, for Laurier's attention – for any indication that he was still needed in public life, that he still had an opportunity to serve his party and his country.

To a certain extent by mid-1913 King had been 'hoist with his own petard.' Having insisted on his right to keep the road to public service open, he was now confronted with the undeniable fact that there was no immediate political role for him. Only if he were no longer actively seeking political office could such a situation be seen as no denial of his merit or his special place. He raised the possibility of abandoning public life on 3 July 1913 in a letter to Violet Markham:

I try to be strong and brave and not shew to others the depression I often feel, and I try to carry the load that is upon me, but I sometimes wonder if I should not give up further thought of public life. This thought presses more and more upon me as I realize that for some years to come we in this country are to be overrun with a jingo-imperialism fostered by an arrogant plutocracy. To fight forces of this kind one has to be free; to attempt to fight handicapped as I am is to neglect oneself, and those dependent on one ...

This was the fourth time in six months that King had raised doubts about his career in this way. On the previous occasions Miss Markham had given him the answer he apparently was seeking; she had confirmed him in his dedication and the decision to remain in public life. His continuing to ask the question in the face of these reassuring answers, however, forces one to consider whether in fact King had had a change of heart. The repetitiveness – and the dwelling on the burdens and demands of his personal problems – may have been a thinly disguised appeal for a way out. Theodore Reik has warned of the need to be aware of nuances in analysis – of instances where the patient/ subject is asking the counsellor to understand something which he is denying to himself to the extent of being unable to put it into words.[8] If Reik's challenge is accepted, it means that King's behaviour must be reinterpreted. The phrase 'the brutal business of money making' may in this new perspective be construed as an appeal for help. It was politics that King had found brutal (in the sense of the crushing blows of criticism, misunderstanding, acrimony), not business. He may have wanted, in the face of all previous denials, for Miss Markham to tell him to take the money. His next move – acceptance of a job with the Rockefeller Foundation – might not have been so attractive had he not already prepared himself mentally for some such change. It was not a position that a man dedicated to a political future as a reformer would have been expected to take.

The invitation, in June 1914, had been unexpected, and at first the possibility of employment with the Rockefeller interests merely added another tension to an already overwrought King. In terms of the immediate issue, it had the advantage of offering an occupation and a generous income. In terms of personality, it offered a solution to identity confusion in a return to the earlier work identity. In this feature, however, it could only be a retrograde step since it involved postponing the problem of finding an effective, lasting solution to his personality crisis. In the short term, it could help avoid a breakdown by 'warding off depression,' but in the long term, because it called for an increased diversion of psychic energy to maintain the defences, it would merely postpone and increase anxieties, which would re-emerge at times of crisis.

It is significant that King described the offer as a 'heaven-sent deliverance.'[9] There were a number of sources of restraint or pressure from which he might have sought deliverance. Financial factors were one obvious area. With an adequate income he would be able to increase his capital substantially and possibly contribute more to the family. It may also have promised deliverance from the self-imposed need to pursue a life of service by political means. There is some indication that King had found the competitiveness of political life distasteful and even the more managerial ministerial responsibilities too demanding.[10] But politics provided the only real opportunity to incorporate his ego ideal of a life devoted to others with the parental drive to wealth and success. Only time and opportunity would resolve this paradox, but for King 1914 appeared to be a time of decision. The wording of the cable he sent to Violet Markham on 9 June revealed the trend of his thoughts: 'Rockefeller New York offers me immense opportunity study industrial peace on Foundation basis would mean life work and giving up canadian politics what would you advise would source affect possible service.' Despite Miss Markham's advice to the contrary, King continued to savour the possibility of giving up politics.

FRIENDS TO COUNT ON

We have already noted King's propensity to bolster his flagging sense of identity and to counter his feelings of helplessness through associations with a significant other, who could provide the supporting role in his life without tying him to any responsibilities. The relationship with Bert Harper had established the pattern, but it ended before the full potential could be realized. Miss Violet Markham provided the next link in the development.[a] His approach to the lady was at first not unlike that which he had already demonstrated towards female acquaintances – earnest discussion, courtesy, uplifting thoughts – but in this case there was an answering spark.[11] Here was someone who seemed to understand, even share his feelings; here was someone with whom he could feel as one, as he had with Harper. The relationship with Miss Markham could begin where the friendship with Harper left off. King was a professional and Miss Markham was merely an enthusiastic amateur in need of his leadership. 'We met again more than once during my stay in Ottawa, and I saw something of Canadian industry under his guidance.'[12] Miss Markham was also well qualified as a supporter-patron. Born in 1872, a daughter of a wealthy mineowner, she had inherited a private income which freed her to devote her life to public service. An ardent Liberal, deeply religious, and devoted to her fellow man, she travelled widely, studying social and political problems, and published extensively on these subjects. She combined the dedication of King's ideal with the practical qualities his parents admired. Such an acquaintanceship could not be allowed to languish.

King took the opportunity to renew his contact with Miss Markham during his visits to England in 1906 and 1908, and the relationship took on the characteristics that were to be the dominant feature of a friendship which lasted for the whole of King's life. To those who see King as an opportunist, who never took a step not directly benefitting his scramble to the top, the friendship with Miss Markham might seem of limited advantage. In terms of practical politics she had little to offer an aspirant to the Canadian prime ministership. She had no connec-

---

[a] The two threads – the memory of Harper and the promise of Miss Markham – were brought together in the year 1905. *The secret of heroism* had been prepared for publication and Earl Grey, the governor general, had unveiled a statue dedicated to Harper in Ottawa. The same Lord Grey was instrumental in King's meeting Miss Markham, an English visitor to Canada who was a guest at Government House. Such coincidences were important signposts in King's life.

tions in Canada other than Lord Grey, and King was already well established in this quarter. She was a staunch Liberal, but the practical links between Canadian and British Liberalism were not strong and Miss Markham was only on the fringes of the British political élite. She was independently wealthy but not excessively so, and King had no reason to expect that he would in any way benefit from this fact.

In terms of personal needs, however, the friendship had a great deal to recommend it. It had a foundation of a common religious outlook; they shared a belief in the deep spiritual meaning of existence, of God's guidance in every life, and of the need to follow 'the way of the cross' with all that this demanded in terms of duty and sacrifice. This harmony of mind was in King's view close to empathy. 'Between us,' he wrote, 'silence is never misunderstood. It would be just the same if we never met again ... our spirits have touched far beyond the mere human sphere.'[13] This was just the type of undemanding relationship that King sought. Their shared interests also carried over into labour relations and social work, and King could feel that at last he could discuss his deepest longings with someone who not only understood but shared the vision.

As important as the non-demanding nature of this relationship was the fact that it was ego-maintaining: there was unquestioning acceptance of the worthiness of King's motives and the selflessness of his aims. King had no difficulty convincing Miss Markham of the steadfastness of his devotion to 'the path.' In this way she reinforced his faith in himself and in so doing strengthened his faith in her. He could not help but be enthusiastic about a friend who could write: 'How greatly I shall rejoice to know that your fine qualities of heart & head have found their proper recognition in this increased opportunity for service.' 'I shall indeed be glad to see you, glad to talk over your great victory & hear of your plans for the future. Above all to talk of those deeper realities which all unseen are the only abiding truths of life.'[14] To this he could reply with conviction: 'I would like you to know that through the battle your words will be a comfort and help to me and the knowledge of your sympathy a real inspiration.' 'How grateful I am for your sympathy & help. I feel that I can write freely to you, that you understand.' 'The sense of your companionship is all that I hold most worthwhile and sacred in life.'[15] Miss Markham reflected King's inner longings and verbalized his romantic self-image: 'I like to think of you as one of Heine's "Knights of the Holy Spirit" girt with the sword of justice, truth and purity waging war against all sin & sordidness.' She was an object onto which King could project the feelings and virtues he sought in himself. 'Yours is a true Christ-like life,' he wrote.[16] The Violet Markham of this relationship was as much a creation of King's own longings as of reality. As with Harper, this friendship involved an intimacy based on distance; only thus could it avoid taxing King's limited capacity for sharing. In this way too Miss Markham was less able to judge the discrepancy between his intentions and his actions and could take him at his own evaluation.

The friendship also provided King with practical assistance. The transition from friend to patron was gradual but crucial. King's friends had to demonstrate a capacity and willingness 'to care' in a practical sense. Miss Markham assisted him financially and acted as a channel through which he could establish further supports in England, connections with people who would sustain his self-image as a social reformer rather than a mere politician. Miss Markham could take King into a world of culture and service that he felt was lacking in Canada. It was also a world of independent wealth devoted to worthy ends, a world which could satisfy his conscious need for worthy people and his unconscious need for pleasant surroundings. The friendship offered King further opportunities for vicarious experience. He could share in spirit the long and arduous ordeal of nursing a sick and beloved mother, the agony of the death of her dear brother, as well as frank exchanges of personal difficulties. All these experiences reflected the manner in which he believed he would behave when faced with similar problems.[17]

Above all it was a friendship which made no demands on his fragile autonomy. Just as Miss Markham was unstinting in her praise and admiration, she also recognized the fact that King needed special consideration because of his greater responsibilities. His visits were tailored to meet his every wish, arrangements altered and re-altered in. anticipation of his needs, and tasks undertaken without hesitation. When he cancelled visits or changed arrangements, he was never reproached. Miss Markham's reply of 18 October 1906 was full of concern and understanding: 'Of course I understand, greatly disappointed though I am. I know full well how busy you must be ... I do hope we may meet in spite of all these drawbacks but I must leave it to you to suggest ... [what] is possible.' She comforted while allowing King to believe that it was he who was comforting and helping her. She was an unfailing source of inspiration for the rationalization of his failures.

As long as King remained firmly established in his work identity there was nothing to mar the harmony of their talks and letters. In their correspondence, King can be seen as he longed to be, but it also revealed a number of characteristics which he refused to acknowledge. Miss Markham, though a loyal and devoted friend, did not refrain from touching on these attributes, although she did so in a way which would only mildly challenge his self-image. King's response was revealing in the rigidity of his denials. Miss Markham could not be wrong but she could be misinformed; her judgments were based on ignorance of the Canadian scene and the trials that it forced on him. Once again King was convinced that access to the facts of the matter would prove him right. It was seldom that Miss Markham put a foot wrong in this way, and in terms of financial support she was able to offer him money in a manner that did not undermine his self-image. King could perceive it in terms of preparing himself for a life of service. 'When we are together we will plan the future somewhat, and you will know that you are helping to make a life, what God meant it to be ... it is only when I see how deeply you share of sorrow and trial that I recognize the common ground which permits me to draw a little more closely to your side. Were it not for the shadow of the cross some of the finest natures in the world would never come to know each other.'[18] Miss Markham's offers, in their recognition of his nobility of purpose, his idealism, and his sense of duty and sacrifice, contributed as much to his personal as to his financial needs.

It was not only in the matter of financial security that Miss Markham played a supportive role in King's struggle. She had also become his principal source of comfort and strength. In times when God's purpose seemed obscure, when his own faith waivered, when temptation was greatest, he could turn to Miss Markham for reassurances. Having stated emphatically in February that he would never contemplate marrying for money, King had to confess on 3 July 1912 that he had been sorely tempted when certain of his friends had been actively encouraging him in this direction:

When I see you I will tell you of what interested friends have sought at different times to do for me. At first, I spurned any and every suggestion, even at the last I could hardly entertain with patience, what seemed to me an intrusion into the inner sanctuary of my life, but I will confess that with the weariness of fatigue, and the knowledge of how all but impossible it is to accomplish anything in the field of politics without some measure of independence, I have wondered at times if I have not been too hasty in turning away from ever considering suggestions that have been made.

Through advice and monetary assistance, Miss Markham helped him win the struggle with evil.

King's relationship with Miss Markham continued unchanged until she announced her engagement in August 1914. Although there had never been any romantic attachment between them, at least in Miss Markham's view, the engagement came as a great surprise and left King feeling particularly bereft. 'The day that we met many years ago brought me the truest, the best, the most sacred friendship my life has known. No one has been to me, in example, in help and inspiration what you have been, no one so constantly in my thought. Hardly an experience has come to me worthy of the name that I have not counselled with you secretly or openly concerning it ... [It] makes me feel now as if something that was part of it [my life] was being taken from us ... I am glad ... [yet] find a deep sadness with it.'[19] Miss Markham assured him of the continuity and unchanging nature of their friendship, but it no longer offered the secure base he had sought. Although King appeared to accept the change and reiterated his great debt to the friendship, their correspondence was never again quite the same intimate exchange of feeling as it had been in the preceding period. They remained firm friends but King withdrew more into himself; he could not share with any equanimity that which he felt was his own. Only in the years after King's retirement, when Violet Markham was a widow, do the letters again take on the tone that they had during this early period. In the intervening years she and King remained friends, but as Mrs Carruthers she was now only one of the group of friends with whom he kept contact, with whom he exchanged political and personal news, to whom he turned for practical aid, praise, comfort, and succour, and to whom in turn he could give assistance, comfort, and understanding. She was one of a number of friends who could be granted only as much time and attention as could be spared by a man burdened with heavy responsibilities.[20]

The opportunity to dominate which had influenced King's friendship with both Harper and Miss Markham was an even more pronounced element of the third relationship to be examined – that with John D. Rockefeller Jr. The possibility of working with the Rockefeller Foundation had created a major problem for King because of his antipathy to big business. He was able to rationalize the decision to accept the position by separating the Rockefeller millions into philanthropic and corporate pockets. He saw the former as 'money held in trust' and therefore untainted by its corporate origins. Thus, he could take it without endangering his credibility or his high moral purpose. In fact he could go further and transform Mr Rockefeller into a social reformer. As deputy minister of labour, King had been concerned to persuade the millionaire minister, Sir William Mulock, to stand forward as the public champion of labour reform, but he had been only moderately successful. The opportunity to guide John D. Rockefeller Jr into a similar path could be seen as a second chance, even though the role of personal adviser to Rockefeller increased the ambiguity of his relationship with 'Standard Oil' money and the 'Ludlow massacre' and gave his actions a different emphasis than a concentration on a wider labour study would have done.

Once his initial doubts had been satisfied King became enthusiastic about the association. He informed Violet Markham (15 February 1915): 'I have found Mr. John D. Rockefeller Jr. one of the best of men and most welcome of friends. He is a man of the finest principles and the highest integrity; a man too of quite exceptional ability. It is to me a real inspiration to be associated with him, and the association is becoming a very intimate and delightful one.' The 'sincerity and public spirit' King believed he had recognized from the beginning, but the judgment was positively reinforced by Rockefeller's enthusiastic response to King and his ideas. King's tendency to see all men with whom he was associated as worthy and above reproach was particularly strong when his own reputation was bound up with theirs. By recognizing King's worth, Rockefeller had removed himself from the despised ranks of big business and had promoted himself to the role of patron of the forces of industrial progress.

It is possible to speculate that King's relationship with Mulock and Rockefeller indicated, in a tentative way, the type of supportive behaviour that King wanted his own associates to follow in later life. King worked industriously to prepare Rockefeller for his testimony before the u.s. Commission on Industrial Relations and coached him on his behaviour on the witness stand. He suggested 'the preparation of a very careful statement of Rockefeller's position which Rockefeller could read into the record,' and even drafted the statement for him.[21] King's political career is littered with examples of his insistence on 'reading into the record' his personal position so that there could be no misunderstanding. He was also alert for pitfalls and active in making contacts and arrangements that would improve Rockefeller's public image. He stood modestly in the background, ready always to argue the importance of his principal's actions and the justice of his cause. Rockefeller's enemies were King's enemies and Rockefeller's successes were King's successes.

John D. Rockefeller's role in King's life was an important one in terms of personal development, as well as in public and financial support. Violet Markham's engagement and subsequent marriage deprived King of the close personal friend and confidant so necessary at this stage of his 'identity crisis.' It was a void that Rockefeller could fill in two senses. Because of his wealth and status, Rockefeller could meet King's needs for a patron and sustainer, not merely in large matters such as salary but in small matters which denoted care and under-standing. 'Mr. Rockefeller has supplemented this expression of good will by granting me ... a month's vacation, and asking me as a personal favour to allow him to defray the expenses of a trip for my secretary ... and myself to the Grand Canyon of Arizona and to California, before returning to Canada. As I am feeling pretty tired ... I have thought it well to accept Mr. Rockefeller's generous offer.'[22] Rockefeller was also liberally endowed with those qualities which King sought in his com-panions – virtue, religious concern, devotion to his family, a strong sense of duty and idealism – as well as the essential attributes of full appreciation of King and a willingness to be led by him. Fosdick, a personal friend of both men, describes the relationship as follows:

But more important than King's professional training was the fact that he was a man signally qualified to influence JDR Jr. 'Seldom have I been so impressed by a man at first appearance,' said the younger Rockefeller later, while King would write: 'I shall always feel that there was nothing of "chance" at our having been brought together at the time we were.' Both men were deeply devout and both sensed from the start their common source of inspiration. Both, too, were strongly influenced by family ties. King was excessively devoted to his mother ... And just as JDR Jr. had idolized his father, so King had, to a certain extent, modelled his life upon the legend of his maternal grandfather ... The two men – King and Rockefeller – were to recognize almost immediately their essential kinship, and what began as a business relationship was soon to grow into a lifelong friendship which would reveal the capacity of each man for affection and warmth.[23]

The fact that Rockefeller was a novice in industrial relations meant that he would not challenge King's status as the expert. The fact that he was ever willing to give King credit also helped. It was most soothing to King's ego to have Rockefeller say: 'I was merely King's mouthpiece. I needed education. No other man did so much for me. He had vast experience in industrial relations and I had none. I needed guidance. He had an intuitive sense of the right thing to do – whether it was a man who ought to be talked with or a situation which ought to be met.'[24] Such statements ensured that the relationship would start on a harmonious footing. Rockefeller's lack of interest in politics and public life further ensured that he would not be seen as a potential rival in this sphere either. On this basis King could build a permanent association comparatively untroubled by the suspicions that often marred his relationship with Canadian colleagues. Rockefeller's aloofness, cautions and his limited capacity for friendship made his openness with King and dependence on him a valuable confirmation of King's worth and special status. That a man so cautious in his responses, so constantly importuned by people seeking advancement, so grudging of his friendship, could write to King's parents of 'his deep regard for the mother and father of the man whom so unreservedly I respect and admire, and to whom I entertain feelings akin to those of a brother,'[25] was praise indeed. King was not hesitant to see more than mere coincidence in their association as his diary entry of 4 December 1914 shows: 'I feel a perfect sympathy in all things as we talk together and have felt it since we first met, it is the more extraordinary as it is the last thing I should have expected to experience. Clearly there is a spiritual or psychic power that has attracted and that attracts and holds.'

King's proclivity to internalize the attributes of his associates and models continued in respect to Rockefeller, although in most instances it merely reinforced existing tendencies. King noted Rockefeller's meticulousness: 'I have observed that in everything that goes out from himself he never lets it pass from his hand until even the commas have been accurately inserted ... I have seen no man in my life's experience more careful and more genuinely honest in the work he performs.'[26] His admiration reinforced a habit which was already an important mechanism of his own behaviour. He noted their shared belief in the value of outdoor activities, such as horseback riding and wood chopping, as a mode of relaxation. Their religious ideas were closely attuned; they shared a belief that the Christian principles of love and compassion were more important than specific theological differences.

Because Rockefeller had a family and a demanding life of his own, this friendship was also characterized by the intimacy based on distance that was so congenial to King. However, moments of crisis could occur if they were together too often, and King came close to real insight into his problems when he considered these aspects. McGregor notes the following: 'King soon began also to advise John D., Jr. on many things which had nothing to do with industrial relations: his excessive seriousness, his method of living, his failure to see enough of his family, his aloofness, his inability to relax and the need for him to get away from detail and to deal with major issues. "The truth is," King admitted in his diary, "I see in Mr. R. precisely the same mistakes which I have heard others complain of in myself".'[27] The fact of their 'alikeness' was always a possible source of difficulty, especially in respect to those characteristics which King was reluctant to even consider in himself. But on the whole the relationship was close to ideal as far as King was concerned. In February 1917 he wrote again to Violet Markham: 'I have found John D. Rockefeller, Jr. one of the best of men and most welcome of friends ... [And] ... the truest follower of Christ ... His humility, his sincerity, his fearlessness, his simple faith, his fidelity to principle – so far as he has horizon at all his one purpose is to serve his fellow men.'

The praise might have been a little less fulsome had King been able to anticipate Rockefeller's lukewarm reception of his 'brain child' – *Industry and humanity*, published in 1918. Rockefeller had been called upon to play the part that John King had so often assumed – reading the proofs and praising the author. But he let King down. Regarding Rockefeller's comments King wrote:

I suppose I was expecting too much, but I felt deeply disappointed. I had hoped for some recognition of the generous attitude I had taken towards the Colorado Plan, what I had done to take opprobrium away from the situation and give the Plan historical significance ... Mr Rockefeller will live to see that in the bold conceptions of the book and its fundamental disclosures there is true originality ... These ideas will have more influence in the course of time than all his wealth.[28]

Although King invited criticism of his work, he did not expect to receive it. When he said, 'speak freely,' he meant, do not hesitate to praise and show how valuable you think my efforts are. Rockefeller's dilatoriness in this respect may have affected their subsequent relationship; King continued to seek the perfect companion, although he remained friends with Rockefeller all his life.

Both these friendships contributed to dysfunctional aspects of King's personal development: they encouraged the retention of a self-image that was becoming increasingly remote from reality. At the same time, the egostrength acquired through this means enabled King to function relatively effectively in a tense atmosphere and to avoid any further personality diffusion. They also provided a mechanism by which he could disguise his aloneness and the increased barrenness of his life. Such supportive others could never entirely meet King's needs, however, and in time they became less important than his religious defences.

ORDEAL BY FIRE

Working for the Rockefeller Foundation put an end to King's financial troubles and provided a satisfactory outlet for his energies, but it could not protect him from his personal problems –especially those related to the family. A further burden of illness was added to that of John King's increased incapacity when Max was stricken with tuberculosis not long after his marriage and the birth of his twin sons. It was now impossible for the family to cope financially without substantial and direct help from King – help he could not refuse but which he was reluctant to give. The relationship between King and his family was becoming increasingly ambiguous in this period of uncertainty. While King visited his parents and had them visit him he never attempted to establish a common dwelling for them all, although the practical need for them to remain in Toronto or for him to be in Ottawa no longer existed. This physical separation was the only dimension of autonomy he had achieved, and despite his exaggerated expressions of love and concern he did not consider any change necessary.

His approach to the whole problem was entirely in terms of self. Even his expressed concern for the family was phrased in terms of the effect on him rather than the consequences to them. '[I] have since been in Toronto with my father and mother. My father has not been at all well, and I am greatly fearing a break up in his case ... My mother bears up well under the strain of everything but that it is telling on her I know full well. Is it not terrible to have no one, but practically all of those with whom one's life has been associated from earliest days breaking down before one's very eyes at a time when one is least able to render the help one would.'[29] King had always promised to devote himself to the care and comfort of his parents at some future time. His decision to join the Rockefeller Foundation in 1914 had put an end to his own financial difficulties and so cleared the way for him to do more for the family. In fact, however, he continued his policy of stopgap aid while deluding himself that conditions in the family were improving.

When he visited Toronto in 1915 he was faced with the reality of the situation – his mother 'thin and delicate,' his sister 'seriously ill,' and his father's blindness increasing – yet his response as reflected in the diary entry for 1 February 1915 seems controlled. 'I was so tired that I slept all afternoon. Tonight I read aloud to mother & father & Bell ... The little glimpse of home was refreshing to my heart.' Rather than directly confront the difficulties his family faced, King preferred to dwell on his mother's spiritual charm and appearance and his sisters' goodness as if he could incorporate these virtues into himself. In particular he refused to accept that Bella's overwork and anxiety was a consequence of the inadequacy of his help rather than a facet of her own nature. It was so much more comfortable to return to Ottawa and to feel distressed and disappointed over a bronze relief of his mother, which he felt failed to do her justice. The illusion that all was well could not be maintained for long; it was in this year that King had to confront the fact that his family could not always be available to sustain his image. The autonomy that they had denied him and the freedom that he had chosen not to accept would soon be granted by forces outside his control.

King was particularly anxious to allay any doubts that he had about family matters in 1915 since he had at last persuaded the Rockefeller Foundation to grant him permission to go to Colorado to investigate the labour dispute there. A decision about the family made on his own responsibility would bring guilt feelings if it proved to be the wrong course. He tried to avoid responsibility by transferring the choice to the family doctor. He was seeking both advice and confirmation that he was doing all that could be expected of him when he informed Dr Thistle:

I have been worried a good deal about the people at home, and am at a loss to know what is best to do.

I agreed to pay the expenses of a second maid wholly regardless of what they might amount to, the one condition that a good one was obtained.

What with the long strain of Max's illness and what it has involved and is involving in financial sacrifice, I find it very hard indeed to keep from worrying over possible increases in this burden.

I realize that someone has to be behind the situation as it has developed both at home and with Max, and I am the only one who can be looked to ... It is not that I am anxious to part with money, for just how it is going to be possible for me to hope to do anything further in public life and continue the obligations I have, I do not know, but if there has to be a choice I prefer to make it in the way of doing my full duty to all at home in the first instance.

There is no sufficient reason why mother should not have two servants and why two servants should not get along as well at 4 Grange Rd. as in any other house in the city; there is no sufficient reason why Isabel should not give up her work at the office for a while and take the rest which is absolutely necessary. Jennie, I know, will help in any way she can. I shall be eternally grateful if you can persuade Mother and Isabel to see the situation in its true light. Unless they do I can see where in my own work is going to suffer through the anxiety I can not but feel on their account.[30]

His anxiety apparently settled, King journeyed to Denver. His sister Bella died during his absence. Despite his suggestion to the contrary, she had continued to work in the bank until a few days before her death. In a letter to Violet Markham, King verbalized his grief, eulogized Bella's character, and rationalized his own inactivity, as he lamented that it was 'just at the moment when I am again able to really lift the burden in a substantial way [that] she has been taken away.'[31]

His statements about his ability to assist the family were always either in the future tense or qualified. At this time his actual contribution had been restricted to a gift to his mother covering the maids' salary for a year, loans to his father and brother, and advice to Bella that she should give up work secure in the knowledge that Willie would provide. It was not an insubstantial contribution if it is accepted that care of the family was the responsibility of the father rather than the son, but it was less magnanimous when equated with the sacrifices made by the family to obtain King's advancement. Bella's reluctance to give up her employment may well have been motivated by fear that Willie's public responsibilities might in the unpredictable future once again ensure that they would be asked to wait a little longer. Her actions do not seem indicative of trust that a loving brother would provide.

King was particularly distressed by the fact that he had not been at Bella's side at the last, though he consoled himself with the observation that he had been in Colorado with Max. He returned to Toronto for the funeral, since the ritual, like the recital of the details of her last moments, brought him comfort and some degree of absolution. 'Did I not believe that in all God has meant me to see more clearly the work he wished me to do for the world, I might feel bitter and resentful, but I do not. I see only the most loving and gracious providence, caring for one and all.'[32] In the distress over Bella's death, King became more anxious about his parents but continued his search for signs of well being – 'all things considered [they] were looking pretty well.'[33]

Although he intended to have his parents with him in August and September, it was actually his sister Jennie who accepted this responsibility. King's one positive act was to apply to the Carnegie Foundation for a pension for his father. His concern for his parents was not such that he was prepared to stay in Toronto. Instead, King returned to

Kingsmere where he was able to renew his inner strength and to lament his situation far away from the cause of his distress:

It was so peaceful here, but I could not get father and mother out of my mind, how I wish they were here too, but for the operation on father's eye they might well be. It is sad to think of them at home with a nurse attending them, mother too weak to be about & father too blind to move anywhere & suffering from a heavy cold as well. May they be spared in strength for time to come and may God grant me the courage to take all the load from them, & make their remaining days & years happy as they can be.[34]

The weakness of the flesh continued to negate the strength of the spirit. In practice, taking the load involved no more than having his parents with him for part of a fortnight while he was electioneering. He had even begrudged having to end a holiday in San Francisco two days early so as to be with Max in Colorado on his birthday; he described his action as 'a real sacrifice to a sense of duty.'[35]

No matter how great the discrepancy between illusion and reality, King continued to rationalize the whole situation in a manner which reflected nothing but glory on himself. In June 1916 he once more sacrificed himself to family duty. This time it involved helping his parents change their abode. After ten days he was able to return to Kingsmere and make a new beginning on keeping his diary with a note on his behaviour: 'I left them both at the door of this beautiful new home with a feeling that the effort had been worthwhile, and that though I may fail in much else I am remaining true to the obligations that home and family have placed upon me. I have at least tried to be faithful to this.'[36] In evaluating his own contribution King gave no credit to Jennie and her husband for the real sacrifices they had made in assisting with the care of his parents. The diary was concerned only with his image of himself; the contribution of others received little or no mention.

John King died two months after this move. His son showed the conventional signs of mourning, and the diary contains a eulogy of his father's virtues and records King's desire to be like him in spirit and heart. It seems likely that the entry of the following year is a more accurate record of his real feelings and actions. 'I almost feared to approach my little cottage lest it might recall my impatience with dear old father on the last Sunday we were together.' At the same time it is possible to detect a strong note of concern for self in the response: 'last night I wandered about alone in Toronto sat alone for a while in Queen's Park, realizing that for the first time in life I had no home to go to.' The concern and attention that had been denied John King during his lifetime was lavished on him after death. King notes, 'I spent most of the morning designing an inscription for the monument recording father's birth and death.' At the same time he commissioned a bust of his mother from an Italian sculptor, an expense justified on the grounds that it preserved 'the inspiration of their lives.'[37]

Beneath the superficial calm, however, there are signs of acute tension. King experienced great difficulty in completing his book, *Industry and humanity*, and in attending to constituency matters. Did his nervous condition and his reflection on this 'dark and difficult time' contain elements of remorse or even guilt? At the conscious level King admitted to some minor faults in his diary (8 November 1916): 'I think much though of the summer, and my impatience with father on one or two occasions. How deeply I regret it now. All might have been saved had I known enough not to resist.' The larger question of whether he had in fact done little or nothing to relieve his father's burdens could not be faced, and it may have contributed to the onset of a psychosomatic illness which King experienced at this time.

From King's point of view, his father's death was poorly timed. The regressive oedipal component had at last reached the final stage, for he had his mother completely to himself. Although he stated that he longed to have her with him in Ottawa and to lavish care and attention on her, other factors precluded its happening immediately: she was in bad health and needed nursing, and he had a book to finish and an electoral campaign to prepare. Isabel King was dispatched to spend some time with the other children.

King was distressed when he arrived at Jennie's home for Christmas and found his mother ill; he blamed his sister for taking their mother out for a drive. King gave little credit to Jennie for her effort on their mother's behalf. He wondered how she had managed to care for her as well as her husband and four children, but he offered no financial aid, although he now had the proceeds of his father's insurance policies to devote to his mother's care. When he had to face the other alternative – caring for her himself – the tone of his diary (23 December 1916) becomes less than enthusiastic: 'My anxiety at present is for mother's health ... It seems to me the only thing is to take her myself ... It is a duty which I must accept & will accept as a privilege.' His concern for his mother's well-being, expressed two days later, is not as strong as his concern for his own comfort: 'It has all alarmed me a good deal as to what to do about taking her to Ottawa. To refuse or delay it would be to cause her to lose heart ... [Her wish] to die where I was, has not helped to make the nervous strain in having her with me less. Still [it is] my duty as I see it ... Thank God I can afford the expenses.' By the end of the year the problem had been solved, his apartment had been rearranged and his mother and a nurse settled in Ottawa. Everything seemed highly satisfactory and he could record (27 December 1916): 'It gives me a very great happiness to have her near me, and now I shall provide for her happiness always. God grant she may be long spared.' In two days the euphoria had begun to wear off and King was finding the reality of his mother's presence more than he had bargained for, particularly when bronchitis threatened Isabel King once again. Her son recorded his response as follows: 'I have sought to get her the things required, fruit, medicines etc. but I find it difficult to remember, and with the cramped quarters doubly hard. I try not to be impatient, but somehow the illness in others is very hard for me to bear. Still I shall seek to be brave in this, and overcome myself, realizing how great is the privilege.'[38]

Nineteen seventeen was to be a year in which King lived closer to his mother than for any time since he had left home sixteen years before. It is interesting to note just how he reacted to such prolonged contact with reality. He began the new year rejoicing in her presence: 'The New Year could have brought no more welcome gift than the privilege of being beside my mother and giving her the first greeting ... How great the blessing that it is possible to have care and comfort for mother at this time of her life, and the best care and greatest comfort she has ever known.' The nature of his pleasure and his fears are revealed in the diary entry two days later: 'It makes my heart sink within me at times, as I fear lest anything should happen to her. I would be very much alone in the world if she were taken away and my life never be the same again.'[39]

The impression that he was finding her presence a burden is reinforced by his response to her suggestion that she should go to hospital: 'it breaks my heart when I think that there is much I might have done which I have not done for her. Still with God's help I shall leave nothing undone henceforth.'[40] By insisting on keeping her with him, witnessing her suffering, and possibly contributing marginally to her care, King was able to maintain the illusion that he loved his mother deeply and had contributed substantially to her well-being.

During her illness Isabel King began to tell her son of her early life, her mistakes, and her difficulties. The details conflicted strongly with King's image of her and he refused to accept them. He dismissed her revelations as imaginary and exaggerated: 'Poor little soul, the very purity of it has made some innocent, small indiscretion in girlhood or early life seem ... "evil" ... – a purer soul never went through this world.'[41] He continued to demand expressions of love and affection from her, and even when he supposed her dying, on 25 January 1917, his diary recorded not expressions of his grief but examples of her love for him. 'During the afternoon three or four times she roused sufficiently to say "dear Billy" & put her arms around me & kiss me.' 'She said to the doctor ... "isn't he a dear son, did any mother have a better son." How often she said "how I love you", & Good night dear Willy, – Billy dear, dear old fellow, & the like. Such pure love – what in all the world beside is comparable to it.' Page after page of the diary recorded this concern for self, the desire that his mother should live for his sake because he needed her love. 'I have just told her I love her more than all else in the world beside, that she is the only one I love, which is true ... I told her I wanted her to live that we might always be together ... I asked her if she wdn't live for me for this ...'[42]

While his part in the care of his mother involved nothing more than holding her hand or holding her in his arms, King was content. When called upon to actually share in the nursing, King speaks of 'the strain on his nerves' and of his tiredness. He was concerned with her pain and suffering but more concerned with the anguish that living without her might be.

Many times she came back to asking me if we could agree to end it now, to let it end now. She asked how long we were going to 'keep up this play' –how long 'this caper' going to last. When she spoke of wanting to go, I broke down this made her draw me to her and say she would get better ...

Two or three times she has said she would like to give up now, that she is too tired, and has asked me to let her, but I always beg of her for her love for me to keep on, and she promises she will.[43]

As Mrs King's illness dragged on the responsibilities and inconveniences of caring for her began to affect her son's behaviour. Although his diary makes no direct mention of this burden there is an interesting little incident that throws some light on the matter. Throughout early March King expressed concern at his inability to get on with his work. After a restless seven days he went to New York where he was tempted by a job offer from J.D. Rockefeller Jr and by the possibility of a closer relationship with the Carnegie family. On his return to Ottawa he once again resolved to throw off the bonds of mammon and rededicated himself to a life of sacrifice and the service of God. When this failed to stimulate a greater output, he spent two days rearranging his rooms – a process which involved shifting his mother from the best room or study into his bedroom so he could have the front room to work in alone.

Henceforth, it would only be possible 'for her to come & lie during the afternoons.' He convinced himself that 'she will be as well with this change' but admitted that it was not a completely unselfish act: 'I long for the sunshine to work in, and less confusion than at present exists.' Was it significant that the new arrangement was as close as possible to the situation before his mother came to Ottawa or, perhaps more significantly, closer to the arrangements that would prevail when she was no longer with him? His feelings recorded on 13 March are open to this interpretation: 'In my own heart I have felt strange sensations today. When the beds were out of my study, and mother in the other room, I felt almost as if I would break down. I have tried to analyze my feelings but find it difficult to know them aright.' Having arranged things so that he would see less of his mother, King felt guilty. 'I feel I am not enough with her, while she is still with me. I shall begin anew.' Yet the next day he noted, 'I have seen very little of mother today.' Nor does his resolution appear to have affected his concern with other pursuits. His visit to Newmarket could be explained in terms of duty to his constituency, but his plan to return to New York to follow up the contact with the Carnegie family is less easily justified. Nevertheless he consoled himself by asserting 'that mother is safe & recovering' and by such activities as giving 'mother a little run in the corridor of the Roxborough, before going to lunch.'[44]

Caring for the chronically ill is not a light task, and it is not difficult to understand that any healthy young man concerned with his political future and his obligations to his employers should find it burdensome. King's problem was that he would not admit to himself that such a response was natural. When he was by her side he was restless and unable to work; away from her he felt guilty. He was particularly concerned that he might be away from her at the last. He knew that the doctors had given her little chance of survival, he believed that his presence and loving care were keeping her alive, and yet he was driven to leave her often. Prolonged bouts of self-condemnation followed any relapses that occurred during these absences.

God has mercifully spared me an affliction the most terrible I could ever know and one I have secretly dreaded for many years – that when mother might be in a critical condition I might be away from her, and possibly selfishly indulging myself, when I should be at her side.

That I could leave her, to find pleasure with others while she is still spared surpasses my comprehension.[45]

This remorse was expressed in such exaggerated terms that one must be careful not to misunderstand what was involved. On 21 April 1917, after his mother had had another bad turn, King wrote: 'I fear greatly for the worst, and was in such mental agony because I had not kept watch faithfully.' He had gone to bed.

King had got himself into an insoluble situation. His unrealistic conception of the duties of a loving son so distorted his judgment that nothing less than a hermit's life would have met his standards. But such a life was beyond his capacity and the demands of his chosen career. Six days later, after an evening of mild, social activity, he noted: 'I have felt so restless, and worried over mother's illness this week ... It reacts on me when she is nervous and restless. I can say very little when I am with her, and anxious when I am away.'

The climax of King's relationship with his mother and the last crisis in the formative stage of his identity were reached later in the year. Despite his words to the contrary, King had not given up all thought of a political career in 1914. He had made no real attempt to renounce the North York nomination and took positive steps to ensure that the contract with the foundation left him free to participate in Canadian politics. The election for which King had been waiting since 1911 finally took place in December 1917. He was still grappling with the personal responsibilities ensuing from his father's death, and on the professional side he was trying to complete a report for the Rockefeller Foundation. His mother's health could have been a valid reason for postponing a campaign, and the circumstances of the election were hardly propitious for a man who had been out of the country for most of the war years. But self-interest and the imminence of Laurier's retirement made his contesting the election essential. The North York riding was still open to him but he continued to vacillate until Laurier told him he must run, thus removing the burden of responsibility.

The problem of his mother, however, remained. To leave her to professional care would suggest that his personal devotion was not essential and would undermine his belief that only his great love for her and hers for him were keeping Isabel King alive. The only acceptable solution was to turn to the family for help, which meant Jennie. It was characteristic of the loyal devotion that all the family gave to Willie that she should attempt to come to his aid. It was equally characteristic that King seemed to have little idea of what sacrifice his demands involved. His narrow focus saw only two things: Sir Wilfrid had said he must run, and his mother needed the family at her side. Although Jennie had her husband, Harry, and children to care for, a house to run, and the responsibility for two young girls who lived in, King did not hesitate to ask her to spend six weeks in Ottawa with Isabel King while he campaigned.

Jennie tried to explain to him her difficulty in meeting the conflicting demands of two families, and she sought to reach some compromise. A letter from her reveals the extent to which she had been called upon to share the earlier burden of John King's death, a fact not revealed in King's own record of the event:

Harry and I have tried to think out some solution of the problem. Of course six weeks is utterly out of the question ... & I hardly think you really expect it ... two weeks is the longest I could possibly go for. Harry says for you to select the time if this would be any help to you, & he will take his holidays then and look after the children. I am sorry to have him do this as you remember how his holidays were spent last year, helping at Avenue Rd when father died & then taking care of the children while I was in Toronto ... I quite appreciate the position you are in & both Harry and I want to do anything in our power to help, but I have a duty here, equally imperative.[46]

There was little sign of understanding in her brother's diary entry for 27 October 1917. 'A letter from Jennie today telling us she could not come for more than two weeks, took the heart out of me for the moment. It seemed to make impossible my leaving mother and entering the campaign. Certainly the odds are terribly against me.'

It was not in King's nature to feel real concern for others or to make any attempt to accommodate the needs of others. He wrote again on 16 November to reiterate his request in terms of his needs and those of his mother, completely ignoring Jennie's difficulties.

I am really most anxious about mother ... I am so worried that I am letting my campaign go and starting off to Ottawa tonight to be with her over Saturday, and posssibly Sunday. I know that it is only because she is left alone with no one near her to help to keep up her courage that she is falling back again. I would rather a thousand times lose the election than lose her. You can perhaps help me to save both if you can see your way at all to get down soon. Please believe that I would not ask you unless I knew from the Doctor, as well as from my own knowledge, how very critical every day at the present time is.

The next day Jennie agreed to assume the burden – 'send word when absolutely necessary for me to be in Ottawa ... I will have to take baby and perhaps John and Jean ... I will shut the house.' Just how little her response was appreciated was soon evident. Once Jennie was installed in Ottawa, King needed to feel anxious about neglecting his duty no longer. Even a telegram from Jennie, saying 'mother wants you. Condition serious,' provoked no immediate response other than the statement that the day train was impossible. King was not prepared, when confronted with the actual choice, to put his mother's health before the election campaign. He phoned Ottawa and was reassured by the servant. He readily accepted the statement that his mother would live through the night since it meant he need not change his arrangements.

Back in Ottawa the next day he seemed prepared to accept that her death was imminent and began to prepare funeral arrangements. His concern did not prevent him from lunching at the Rideau Club and later taking supper with his brother-in-law at the golf club. By the time he was due to return to the riding he had dismissed from his mind the possibility of her death: 'I asked her if she would be all right while I was away & she said "Yes not to be anxious."'[47] With these words his mother had relieved him of the responsibility of deciding whether to go or stay, and he could confidently write from the constituency on 3 December of 'looking forward with all my heart to the time when we will be together.' Once again, for the last and fateful moment, intention diverged from action and he wrote again to say: 'It will probably be necessary for me to stay here longer than Monday [the election day] over Tuesday anyway & possibly Wednesday of next week. If Jennie could stay over until Wednesday night I would be grateful.'[48] The consequences of the delay were traumatic: his mother died while he lingered to deal with post-electoral pleasantries.

The last week of 1917 thus became a time of critical self-examination. The election, apparently providentially held on his birthday, had resulted not only in personal defeat but also in his being away from his mother's bedside at the time of her death. The guilt feelings associated with her death were particularly strong as a consequence. In February 1917, when his mother's physician had giving up hope of saving her, King had dismissed the doctor, taking upon himself the role of expert and physician. In October he had declared that even the probable loss of the Liberal leadership would not affect his resolve to be 'at mother's side, come what may, until the very end.'[49] But he left her and she died. Could he ignore the possible cause and effect relationship in this event without denying the earlier belief that he had kept her alive? King found it necessary to maintain an illusion of unbroken care when he described his behaviour to Violet Markham on 2 January 1918. '[My] vigil at my mother's side was much like your own ... only that your watch lasted for two years and mine for only one ... during that time, with the exception of the period occupied by the campaign in North York, I never left her except to pay one or two necessary and very hurried visits to New York. I was not with her at the end. This will ever be a sadness to me.'

The ambiguities and complexities of King's relationship with his mother did not end with her death. The relationship had been essentially regressive in its oedipal nature and in King's great reliance on the mother image while having an insecure attachment to her. King's already pronounced difficulty in establishing intimate relations became completely entrenched. His plans for marriage, revived immediately after his mother's death, came to nothing. Over the years King's memory transformed the idealized Isabel King into a fantasy of truth, goodness, purity, and beauty. His yearning for the love object could be met only by becoming himself the substitute love object. Adolescent narcissism remained a strong thread in King's adult character; he continued to devote to himself the attention and loving care which he longed to have another bestow on him and which he believed he had bestowed on his loved ones.

Neurotic defences: Shoring up the foundations

4 The neurotic self

Before examining the impact of King's personality on his political life, the basic features of the personality as it existed on the eve of his return to public life must be established. In particular we note the increased prominence of patterns of behaviour that can be identified as defence mechanisms. These patterns became key elements in his political behaviour and help to explain such apparently bizarre phenomena as King's dependence on spiritualism and his financial dealings with John D. Rockefeller Jr.

INTERNALIZING THE FANTASIES

The idea of the family as a refuge had been a key element of the King myth and, despite the extended struggle for autonomy, it remained a dominant feature of the neurotic and later the politicized self. The death of Isabel King marked the end of the King family as a real unit. For a short time Willie attempted to play a paternal role with his brother and sister and maintain the illusion of a common purpose in their lives. In reality he was unable to show any real concern for their problems and lacked any true understanding of their situation. Unmarried himself, King was unable to grasp the difference that marriage had made to his siblings. He unrealistically expected Max and Jennie to maintain a group cohesiveness which excluded their spouses and gave prime consideration to his needs. Despite his dependence it was as a wise, all powerful, substitute parent that King sought to advise Max and Jennie, a role that increased the misunderstandings and resentment on both sides.

After Max's death on 18 March 1922 King's contacts with his remaining relatives became highly stylized. The idea of loving family ties could be sustained only as long as he had little contact with them. Two incidents from the mid-thirties show how his responses were repeated in the third generation in a way that echoed his earlier inability to give of his time or money. When Jennie's son Arthur suggested a Christmas visit, King's response was less than enthusiastic:

I told Arthur I did not think I could arrange to have him as it was so near the time prlt. wd. be assembing & that I had to cover much on Xmas Day myself. I spoke of the need for rest & quiet, when these moments came. I just felt I must have him & the others know that my life does not permit of my giving up time to looking after young people during the holidays. I said I would have to choose the time to have them down & let them know ... It seemed selfish, but before my conscience I know what I can & cannot do ... I shall keep an eye out for what I can do in other ways & feel the last (best) thing is to hold as much in reserve as possible – causing the boys to feel they must make their own way.[1]

He was similarly unwilling to assist Max's sons in any open-handed way. The tone of his thoughts in 1936 was strongly reminiscent of the early part of the century: the time 'was coming to help to educate Lyon & do more for the others in that way,' but it never arrived. King held back 'against the day of need – to teach the value of money.' When Lyon suffered a breakdown in health, his uncle was full of remorse, castigating himself for spending so much 'on old furniture – when there was a young life needing help.'[2]

King did not find it difficult to justify his actions, however, even when confronted with the consequences of his procrastination. He had meant 'to send him [Lyon] $100 as a gift on graduation' but had delayed so as to be able to write by hand. He assured himself, 'it is not lack of intention or desire, but simply the pressure from day to day ... [of] public duties crowd[ing] out all personal "family" obligations.' He resolved to do better in future in recognition of the fact that 'if I had taken steps in time Lyon might have been spared the collapse,' but as in earlier circumstances his intentions were stronger than his capacity to act.[3]

His lack of closeness with his family had made it imperative that he establish a family of his own if he was to retain a grip on reality, but he was unsuccessful. His endeavour to find a life partner while at the same time exercising complete control over profane thoughts set up considerable conflict. Nervous exhaustion drove King to seek a complete physical check up in the course of which he asked for medical advice about his sexual problems: 'I outlined the conflict in my thought between spiritual aspirations and material struggle & conflicts, the fight within myself. This he explained was unnecessary and wrong that all the phenomena I had described to him were natural enough, the circumstances mentioned being considered, that what was health, I was mistaking for an evil passion.'[4] Dr Baker told King that he 'overexaggerated [the] significance of perfectly natural phenomena, that there was danger in doing so by a healthy man,' and he advised him to reconcile 'in thought, any conflict between the animal and spiritual nature.'[5] (This was not a temporary phenomenon; King was still consulting his physician about the problem of the 'forces of the night' as late as 15 September 1939.) He found it difficult to take the doctor's advice because of the dysfunctional relationship with his mother. Although it may not be possible to make a categorical statement about King's sexual activity on the evidence available, the most satisfactory conclusion is that King, throughout his life, was psychologically a virgin, unable to reconcile himself to his masculinity or to establish satisfactory intimate relationships with individuals of either sex. This sexual ambiguity influenced his personal and political style. King's established behaviour pattern was closely akin to the nurturant female role, as his passivity and his desire to serve the poor and the needy demonstrate. But when he was confronted with any acute physical or emotional crisis, a more competitive masculine style manifested itself until the crisis was dealt with; he then returned to the established pattern. The female style closely resembled that of the ideal mother, one who supports, protects, and heals, providing safety, security, and strength. The crisis style, modelled more on the real mother, was intrusively aggressive, dominated by concern for self, and demanding support from others rather than providing it.

Isabel King's death produced no real change in behaviour. King continued to think about love and marriage but in terms which suggested that the whole matter was something outside his control:

I feel so lonely that no one knows what it means to hear a little music and to enjoy the society of a young girl who has charm and goodness. Why can I not have a home of my own! My heart yearns for it more than ought else on earth now. God grant it may come soon.

If I had a wife to share what there may be of service, or happiness or disappointment in the whole procedure. It is essentially a venture of faith, a belief that it will be the right thing in the end.[6]

Between these two entries King had begun another romantic venture which was in effect a repeat of the earlier incidents. This time the lady was much more suited to an ambitious man since she was a friend of the Rockefellers.

The diary entry for 21 February 1918 covers familiar ground:

> I see in her all that I most wish to find in a woman – more than I believed I should ever find in anyone – though God knows how I have sought and prayed and patiently waited that some day a woman whose nature was akin to dear mother's might come into my life, some one to whom religion was the greatest of all realities ... some one whose nature could strike upon the depth of my own ... Someone who could part the gold from the dross in my being and make me the noble man that I know I am capable of being with someone who understands and inspires.

This time he was not being impetuous; he had known the lady for two years before taking the first steps towards a closer friendship and was prepared to wait ten years to win her. He drew the same parallels between her life and his own, between their ideals and shared experience, that he had drawn in earlier incidents. Now, however, he could assure himself, without fear of contradiction, that she was 'what father & mother would have wished for most.' In fact he could go one step further; he decided that they not only approved but that the lady in question had actually been sent to him by his mother.[7]

Despite this sign that she was indeed the one for him, King showed the same anxiety reactions already noted. He wondered whether she would write, whether he was worthy of her, and whether in fact it was God's will. He sought to quiet these worries by asserting that 'she truly is the woman I have prayed God to send into my life, if I win her, she will be in my belief the answer to my own and to my mother's prayer.' Thus, the lady could prove, by refusing him, that she was not in fact the intended one. The diary entries for March 1918 are a replica of those of twenty years earlier though the later entries are less emotional. Mr Rockefeller tried to persuade King that the lady had no thought of marriage, suggesting that King was apt to 'interpret her actions in accordance with [his] ... own wishes and feelings.' The advice fell on deaf ears. King only accepted advice that confirmed his perceptions. Fantasy or not, the correspondence and the dreaming of a successful outcome intensified the problem of control: 'It is a frightful thing to be plagued with a continuous fight against the passions of one's own nature. Some times I feel as if there could never be peace through subjugation. It is this unnatural way of living alone. It makes every endeavour at high resolve almost fruitless.'[8]

He was particularly concerned with the issue at this time because he had come to believe that his inability to subjugate his masculinity was keeping him from his loved ones beyond the veil. His difficulty increased because of this need to be close to his mother after death. At Mt Pleasant Cemetery he prayed that 'he might overcome his weaknesses and longed to stay by the graves of those [he] ... loved.' He mourned in a strongly dysfunctional manner: 'I could have lain down there with a will to rest for ever at dear mother's side, but I prayed for the will to do & to be. I sang over the little songs "Backward turn backward" & "What are the wild waves saying" – which as a boy I used to hear mother sing ... Oh that I had someone to love with whom all that is most precious & sacred in my nature could be shared.'[9] The tale the wild waves were telling was of mother love! It was not possible for King to make this linkage for himself. He continued to worry over the difficulty he faced in reaching this most desired goal, a wife and family of his own. 'The problem of marriage perplexes me constantly. Why can I not solve this problem aright. The solution I suppose lies beyond me, and yet in some way I must seek and find. One seems so helpless against great contending forces.'[10]

There was a practical as well as a personal concern behind his worry for he felt sure that 'to go into politics without marrying would be folly.'[11] He even went so far as to run over in his mind the list of current possibilities but clearly he lacked the capacity to take the necessary initiative. 'I shall learn soon which one I love – if it is to be one of the three. Then perhaps the solution of this problem will be made as life itself thereafter will be made a thing of joy and service in which two – and no longer one –together.'[12] It was a problem he never solved, and it was important because it sapped his energy, cut him off from the common experience of the people he sought to serve, and led to his becoming increasingly neurotic in his old age.

In the light of King's failure to marry despite his frequently expressed desire for a home and family of his own, it can be suggested that in practice he took his mother's advice more literally than she intended when she said: 'I would be the last to tell you to live the lonely life of an old bachelor. I would tell you to consider before you step into matrimony.'[13] It is possible therefore that we should consider the foregoing not as a search for a wife but for a mother substitute, a supportive other resembling the ideal rather than the real Isabel King. This he finally achieved in his friendship with Mrs Joan Patteson of Ottawa.

Joan Patteson was more than a mother substitute in King's life. She embodied most of the virtues which had marked earlier friendships but had less of their disadvantages. The key dimension of the friendship was that it was not demanding on King. It committed him to nothing in the way of personal obligation. If he had married, King would have had to support his wife, but Godfroy Patteson supported Joan and provided for her personal needs. A wife of his own would make demands on King's time and energy and might expect to be consulted, considered, or entertained; with Joan Patteson these demands were someone else's concern. King was particularly sensitive of any intrusion into his life space, particularly physically. He disliked the disorganization and selflessness that visitors to his home necessitated. But Joan Patteson had a home of her own, both in Ottawa and later in Kingsmere. Close and frequent contact with her therefore involved no personal costs in terms of comfort, and Joan Patteson revealed an awareness of these facts in her behaviour.

A compulsive talker, King rated highly the capacity to be a good or at least a willing listener. Joan Patteson was in this respect much more satisfactory than Isabel King had been, taking an active part in discussions, reading the books that King recommended, and actively concerning herself with his interests, always in a non-competitive way. This non-competitiveness was an important element in the success of the relationship. The other friendships discussed above had proved only partially successful in terms of image-maintenance. Violet Markham's active involvement in British politics and John D. Rockefeller Jr's extensive financial responsibilities forced them occasionally to take stands critical of King's views or responses. King resented these occasions.

Only in Joan Patteson's care and admiration could King find a mirror that reflected the true self of his self-image. She had no independent status, either in her own right or through her husband's position. Any prestige or influence that she had was a reflection of King's friendship and dependent on his continued support. There was no element of challenge in this relationship and therefore no drive in King to prove his superior worth and his dominant role. The absence of any note of rivalry or repressed animosity in the friendship would suggest, however, that the mother substitute dimension should not be overrated.

A sympathetic ear was not enough to ensure the continuity of King's regard. King demanded of all his associations practical care. Other friends had partially contributed to the satisfying of this need – Harper in terms of help in the Department of Labour, Miss Markham in financial terms, and Rockefeller in job opportunities – but they were of limited duration. From Joan Patteson he demanded and got daily care and support in the burdens that he had to bear. Such support ranged from help in domestic and social responsibility to aid in preparing speeches for important public occasions. It was in doing things for him that individuals could most clearly show themselves worthy of his trust and friendship.

These qualities were the bricks on which the friendship was built; their shared interest in the 'life beyond the veil' and their joint participation in experiments in the occult sciences formed the cement that kept the relationship standing firmly. Because of the intimacy and the introspection involved in their searching, the friendship was put under considerable strain. In sharing the deeper longings of his soul King was reaching out for a communion with another that he had been unable to effect in intimate personal relationships. If talk was a substitute for sexual activity, then intense personal talks and associated activities must bear overtones of this original tension. However, too much attention should not be focused on this dimension. The factors that had prevented King from entering into the matrimonial state he so fervently desired also served to prevent any overt expression of this tension. Although he did talk about 'storms of passion' in regard to the relationship, it is most likely that the expression referred to an intense emotional experience more closely akin to spiritual ecstasy than to any physical interaction.

IN THE STEPS OF THE MASTER

The second decade of the twentieth century, with its dramatic changes in fortune, had undermined King's sense of security and reinforced his feeling of powerlessness. The family offered neither refuge nor confirmation, and his close friends had other interests and responsibilities which prevented their devoting themselves wholeheartedly to his cause. The only satisfying solution to the problem lay in a closer and meaningful relationship with the all-powerful creator of the universe. Harnessed to God's service and confident that the Lord had a purpose for him in this life, King could shoulder the burdens of political office much more readily.

The importance of religion to King, and to an understanding of his political career, must be emphasized. Without comprehension of the nature of his beliefs it is difficult to grasp the essence of his motives and actions. Brought up in a conventional Presbyterian way, King had soon developed an evangelical fervour. In keeping with the evangelical tone of his beliefs was the consciousness of his own unworthiness and the need for God's grace. King was not always satisfied that he had fulfilled his desire to be a good Christian, but he never waivered from his commitment, and there is no reason to assume that he was anything but sincere in his Christianity.

One of the earliest letters kept by King was from a former Berlin clergyman who wrote: 'I am very interested in you ... and if I am spared I shall watch your course with deep interest. I am particularly anxious that you should be a good man ... that you will do right always no matter what other boys or young men may do. What a great comfort it would be to me to know that you are a true Christian.'[14] It is interesting to note an echo of this letter in the diary entry for 31 December 1925 in which King declared 'above all else I want to be a good man.' Neatby has suggested that 'Mackenzie King never outgrew this Sunday School version of Christianity.'[15] In this respect it is important to consider Allport's observation: 'Evidence shows that the very subjects who accept religion unreflectively and uncritically tend to react in an equally unreflective way to their parents, to political issues, to social institutions. Their sentiments seem uniformly immature. They are found usually to have repressed conflicts.'[16] Evidence of King's unreflective attitude to his parents occurs throughout his diary. Taken together with his immature religious perspective, it might explain the rather simplistic ideas that King held on industrial and international affairs and his attitude to his party and the British connection. To accept his political beliefs as immature sentiments is to establish a more appropriate framework for considering his basic political stance.

Equally prominent in early years, but of less import in subsequent development, was the desire King expressed to forsake material things in a closer association with the life of service. 'My thoughts have been running in a higher sphere,' he wrote. 'I have thought more of "right & good." I have thought of entering the ministry.' This inclination was strengthened by a series of revelations through random Bible selections: 'Last night I had a sort of revelation for 3 nights in succession I have opened my bible & read Chapters in which I found some verse which spoke of my going into the ministry.' The revelations continued for seven successive nights, a sure sign of the hand of God at work. Or was it? Two months later King asked: 'What course am I to take in Life. I have decided I might say on the Ministry and yet I have a very great desire to go into politics ... I will leave it to my maker. He has guided me in the past and will open up the way for me in the future.'[17] Although King was to continue to express this desire right up to the thirties, family pressure and psychological needs were to ensure that 'guidance' would lead him away from the Ministry.

King's commitment to a Christian life is the frame on which his self-image and his world view were woven. It also became an important dimension of his defences against his neurotic anxieties and the tensions and stresses of public life. Isabel and John King had left their son in no doubt about the threatening nature of the outside world. At the same time they had underlined consistently the inability of the earthly father – John King – to provide protection. The consequent anxiety could be placated by belief in an omnipotent God who controlled all things and could guide and protect the faithful. Through signs and portents this all-knowing God can also confirm an individual's trustworthiness and remove doubts about the worthiness of actions and responses.[a] If God could favour him over others, could try him and not find him wanting, then he was undeniably worthy. In periods of self-doubt, signs of God's love, God's intentions in his life, God's helping hand were essential. Without them his mistrust of others might recoil on himself.

Public service was for King a vocation. He went into politics in the same spirit and with the same sense of mission that he had sought to go into the church. But because he believed that the path God desired him to follow was the path of public service, he could only be sure that he was correctly interpreting God's purpose by succeeding in the public sphere. He felt that failure and suffering were God's way of testing his mettle: 'This has [been] sent to help to lead me closer to Him, to increase my faith in Him, to make me like I see the Christ in the painting over mother's bed to be "a strong son of God." This is my wish

---

[a] During the adolescent period King continually sought verification of his inner worth through recognition of his highest aims and motives. He was driven to seek publicly acknowledged success as a measure of this worthiness. No matter how often he declared his scorn for the tawdry symbols of status, they had become an essential element of his self-verification though they left him feeling dissatisfied. He had to reconcile his need for recognition with his belief in his own trustworthiness. Self-doubts had to be rationalized in a manner acceptable to his self-image. Thus he expressed fear of being inadequately prepared for the task, fear that he was not making the best use of his time, and fear that he was unworthy of the high place he had been chosen to fulfil, but he could never consciously admit that he feared his own trustworthiness. His belief in an all-powerful God who had a purpose in his life provided a mechanism for quieting doubts and establishing a higher regard for his own trustworthiness than for that of others.

my aim, in this world ... This is my mission. To reveal the Christ in public life and service.'[18] Conversely, success could only be a sign that he was truly on God's path and fulfilling God's will. What might appear to others to be ambition and egotism (for example, clinging to office at any cost) was to King only confirmation of submission to the will of God.

The only acceptable agent for interpreting God's will was King himself. His frequent self-examinations were directed towards establishing the degree to which he had kept to his ideal. As part of this process he could make emotional criticisms of his own behaviour: 'careless indifference to so much in life'; 'I seem to have let go many of the ideals which I had'; 'I have not been strong enough to hold out against the tide around me.'[19] But it was a different matter if someone else reflected adversely on his character, especially during periods when his work identity was threatened. Miss Markham approached the task of offering a gentle warning with the greatest delicacy despite King's frequent assurances that he valued her opinion above all others. Not even the most intimate friend could voice doubts about his position without negative reaction. After declaring that the 'path of a public man is beset with trials and temptation,' Miss Markham continued: 'I would ... ask you to guard against two tendencies which might if they develop destroy something of your wholeness as a man. Don't become too partisan, seeing your fellow men exclusively in terms of Liberalism & Conservatism ... Still more would I urge you to guard against the assumption that spiritual truth is with your own beliefs & your own beliefs alone.'[20] Gentle or not, it was criticism that King was not prepared to accept. Those who were not for him were against him, and those who were for him were for him in everything; there was no room for half measures. To deny these accusations would involve considering the possibility that they might be true, but they could not be ignored for the statement was too direct. King's response was to present Miss Markham with an alternative picture of himself, which supported the righteousness of his position, and allow her to retract the criticism.

A similar pattern of reaction marked the termination of King's association with the Rockefeller Foundation. When doubt was raised as to whether he had fulfilled the terms of his service with the foundation, King responded with a bevy of self-praise:

In the matter of *service* I feel sure I have done much more for the Rockefellers & the Foundation than they have done for me. When one recalls what the

Colorado situation was, what the attitude of the public toward Mr. R. Jr. was when I took hold, and the change there has come about in both, I can say honestly, due to what influence I have exerted on Mr. R. Jr. & work actually done there, there is no sum of money that could cover the evil that may have been saved and the good that may have been achieved as a consequence.[21]

Even Rockefeller had to be repudiated when he in his turn failed to give King the absolute assurance of support and confirmation that he sought. 'He has been wonderfully considerate, but has revealed selfishness in his motive ... How can we deceive ourselves! I am not in the position to help to let him see perhaps the error of his ways, and that there are men in the world whom the Rockefeller millions cannot command.'[22]

Because of his close association of religion with the sense of trust, religious beliefs cannot be dismissed as incidential to an understanding of King's behaviour. Because of the fundamental importance of his religious outlook to his politics, it must be asserted that King could not have been as great a compromiser as he is often alleged to have been. Although his faith in God's guidance and God's purpose enabled him to overcome any uncertainty and diffidence which problems of trust might engender, it also restricted the degree to which he could compromise, particularly when matters of principle were involved. His faith would not allow conscious compromise. As a servant of God, he had to bring light into darkness, to substitute harmony for dissension. This required that he strive to establish a consensus rather than give way on principle by making concessions. Conciliation involved bringing all parties to the truth. His stance restricted his conciliatory moves to strict and narrow limits. While others must be prepared to give a little to gain a little, he could only give time – time to reconsider, to see the wisdom of his position, to follow the path of his choice.

King's religious development exhibited three strands, social, practical, and spiritual, and each contributed to his subsequent identity and behaviour. His church going, his commitment to Christian idealism, his drive to establish a personal conceptualization of his faith all constituted important elements in King's attempt to avoid the worldliness and opportunism underlying his family's approach to life. A number of characteristics of this simplified Christianity dominated King's world view. One strongly developed feature was an apparently literal acceptance of the Biblical relationship of father and son and the Biblical injunction to follow the way of the cross. Throughout his correspondence with Miss Markham and in the diary, one of the most consistent themes is the sacredness of the passiontide: the call for sacrifice, even martyrdom, which being a true Christian involves. On 5 November 1908 he had told Violet Markham: 'The way of the cross is a hard way, but it is the path of progress and of life, sacrifice is the law of growth, immortality is born of travail and of pain ... its truth and reality is borne in upon our deepest consciousness, as we share the companionship of that Life which trod the path that we are called upon to share at times.'

King was not unaware of his tendency to fall by the wayside in attempting to practise these ideals, but he had no difficulty in rationalizing these failures. While he acknowledged that the path was not without its thorns, when it came to bearing the 'pricks' he was constantly forced to confess his lapses: 'You are quite right. There has not been with me the entire submission of will, the consecration of life without reserve to the purpose and service of God which there should have been ... I have learned with the weariness of battle how fraught with meaning and understanding of human life are the words. "The Spirit is willing, but the flesh is weak!"' Just how weak can be seen in the type of issue which was worrying him – 'making up laundry lists, rigging up clothes presses etc.'[23]

Despite an intellectual approach to religion, King's basic outlook is more dominated by faith rather than by reason: 'It is taking all of life on Faith but some how or other that is the only way I can take life and be happy, and that is one of the ways I become more conscious of the presence of God in the world, and of his purpose in my life. Your faith has helped me greatly ... Perhaps that is what God wishes me to reveal to others.' Another theme repeated in his correspondence is the interplay of light and darkness and the use God makes of darkness to reveal Himself. This essentially Christian theme allowed King to see both success and failure as the presence of God and as signs of God's special purpose in his life. Although King rejected the Calvinist doctrine of predestination intellectually, he accepted its implications to the extent of seeing God choose people to work for His purpose: 'There are some events in life which give us a faith in a personal God who has an individual purpose in our lives and His own chosen instruments for the working out of his will, and manifesting His loving tenderness towards us in a very special way.'[24] This aspect, the sense of being chosen, of being an instrument rather than an individual with freedom of choice, could be a source of great security. '[It] seems to say to me that if I will but hold to what I know is God's purpose in my life, He will send His angels to minister to me.'[25] Thus, those who help King became agents of God's will and those who oppose him are the minions of the devil.

Two other important issues involved in the religious outlook are directly relevant to King's political behaviour. One concerns the question of whether his professed dedication to Christian service and religious zeal was mere bolstering of low self-esteem or even hypocrisy. The second relates to the question of whether his religious expression came dangerously close in later years to neurotic blasphemy. In the latter connection some writers have drawn attention to King's equating his burdens to those of Christ.[26] Like many Christians of his time King was in the habit of verbalizing his feelings and describing his actions in terms of Biblical analogies and identification with the great Biblical figures; Moses, St Paul, and Christ were regularly referred to in this way. Such practices had roots in custom and Christian doctrine. In terms of King's strong tendency to internalize the things he valued, however, there was always the danger that such identification would come to mean more than a mere figure of speech. King had already internalized many of the features of the original protecting figure – his mother. It is equally feasible that he would in times of great stress internalize features of the religious figures important to his faith.

In regard to the question of hypocrisy, King was confronted with what theologian Pierre Teilhard de Chardin has identified as a basic Christian problem – the sanctification of action. He asked: 'How can the man who believes in heaven and the Cross continue to believe seriously in the value of worldly occupations? ... Perfection consists in detachment; the world around us is vanity and ashes ... How can he reconcile them with the other counsel that he must be an example unto the Gentiles in devotion to duty, in energy, and even in leadership in all the spheres opened up by man's activity?' Teilhard suggested that when men faced this apparent contradiction, 'a tension between ... God and the world,' they usually follow one of three possible courses:

Either the Christian will repress his taste for the tangible and force himself to confine himself to purely religious objects ... or else, harassed by that inward conflict which hampers him, he will ... decide to lead what seems to him a complete and human life; or else ... he will give up any attempt to make sense of his situation; he will never belong wholly to God, nor ever wholly to things; incomplete in his own eyes, and insincere in the eyes of his fellows he will gradually acquiesce in a double life.[27]

It is clear that King found himself in the latter category. The word 'found' is used deliberately, for it is evident that there was no matter of conscious choice involved. His 'double life' interlocked closely with two levels of his identity – the conscious desire to be wholly a man of God and the unconscious drive for earthly success and material achievements, both combined in the concept of service to his fellow man and to the will of God. King was not unaware that there was a problem to be reconciled, but he apparently could not accept the fact that he had not solved it. This was revealed by his response to Violet Markham, 28 August 1912:

With fatigue and a sense of great loneliness I have sometimes felt that the subtle and constant beleaguing [sic] of the citadel of one's being which public life exposes one to, makes its prizes and its opportunities of service to be gained at too great hazards, in hours such as these my thoughts have turned to the cloister of the church or the college, where the soul is aided by inspirational forces not wounded by the rough and rude hand of the world, but they have seldom dwelt long on this prospect without a sense of shame coming over me ... What we have withstood rather than what we have escaped must be ever the test of noble souls.

Although it is not commonly accepted by his critics, it is fair to say that King's actions have to be interpreted in the same tenor. Our modern secular society appears to accept and appreciate religious motivation only when it leads to failure or when the politicized Christian forsakes the teachings of the church to concentrate on practical social reform. It is more confused and less charitable in its judgments of politicized Christians who achieve worldly success.

King's rationalizations were not mere self-deception; his process of justification was consistent with standard theological directives, as was his dedication to the Christian duty to fight evil. This was the burden that King was anxious to assume. The difficulty for the individual lies in identifying evil and in finding the voice of God. Where the individual is not governed in this respect by an authoritarian system, he is always in danger of confusing God's will with his own psychic needs. When the doctrines of the person's church favour such individual wrestling with the issue, and the belief is held that God chooses men for his purpose, calls them to his service with messages, and answers their prayers in signs and feelings, this danger becomes particularly acute.

The search for God's purpose in his life and the tenets of his religious belief were further joined in that aspect of King's world view that can be identified as the concept of the enemy. As a Christian King was aware that man had been conceived in sin and that temptation and error were his constant companions. In his concern with his own minor shortcomings he frequently referred to this problem: 'What you have said on one or two occasions of the roots of good and evil being so closely intertwined has been a helpful discovery in someways to me ... there is latent somewhere the springs of all human action and whether they be good or evil will be determined by the intention and the will.'[28]

In King's attempts to deal with the problem, one can see elements of distorted perception and the full gamut of ego defence mechanisms at work. It is not unusual for individuals to want to see themselves in a favourable light, but in King's case the tendency was so exaggerated that he found it difficult to accept the existence of both good and bad in himself. As a counterpart of the perfect 'idealized' self, King had developed the idea of the enemy as an object onto which aggressive feelings and negative features of the self could be displaced. In exploring the dimensions of the enemy, one finds further evidence of those aspects of selective perception which Milton Rokeach has characterized as closed-mindedness. Undoubtedly King viewed the world as a threatening place; in 1916 he had written 'how sinister & cruel the world is to those who would befriend it.' He also tended to make absolute judgments about the motives of those who opposed him. His feelings were generally hostile towards those who would not accept the idealized self as real and those who refused to give him active support. Thus, King saw the absence of whole-hearted enthusiasm as motivated by hostility towards him.[b]

Opposing the enemy were the forces of good as personified in the heroes of King's romantic idealism. Because service to the working man was an important element of King's work identity, men who made their mark in the field of Christian service were particularly favoured by him, for example, the young English social reformer, Arnold Toynbee. The most politically significant example of this phenomenon, the identifying of Tory parties in Canada and England and British imperialists with the forces of evil and King's Liberal party with

---

[b] The process whereby the world was divided between the forces of good and evil dominated King's approach to labour relations. Although King generally took a pro-labour and anti-business stance, his outlook was affected by his need to justify his own limited response in terms of the enemy. At Rossland, B.C., he had been forced to view the union leaders in this way because they had refused to cooperate with him and had denied the well-intended element of his approach. He showed a similar reaction when confronted with union criticism while working with the Rockefeller Foundation and with the antagonism of the chairman of the U.S. Senate commission investigating the industrial unrest in Colorado.

the forces of good, will be considered below. The phenomenon represents a natural integration of King's religious beliefs with his political action. His defence mechanism was to become a useful political tool.

THE CULT OF MONEY

The most prominent and least recognized of King's neurotic defences was his handling of his personal finances. His insatiable need for affection was matched only by his acquisitiveness. One of the roots of King's attitude towards money can be found in Isabel King's need for financial security. King's recognition of the fact is reflected in his statement: 'I have known poverty at first hand because my mother had often gone to bed hungry in exile.'[29] Given an initial predisposition to fear financial insecurity, subsequent events could only deepen the reaction. Although it is not possible to reconstruct the family's exact financial circumstances during the period spent in Berlin, it would seem that they passed through stages of feast and famine at regular intervals – a process marked by the appearance of governesses or the disappearance of servants.

The financial worries became obvious once the family moved to Toronto and John King faced the additional problem of a university education for his sons. It was not long before extra expenses, such as those incurred during Max's illness in 1894, forced John King to mortgage the pictures and to struggle against a persistent state of indebtedness thereafter.[30] It is also clear from King's diary that his father discussed all these financial difficulties with him at least as early as 1895 and at frequent intervals after that. Not only did King have direct evidence of the consequences of imprudence before his eyes, he also received advice from his father on how to avoid a similar state. 'If I had to live my life over again,' his father wrote on 1 May 1898, 'I would commence to save at the very outset, lay up a store for the future.' Such advice was unnecessary. Two years before King had recorded his first savings – $1.15 in a Post Office account – and his resolve to 'save in every possible way for the future.'[31] He took to this task with enthusiasm: three months later he had $100 put by and the amount increased steadily for the rest of his life. The diary for 1896 also records the meticulous accounts that King had begun to keep of income and expenditures complete to the last cent.

The main characteristics of King's approach to finance were quite clearly drawn by the time he took up his career as a civil servant in Ottawa. He was prepared to turn his hand to any honest toil which would bring a reasonable reward. He worked his way through university by tutoring, lecturing, writing articles, and preparing government reports to supplement scholarships and fellowships, He cheerfully took working holidays since they enabled him to combine financial gain with enjoyment. Nor was he afraid to accept 'the perks' which would allow him to avoid spending. For example, he secured through his employment at the Toronto *Globe* a railway pass for his journey to the University of Chicago – just one of many occasions when some kind 'friend' was allowed to foot the bill. He seldom paid the asking price or missed an opportunity of bargaining for goods he bought. He demanded quality but preferred to pay basement prices and often got them. While at university he changed his boarding arrangements several times to save a few dollars. Nothing was too small for his close scrutiny. It was not mere miserliness; every cent spent was a cent that brought a direct return. He was always conscious of the fact that 'money matters had spoilt his father's life' and deprived his mother of the trouble-free life she deserved.[32]

At the same time he was not prepared to make financial gain the dominant motive of his life; he refused to countenance a wealthy marriage although this course was quite acceptable in the circle to which he aspired. Once money was acquired, however, King showed great reluctance to part with it except as a last resort. To be in a situation where he could save most of his earnings was a state fervently to be desired. 'If only all debts were cleared off we could be saving money and having seemingly no cares.'[33] If saving was a virtue then debt was abhorrent. In this regard one should note King's near panic when faced with the need to incur an obligation to pay for lodgings at Harvard. He was forced to ask one of his professors to go surety for the money, and rather than rejoice that the man had such confidence in him he reacted violently: 'if I can only get the oblig^n of Prof Ashley off I shall never undertake another ... I would give all I have never to have undertaken it.'[34]

The clear objective of all King's financial dealings was accumulation, and no activity which involved depleting these reserves could be contemplated without anxiety.[c] For King, savings were like energy: they could be transformed but not destroyed. Acquiring good quality

---

[c] Note King's response to approaches from his father for aid: 'I sent up $10 which is all I can spare.' Two weeks earlier he had paid off $20 worth of debts for his father but at the same time he spent large sums of money ($80, $75) on furniture for his library. In fact the money which passed between them was later revealed to be a loan covered by having the debt assigned to King. Diary, 19 Sept. 1901, 3 Sept. 1901.

possessions was one form of indirect savings that he practised throughout his life. But giving money without direct return was unbearable since it reduced capital. Consequently King could only give in a manner which allowed him to perceive no loss. Hence his need to accept assignment of debt from his father for sums as small as $20: assignments could be recorded among his assets. In this way King could list among his savings in September 1907, $1500 in mortgage-secured loans to his father.[35]

His personal predisposition to husband all available resources, rather than send good money after bad in looking after his father's debts, was reinforced by the advice he received from men of position in Ottawa. A political career had always been one of the possibilities that King felt the future might offer him. He had listened readily to Mulock and Laurier when they warned him of the dangers of a life in politics without personal resources. Thus he had to follow the advice he had given himself years before: 'the only way to do is to be clear of all obligations, keep deposits of savings, and then live so as to always save a little.' Further, because of the interlacing of the problem of debt with his attitude to his parents, the capacity to save acquired heavy overtones of virtue and self-esteem. With the arrogance of a relatively pampered, young man, King declared, 'I can not understand the incurring of debt where one has competence, it is inexplicable with true manhood.'[36]

A desire for the security which savings can bring is not unnatural; however, it has to be suggested that in King's case the response was excessive and must be considered as a positive clue to a neurotic solution of a personal crisis. Further, his attitude towards saving demonstrates an extended time dimension later carried over into policy issues. As early as 24 January 1901 he believed that 'a man shd. save while the opportunity is present, lay up not only for middle life, but old age & now is the time for me.' King's life was to have a monetary as well as a policy chart. Before he could even begin to spend his resources he must accumulate enough for all future needs to the end of his life. In this context 'enough' is an infinite objective. When it came to using these resources, the only possible answer to the question 'is it time?' was 'not yet.'

No single sum of money could fulfil the conditions of enough. Consequently, it is impossible to accept King's statements about his own financial condition at face value. On 20 September 1908, for example, he wrote to Miss Markham, 'I have resigned my position ... and with it all I have in way of ... means of livelihood.' She took the statement literally and hastily offered him money to carry him through. He accepted $200 a year even though his savings were at this time close to $10,000 and his resignation the prelude to his election to parliament. The difficulty was that he could only feel secure when he was able to meet all demands on his purse out of current income and add regularly to his nest-egg. Any break in this pattern caused acute anxiety and stress, out of keeping with his actual financial state.[d] No actual sum of money could ever allay his anxiety. It was his ability to withstand what he saw as the temptation of public life that confirmed him in his self-image and idealism. He did not seek to be wealthy but he needed to be financially secure. His idea of what was security, however, was influenced by the fact that in the circle in which he moved great wealth abounded, so that although he despised 'mere' wealth it was against great philanthropic riches that he measured his own resources.

Changes in King's actual financial stage produced no corresponding changes in his financial dealings or his attitude towards money. He continued to haggle over prices and to seek to avoid having to pay out money on anything that did not involve a visible increase in assets. He continued to make a minimal contribution to his family's need while denying himself nothing.[e]

The essence of democracy is responsible government, a process by which the politician is publicly accountable for his actions before parliament and to the people. The way in which an individual reacts to criticism is therefore an important part of his political style. It has already been suggested that there is a close correlation between King's attitude to personal finances and his attitude to policy making. It is important to examine his behaviour just prior to assuming office in great detail, for it explains much that has generally been considered inexplicable. During this period he had assumed new responsibilities as head of the family. These responsibilities involved money and a need to portray his own actions in this area in a way which produced no feelings of shame or guilt.

John King's death meant that King had to spend some time settling

[d] External factors also contributed to King's uneasiness at this time: his father's increased blindness, the poor health of his mother and sister Bella, and Max's illness. But they were not the main consideration. While crying poverty King did not even consider employment opportunities offering salaries of $3000 and $6500 a year.

[e] For example, in August and December 1915 he gave his mother $25 with great flourish and expected much thanks, but in October of the same year he paid $300 for a piece of sculpture for himself. Money advanced to his father and Max was secured by notes wherever possible. Even outright gifts were often financed from other sources – for example $500 to Max to buy a small car came from his sister Bella's estate; in another case King used money advanced by Miss Markham.

the estate, an activity that could only strengthen his resolve to avoid debt. It also provided an opportunity to exaggerate his own contribution to the family and his own virtue compared to his father's: 'As I go through father's papers it is sad to realise what a struggle he had with finances all his life and how he lived on the margin ... All these obligations I helped to clear off ... Then the practise of borrowing was stopped, the drain of interest payments ended, all creditors were satisfied, and current expenses met with assistance from time to time.'[37] In fact all King had done was make a series of 'bill-payer' loans to his father. Although this contribution should not be dismissed as negligible, it should not be inflated in such a manner as to give a distorted idea of King's actions. Such a process of inflation pervaded all King's statements on the matter, as it was later to characterize all his statements regarding Liberal party policy.

The detailed work on his father's estate was not pleasant. He spent several days in a deep scrutiny of his own financial affairs, and his reflections demonstrate his need for security and his reluctance to take risks.

I am trying to clear the slate absolutely of all anxieties ... to get finances out of precarious position where investments are doubtful ... I have interest on investment netting nearly 4,000 per year ... it shews how money if it can be kept invested will rapidly increase once past a certain point.

I feel it better to put much of money into Govt. annuities & securities, to protect me against the risks of industrial disaster & political misfortune, and to make sure of security for advanced years whatever obligations come in interval.

So far as I am able to do so I intend to change my stocks into Government Bonds and like securities, also to get annuities where possible. This saves the temptation to use the principal for special needs, ensures against bankruptcy & poverty in old age, and against the perils of a political life.

Was this reaction mere prudence or undue anxiety? The need to avoid any further obligation was a prominent element in his thinking. 'So far as I know I owe no man or woman living a letter or a cent,' he declared. But there was no real fear of debt with 'total savings of over 80,000.' King was not being unduly optimistic when he declared 'by living inside this income I should be able to continue to put enough aside to fix me pretty securely for the future.'[38]

What then was the reason for his anxiety? Was there cause for shame and guilt in his conduct? King had been able to win and keep his mother's affection by his success and the added financial rewards that it had brought. He had observed also the 'shame' and the 'contempt' which had followed his father's inability to provide. The need to disburse his resources to gain affection had to be balanced by the need to guard his reserves to avoid being an object of contempt. These two conflicting drives were highlighted in a misunderstanding which arose during this period over his mother's estate.

King was by 1918 a moderately wealthy man, yet he remained neurotically secretive about financial matters. Further, the obsessional defences that he had established to deal with his anxiety conflicted with the need to spend money to help the family and to deal with the family estate. The specific provisions of Isabel King's will introduced greater tensions; instead of providing for each of the surviving children, she left the estate to Willie, a situation that caused Jennie considerable concern. On 13 January 1918 she wrote to her brother: 'After reading the wills I didn't wonder that I had had to request repeatedly before I was allowed to see them. In the light of them much is clear which before I could never quite understand. I don't wonder dear little mother didn't want to die in Walkerton. Poor little soul! I thank God there is nothing on my conscience which can come between me and my loved ones.' In his reply four days later, Willie took refuge in righteous indignation. 'You have evidently chosen ... to deliberately misinterpret ... the whole of my endeavour of many years to safeguard and protect their interests and the name and interests of each member of the family. You seem, too, to be eager to reveal a distrust and to impute motives which are hardly worthy of you, and which I find it impossible to comprehend.' Jennie had questioned his motives and had therefore shown herself to be suspect. It was not just a simple incident; as King had told her on 7 January, 'unfaith in aught is want of faith in all.'

The matter was further complicated by the existence of a separate financial agreement between John King and Willie. This agreement affected the amount of the estate which passed from John King to his wife and her estate. King tried to explain the situation to Max in a letter (25 February 1918):

I have tried to make it clear that the agreement between father and mother and myself, and everything pertaining to it, is in no sense a part of father's estate. It is wholly independent of it. The estate is what is left by father's will to mother, and by mother in her will to me. This was clearly an estate in trust willed absolutely to me, it differs wholly from the agreement in that the agreement was based upon consideration, whereas the bequest in the will was a bequest which was made, as I have said all along, on the understanding to use mother's words, that 'Willie would do what was right.' My interpretation of doing what is right, as respects the Estate, is that you, Jennie and I, should share equally.

Such a provision left King virtually in control, with the power to do what he believed was just in the distribution of the assets of the estate. In such a role King was a stern and demanding guardian, jealous of his prerogatives and rights, capricious in responding to his siblings' approaches, but certain that he could be trusted to do the best for all. Jennie and Max were required to trust so that they might be trusted; their doubts, especially those raised by Jennie, were so threatening that King could not countenance them.

The fact that he needed to make such issues a matter of trust suggests that shame may have been a factor. It is common to find individuals ashamed of being poor. In King's case, however, the shame was related not to poverty but to wealth or, more specifically, to the discrepancy between the image of himself as without resources and the facts of his steadily increasing bank balance. If he was not poor, then the limited assistance he had given his parents and the assignment he had taken from his father constituted rank ingratitude. The existence of doubts and tensions was revealed in the controversy which arose when Jennie sought to break through the barrier of secrecy with which King had defended his self-image.

Finding herself confronted by a seemingly impenetrable wall of silence, Jennie enlisted the aid of Max and a voluminous three-sided correspondence ensued over a period of six months. The basic position was set out in a letter from Max to Willie on 25 February 1918.

Jennie tells me that, since Father's death, she has requested you on several occasions to show her Father's will because you have told her nothing voluntarily. She says that you always appeared to avoid meeting her request ... apparently non-compliance with her request created a suspicion in her mind that you had some good reason for not giving her the information. I must confess, such information, as what was paid out of the estate for the family monument, etc., would be a matter of very great interest.

The question raised by Jennie carried with it a reminder that Willie had not in fact carried the burden of the family misfortune alone, but the second point in this letter raised the possibility that King might even have profited from the arrangement: 'I had the impression ... that you were meeting the expenses of Mother's illness almost entirely out of your own pocket. Seeing that there was what might be regarded as a fund for that purpose don't you think it is only right that Jennie should be reimbursed for such travelling expenses as she incurred purely for mother's benefit?' Such a suggestion could not be countenanced or treated in a rational manner. If they could not be ignored, the people expressing the idea could be repudiated as unworthy. Isabel King had shown the kind of trust that Willie sought when she had left everything to him, confident that 'Willie would do what is right.' In practice, however, Willie tended to do what he thought was best and the others would share in the result. Thus he could happily spend money from the estate on the purchase of additional ground for the family plot at Mount Pleasant Cemetery and for the erection of a distinguished family monument because these things were important to him, ignoring the fact that the young couples with family responsibilities might have felt that these were luxuries they could not afford. A similar pattern of behaviour can be seen in King's political career when he refused to be bound by commitments and expected others, for instance the French Canadians, to accept that 'King would provide.'

It is obvious from his reluctance to provide Jennie with an accounting that Willie had begun to suspect that it would reveal that his outlay for his parents' expenses would not equal the money he had received from the policy on his father's life. He vacillated between denying that there would be any money left over and stating that, even if there were, he had never been motivated by any desire for gain or sought in any way to profit from the transaction. It was a fine line between seeking to profit and profiting, but it was one King was prepared to draw. The important thing was that his intentions were honourable.

It is probably significant that he was suddenly taken ill and had to go into hospital. He gave his own diagnosis:

The situation is due in a measure to fatigue and exhaustion ... Mother's death and all that it has meant of a tax upon my sympathy, coming on top of the strain of absence during the election and the elections themselves, render my system liable to any infection – one way or the other. Besides, since mother's death I have not slept as well as formerly, and have feared a return of the nervous trouble I had at the time of father's death.[39]

Peace of mind required that the fearful doubts be allayed and his probity accepted. If there was a culprit to be found, it was Jennie whose persistence had caused all the anxiety: 'I really think the shock I got at Jennie's letter and attitude, coming so suddenly after mother's death had more to do with this thing coming on than anything else. Her action was such a surprise to me and seemed so unnatural.[40] The irony of his position had been revealed in his previous letter:

Jennie's hasty judgment would be amusing if it were not for the pain which such an assumption must have brought herself, as well as for the injustice which it does all others concerned. However, I hope I have long since learnt to make allowances for limitations, whether of environment or otherwise, and to excuse rather than accuse. The truth is, Jennie has known so little about the home problems, saving those of her own home, that she has really not been in a position to appreciate the considerations of which it has been necessary to take full account.[41]

Taken at face value, the assertion that Jennie, who had undertaken most of the positive care of their parents and had shared the economizing necessary to support the boys' education, knew nothing about their problems was absurd. King was forced to spell out his meaning to Max in a letter on 25 March 1918.

Had Jennie been willing to share with me, through Harry or otherwise, the obligation which I was assuming in its entirety at the time the agreement was made, I should have been mightily glad to have her or anyone else a party to it. Being unwilling or unable to share in an obligation it ill becomes her not only to seek to profit when an obligation no longer exists, but make all the trouble possible, where at least something in the nature of an expression of gratitude might have been expected.

Max had the unenviable task of trying to confront Willie with the illogicality of his rationalization and he did so in a way that would increase his brother's anxieties and strengthen his denial:

It pains me to write of what you have said about Jennie and the assistance she has given the home. However, I consider it only right to tell you that I regard your words as unfair, unbrotherly and unmanly in the extreme. Jennie may not have had the monetary advantages that you have had, but, burdened as she was with the duties of her own home, when opportunity permitted she gave her all to Isabel and mother, and moreover she gave it without thought or expectation of remuneration. If you reflect you will realize that any words or actions of hers which have stung, have emanated from what on your part in all fairness may be termed an unnatural and autocratic secrecy in the family affairs.[42]

This argument was not acceptable. In King's view those who did not give money did not give at all and those who had been prepared to make financial sacrifices had the right to receive the reward. If we apply this judgment to his attitude to the family, we arrive at the conclusion that because his father had not provided adequately for Willie's need John King had no right to expect anything from Willie. If Willie in fact had made a profit from his father's financial incompetence, this was the reward for good management. Such a trend of thought, if it did exist, would of course be deeply unconscious. Carried over into politics, the position can be seen in the view that those who paid with their votes (by electing Liberal candidates) were entitled to share in the government. Those who were not prepared to pay (those who voted Tory) did not deserve 'one cent.'

Although King could not recognize the deeper origins of his disquiet, he was aware of the issues that had to be avoided. He had explained his plight to Max on 4 February:

My brain is anything but rested, and I must for some time avoid those things which stir the emotions unnecessarily. I can not harrow my feelings by dealing with those matters which have very sacred and tender associations until at least a little time has passed. Indeed, I must stop altogether writing or discussing these matters further until I get properly rested. Nothing breaks me down so completely as being crowded with obligations and work combined, and having to go over matters that have cost me no end of pain and concern of recent years.

Later, in an attempt to remove pressure and to win Max to his view, King offered to regard Max's debts as fully paid in return for Willie's being relieved of any necessity to account for moneys involved in the estate. Max rejected the offer: 'In fairness to Jennie, I can not see that such a settlement would compensate her for not receiving full particulars about the estate. Indeed it would involve a sacrifice on two accounts on her part.'[43] This may have been the goal that King unconsciously sought, but it was a thought which he preferred not to confront. In his rationalization of the offer, Jennie had been given a chance to redeem herself through accepting the burden of helping finance Max's illness.

The debate was obviously getting nowhere because of King's obsessional response. Max had revealed the crux of the whole issue when he wrote: 'according to these arrangements the rights of each depends on your interpretation.' Willie's only response to this accusation was increased self-pity. 'Happily, however, I am possessed of a sense of humour as well as a sympathetic understanding, or I might be at a loss to account for the degree to which my well meant and generously meant intentions seemed to have wholly miscarried in their purpose.' The need to maintain his defences prevented his letting the matter drop, however. He concluded that the misunderstanding with Max was due to the fact that they had not met face to face.[44] King's faith expressed in the value of personal contact in labour relations and in international relations would also be demonstrated in personal matters.

In his deep hurt and tense bewilderment, King hit out in every direction but particularly at Jennie who, he felt, had been responsible for the whole confrontation and the deterioration of his relationship with Max. To the latter he wrote:

I had reason to feel very deeply Jennie's attitude toward myself. That, I am quite prepared to forgive her. I doubt, however, if I shall ever be able to wholly forgive her opening a correspondence with you calculated to do injustice to me and to injure in no slight way your own health. However, that she may live to regret herself, and I trust I shall be granted the power to forgive and forget that as well. You however must choose between believing her or believing me.[45]

Jennie had cast a harsh light into his fantasy world and he could not tolerate the suspicions thus exposed.

Max saw the realities of the situation more clearly:

I took up the matter from a genuine desire to do you justice. I saw from the beginning and I still see that a statement of figures was the easiest means ... and the only means that would effectually clear up bad impressions ... Quite evidently, however, you have viewed my letters in the light of an attack and, instead of a sympathetic desire to get together on the matter, in every possible way you endeavoured to put me on the defensive ... If I say this matter must not be discussed when you come to Colorado, it is because I realize that any explanation that you will make will be entirely outside the figures and limited to just what you are willing to have me know ... It is not a question of what was desired but of what actually happened. To argue about this sort of thing is utterly unproductive of anything other than fatigue and unhappiness.

Having held a mirror to Willie, Max went one step further and offered a world of warning: 'Just one word more dear Billy of brotherly concern. Probably you will resent it now but at some future eastertide you will remember my words and they may be of good influence. Beware lest your passion for obtaining credit leads you into paths of dishonour.'[46] King replied on 9 April: 'No I am not likely to forget those words at any eastertide. I grieve to know that they express what the five intervening years have meant to you ... I appreciate the force of all the words you use ... and this with passion for credit and paths of dishonour are what the five years have brought! May God forgive you your words and may they never cause you pain.' It can be suggested that King's personal unity was so fragile and tension-ridden that he was no longer able to accept criticism from anyone and that he was unable to make a realistic judgment of his own actions. Further, he could not distinguish between queries concerning impersonal matters and personal criticism. This was to be a difficult defence mechanism for a man who was later to become leader of a minority government in a parliamentary system where he was required to face a continual barrage of institutionalized opposition.

The dispute continued into mid-year. King's work was falling further and further behind; he could not concentrate on his book when such matters were troubling him, a sign in itself of the degree of his anxiety. King's generative impulses directed towards Max and those directed towards his book were intertwined. In his book, he was attempting to reveal his innermost thoughts on matters relating to industrial affairs, his ideals, and the motives by which his life was governed. He could not write freely about such things at a time when his very essence was being challenged by the treachery of his brother and sister. To escape these tensions, he abstained from contact with them – a visit to Colorado was postponed and plans to spend Easter with Jennie were abandoned. His lack of progress in winding up the affairs of the estate forced an extension of his isolation. In reply to Max's query about his silence he wrote (11 May 1918):

If I have failed to say much about my own movements of late, it is because I so strongly believe that lack of faith in the most vital relationships of life must bring of necessity a want of faith in everything; and it is difficult for me to see how, entertaining the views and feelings expressed in some of your recent letters, any of the interests of my life could be a matter of real interest or concern to you. Naturally, one does not find in the mind of another doubt and mistrust with regard to the most sacred obligations of life, and feel that minor concerns can be of any real interest.

However, let me say, dear Max, that I have never allowed your words to bring with them the significance and meanings which are usually attached to expressions such as you have found it necessary to use. I have realized also that, being ill, and possessing of a very meagre knowledge of all the facts and circumstances, you have judged too hastily and on too narrow a basis. Did I not believe that at heart you cherished a love for me as real as my own has ever been for you, I should feel very differently than I do. As matters are, however, I hope I am broad enough not to misunderstand your attitude, or to give it any significance which it would be unfair to you to give.

This important statement of King's views would seem in some respects to be a rationalized version of the more forthright letter of 9 April. In the 11 May letter he outlined a method he was to practise extensively during his political career which, although it caused his actions to be misconstrued and provided an excuse for procrastination, contributed to his effectiveness as a party leader.

Once again, however, I should like, if you will permit me, to point out the great danger there is in imputing false or ignoble motives or purposes to any one, or of forming judgments other than such as are charitable, especially of those that are near and dear to one. However much one may feel prompted to any course of action from a sense of either right, duty or self-imposed obligation, it is always well to remember that it is never wise to form a judgment concerning any person or anything until one has a knowledge of all facts and circumstances; and that the only attitude which ever succeeds in a noble way is the one that believes in the good, rather than in the bad of others, and cherishes rather than destroys the tender outreachings and aspirations of love and faith.

Jennie, having been consigned to the ranks of the ignoble, was not to be allowed to redeem herself; her offer to pass on to Max her share of the money received from the estate was scorned as impracticable now that it came from her and not Willie. In effect he told Max (3 August 1918) that she was incapable of managing her affairs and must be sick: 'her condition is really more serious than she knows herself, or than either of us believed. It would be wholly impossible for her to have misjudged me as she has were this not true.'

The disposal of the estate continued to occupy the family for the rest of the year since Willie persisted in avoiding a full accounting. On 3 September he offered Max alternative financial aid to the money due from the estate: 'I received tonight the first money I have earned from any of my 'new clients' a cheque for $1,000 ... I am endorsing over this cheque to you ... You understand that this one thousand dollars represents the one thousand which came to you from mother's estate and which you endorsed over to me in repayment of part of previous advances.' Max understood nothing of the sort and refused to accept the money. Willie settled his own conscience by issuing a receipt which recognized that Max's share of the estate was to be used to repay his indebtedness to Willie. King's draft of the receipt prepared 3

December, ended with the statement: 'This receipt is given with genuine admiration and appreciation of his desire that all property to which he is entitled under my mother's will should be used in the way of repayment of money advanced.' This occurred during the year in which King earned $22,000 over and above expenses for his part-time work as an industrial relations counsellor and the month in which he was to receive an offer of a directorship of the Carnegie Corporation at $25,000 a year. But King's concern was not so much for the money, although he could never actually bring himself to refuse it; he was concerned that his original position be recognized as just. Thus Max must be persuaded to acknowledge that he trusted Willie not to profit from the provisions of Isabel King's will. Yet this was what he had failed to achieve.

Max on the last day of January 1919 made a further attempt to re-establish the old relationship. 'Sometimes I feel you would be less lonely and we should feel much closer, if you would take me a little more fully into your confidence in matters such as these.' But this King could not do; he maintained the veneer of friendliness, concern, and pseudo-intimacy that was his defence against isolation, but he had withdrawn from Max in terms of real intimacy.

It should perhaps be repeated here that King's behaviour in regard to Max's indebtedness and that of his father was a projection onto the family of his own desires for autonomy and independence. This repetition of a concern that he had expressed so adamantly ten years before bore no relationship to his changing circumstances. It was a subject which was to continue to worry him to the end of his political life. Yet his reply to Max of 10 February revealed just how unnecessary this concern was: 'I am fortunate in having many good and influential friends who, I think, believe in me and my purpose, and who, should I ever become bankrupt through the effort to serve my country at the sacrifice of a life of less strain and larger remuneration, will help me to get on my feet again.' This was a realistic appraisal of his situation. He was indeed fortunate in having influential friends ready to contribute to his welfare. But he continued to parade the spectre of poverty and financial need because economy and financial security had become the dominant element of his unconscious defence and of his self-image.

OBSESSIVE-COMPULSIVE NEUROSIS

The debilitating effect of King's upbringing and subsequent life experience can be seen in the emergence and maintenance of obsessive rituals. Although it is not possible or necessary to locate the origins of these defences, the repetitive patterns of behaviour and the beginnings of obsessive rigidity are apparent by the time King began his diary. In addition from the start of his university career King had subjected himself to rigid timetables and routines. He concentrated on précising his lectures, and reading was a matter of making summaries which he learned by heart. On 7 January 1899 he had resolved: 'this term I will seek to memorize everthing I read. I am going over my work carefully ... learn everything as I go.' He showed very little spontaneity in any aspect of his intellectual life; even at home, books were catechized rather than read for pleasure. Any lighter activity was followed by self-castigation: 'After dinner, I went out and walked about , called ... and spent an hour talking ... This is all a mistake ... I should overcome self & this restlessness, I need more self discipline more devotion etc.'[47]

Even his thoughts were not to be freed from this drive to control and eliminate spontaneity. 'I have tried to be more careful of my words & thoughts today, but find it hard to do 3 things, (1) not to allude to self, (2) not to say or think ill or cynically of another, (3) not to smile or at least to speak disproving [sic] of some light remark or improper word.'[48] His personal fastidiousness, his distaste for the 'rough' life, and his constant self-analysis all contributed to the strength of this solution. He not only imposed a rigid routine on himself but also endeavoured to do the same to others. In a letter about study methods written to his brother Max on 16 October 1898, King said:

If you decide to work till ten at night do not stop at nine thirty and do not work till ten ten stop at ten sharp. If you do this you will see at the end of a week you can look back on the work you have done and find it fitting into squares, each bit of it will stand out almost as a distinct block – there is no sensation of the mind to equal the pleasure of this except perhaps that which comes from complete concentration ... These little squares mount up and I find that the pleasure comes when one sees his duty well done.

The aura of religious sanction gave added strength to patterns of behaviour which might otherwise have appeared meaningless. King's habit of organizing his academic work in rigid blocks was evident in the rest of his activities. Rituals, such as his obsessive noting of the time and his commenting on the symmetry of the hands of the clock, were a mark that a specific task had been accomplished or a particular span of time duly passed. In some respects King's whole life was like the chart that schoolboys prepare as the holiday season approaches or like a record of a prison term served. This concern for boundaries, the desire to organize the whole life into manageable segments, carried over from the clock to the calendar. Particularly significant boundaries included the end of the year, birthdays, and great religious festivals. Each marked the passing of another milestone, a time when the events of the previous twelve months could be recorded, weighed, evaluated in terms of fidelity to God' purpose, and then put aside so that the new year could be faced with a feeling of omnipotence based on the culmination of a successful year's endeavour towards the ideal. For such occasions King had evolved rituals as important to his peace of mind as those of his church were to his spiritual well-being. He described the process to Violet Markham on 1 January 1911 in the following terms: 'I wanted to send you this wish last night to let you know that you were much in my thoughts as the old year passed away, but in my effort to have every letter in my department answered and my work complete ... I was obliged to remain with my secretary at the office.'

The same ritualization with religious overtones was also characteristic of his devotional and recreational reading: 'I read aloud to my mother ... we had a great deal of pleasure in going over its chapters in a sort of shorter catechism fashion after each was read.'[49] This shorter catechism approach occurred both in intellectual and religious matters. It reflected in part a drive to exert control over his material – control through segmentation, review, and digestion – which was the corollary of the control he sought to exert over his whole environment, his intimates, and himself. The conscious motivation for this rigid control came from his anxiety about the impetuosity of the Mackenzie strain, and the fear that its powerful emotionalism, creative rhetoric and persuasive oratory would lead him to his grandfather's fate. One strand of his defence mechanism was thus always involved in this struggle, with God's help, to control the inheritance of his blood through routine and ritualization. This control also served as an ego-enhancing rationalization to justify actions that might otherwise have been considered pique.

The obsession with control and repetitiveness can be seen in King's adult life in his predilection for signing important documents on anniversaries, the compulsive noting of the time at which even the most trivial event or action occurred, and a tendency to govern by the letter rather than the spirit. It increasingly influenced the practice of his religious beliefs where ritual became a substitute for essence. His daily reading of the Bible and other religious tracts had more an element of routine control of behaviour than a deeper communion with God. Later he came to distort the process further by forcing God's will to be revealed at regular intervals through passages selected at random from the Bible.

King appears to fit very well into McClelland's definition of men who 'feel powerful through the accumulation of possessions and the control of things especially money.'[50] This tendency appears in several dimensions of his life, for example Kingsmere. The development of his property at Kingsmere not only signified that he had 'made it' through possession of a symbol of élite status – a country estate – but also established a further triumph over the rival father. John King had never been a landowner: Woodside, the childhood ideal, had been rented. Kingsmere, so fortuitously named, was possessed as a extension of self, and every increase to its size or worth was an enrichment of self. In lavishing time and attention on Kingsmere King was indirectly lavishing attention on himself, and the grandiose aspects of the estate – the mock classical ruins, the stone from the British parliament buildings – reflect the grandiose dimensions of the self.

The need for continual self-examination encouraged by his religious beliefs and incorporated in his diary-keeping was also distorted by this trend. The annual accounting served as an occasion on which he could gloat over his possessions and revel in their increase. His tendency in his political career to have long recitals of his actions and achievements read into the parliamentary record was an extension of this need. In fact it might be argued that he was more concerned with providing the basis for an historical accounting than with any other objective.

A third dimension of this need to feel powerful through self-control pertains to knowledge or insight. As a student King was attracted to those areas of learning that concerned human development. His intellectual curiosity regarding the nature of the universe and man's relation to the infinite was one of the strands that led him towards the more ritualized forms of spiritualism. This progression was reinforced by his inability to submit totally to authority, to let God's will take its course; thus King failed to find the release and the sense of power and purpose in religion that others did. Instead he was driven to more and more restless searching for the certainty which would allow him complete control over his destiny.

The inadequacy of orthodox religion to deal with King's emotional crisis following the virtual disintegration of his family drove him into less conventional channels of support. Such channels, for instance the spirit world, did not make the same sort of demands as earthly supports. Except through dreams and visions the spirit world communicated with him only when he made overtures to it. And even dreams could be interpreted in such a way as to preclude their bearing messages at a time when he did not wish to concern himself with such things.

King's lack of basic trust made the separation from his 'loved' ones particularly threatening as freedom from family duty meant aloneness. A Christian may take comfort from his faith in a life after death, but King's need for such consolation was particularly great. On the loss of his mother he had written: 'somewhere her spirit dwells, not far from me here. Did I not cherish that belief I should be unhappy beyond words.'[51] His anxiety was such, however, that mere belief was not enough. Just as he had constantly sought signs of God' purpose in his life, he now needed signs of the presence of the 'loved ones beyond the veil.' Since spiritualism claims to help in this search for the dead, it is possible to locate the roots of this facet of King's personal beliefs in this process. (There were a fair number of believers in the spirit world among King's early associates and their support may have confirmed King in the validity of the approach.)

The fact that all his loved ones died when he was away from them meant that he had not witnessed the moment of death. In spiritualism there was a 'denial that the love object [was] permanently lost.' Thus King was able to continue his life as if death was a remote occurrence and to avoid the readjustments which recognition of his 'aloneness' and 'loneliness' would have involved. Instead of experiencing the 'lonely heights,' he passed his span of duty in the company of those 'beyond the veil' whose approval he could count on and whose advice and counsel would always be what he wanted to hear. This interpretation seems to be supported by an incident King had described to Violet Markham on 28 August 1912:

As I was coming into Canada on my return ... I had a very real experience of the presence of my friend Bert Harper. It seemed to me that he came to talk with me and assure me of his continued interest in my life and welfare, and his continued existence. It was as if I had gone to England to be asked a question, and he had come to answer it on my return ... His presence has been real to me ever since to a degree I have not known for years – never I might say since his death.

It should be noted that 1912 was the first time since Harper's death that King was faced with failure rather than continued success. A detailed analysis of the diary and a matching of responses such as the above with events in King's life would be necessary before any complete interpretation of the meaning of spiritualism to his life could be made.

The utility of these beliefs should not be denied, however, merely because it is a form of response uncommon among political figures.

Spiritual contact with the family beyond the grave also helped mask the inadequacies of relations with members of the family still in the world of the living. The disadvantages of these real contacts compared with those associations beyond the veil was that the former could make demands on him. Turning the latter for support did not involve any chance of involvement. The nature of this preferred form of contact can be seen in King's own interpretation of his visions: 'It was to assure me that mother's love & care is about me ... that I am being cared for & loved & guided & to have no fears but rest secure.' He in turn could lavish the care and attention he craved himself on an undemanding substitute – his dog. 'I began assuring him of the love I had for him, calling him 'my boy' and telling him he was safe & secure & rejoicing in his complete confidence and trust.' From these two sources King could find the absolute response that he needed.[52]

In his early spiritualism King had combined many of his religious and personal rituals. He had always thought that he could find personal messages in the Christian record, and indeed this belief was accepted widely in the denomination to which he belonged. This process, which had led him to write in 1896 'at times I wondered whether I was taking a wise step. I took down my Bible and read a few chapters which assured me I was right,'[53] would also lead him to attempt to interpret other coincidences and happenings in terms of God's purpose in his life.

A political career can be particularly hazardous for an individual who has pronounced feelings of insecurity and vulnerability. There are many aspects of the political environment that deliberately create conflict and are likely to produce feelings of shame, loss of pride, weakness, and insecurity in an individual who is already over-anxious. Obsessional defences that utilize devices to establish control over the self and the external world have their counterpart in religious practices such as crossing oneself or such ritual phrases as 'thanks be to God,' 'by my lady,' and so on. In King's life we note the recurrence of phrases, such as 'if it is the will of Providence' and 'if I am spared,' obviously in the same tradition. Not so obvious, but possibly similar in origin, is the ritual recitation of the names of loved ones beyond the veil – a technique to placate the forces of the spirit world rather than any true indication of his feelings.

Elections are particularly traumatic for insecure political leaders, and it is not surprising that some of King's spiritualist activity was concentrated around these times. Similarly, the period he spent in opposition in the thirties was a testing time for King. Opposition was not a role that he could easily accommodate because it threatened his control, and once the floodgates were opened the dangerous passions of the Mackenzie inheritance could destroy him. Spiritualism and other research into the unseen world allowed him to fill his time with a semblance of purposeful activity, which masked the aimlessness of the early years out of office. In January 1931 he had expressed a 'feeling of isolation & inadequacy to present tasks,'[54] and the situation worsened as the session progressed. In a personal sense his need for reassurance was far greater at this time than later. He had always felt uncertainty in situations in which no one was closely concerned with his activities – 'I feel a great loneliness no one interested in me and no purpose in my work,'[55] he had written. His colleagues had all but deserted him, the future of the party was not clear, and once again a radical force was rising on the prairies.

When he returned to office in 1935, the whole picture changed. It was not merely lack of time that produced a decline in spiritualist activity, it was also a reduced need. When King was surrounded by the formal trappings of government, his aloneness was not so obvious. In the aftermath of the Liberal victory, doubts about his leadership were reduced, and the support of his colleagues more forthcoming. At the same time any need for 'otherworldly support' could be found in dream interpretation.

A great deal of attention has been focused on King's spiritualist activities, but interest in his 'visions' and the extensive amount of time he devoted to recording and interpreting his experiences has been relatively small, although they constitute the more regular of the two types of activity. The role of psychic phenomena in King's life was multi-dimensional one. At the most practical level, there was a close connection between King's research into life after death and his religious beliefs. King believed that God's hand was guiding him and that the 'cloud of witnesses' who communicated with him from beyond the grave were agents of this purpose and a 'guiding presence' in his life.[56] Further, King believed that through spiritualism he could increase his understanding of life's great mysteries. After a session with a new medium he declared: 'The scriptures will take on new & literal & clearer meaning; the world itself will evolve to a higher plane – one can see a new significance in 'the second coming' and its nearness, but in a way a little different from that accepted by many.' This belief was particularly strong in his acceptance of visions. These, he declared were 'the highest form of mediumship – recognized in the Bible, both Old and New Testament.' It was not obvious from the record just what distinguished a vision or revelation from an ordinary dream; the most frequently recorded qualification was that visions were clearer than dreams.[57]

Visions and messages from beyond the veil fulfilled several other needs in King's life. He derived a great deal of reassurance from the unseen presences. Praise from Sir Wilfrid communicated during table-tapping removed anxiety about his performance. Awakening to the sound of the celestial choir, King noted that 'it was a real communion of spirit and assurance that we were together and at one with God. I faced the speeches of the day without fear.' When he missed his visions through fatigue or overwork, he 'prayed for guidance from the loved ones "Beyond".' In particular he looked to 'dear mother' for assurance of her consoling presence.[58] Isabel King did not have to be actually present in the vision for her son to feel her guiding hand. After a vision about a search for a Bible box King observed: 'I am sure all this vision was to make clear that mother was with me to comfort me. – I felt last night completely exhausted, & discouraged, fearful. I wondered if I really had the strength to go on ... '[59]

King turned to the visions for guidance as part of his desire for omnipotence and his wish to cleave to God's purpose in his life. He dreamt of George Graham speaking of King's fifty-four years of public service and wondered if it was prophetic. He dreamt of snakes while attending the Port Hope Conference and 'wondered if it could mean that by any chance my hosts [the Masseys] ... were not to be trusted.' He dismissed the thought as unworthy but the next day observed, 'I trust the visions in their warnings.' King was not merely naïve in his approach to spiritual matters; he saw himself as a true student of the mysteries. He was aware of the dangers of interpreting the promptings of memory or his subconscious as messages from beyond, and he sought evidence to justify his belief. In the matter of evidence, however, he fell back on an easy rationalization. Factual errors detected in the spiritual record were the work of 'evil influences' and of 'the lying spirit,' particularly during 'conversations over the table.' Consequently he believed that he was less influenced by the latter than by his own interpretations of his nocturnal experiences. In practice, his need for guidance was an extension of his need for reassurance. The valid messages were those that reinforced his expecations or his chosen course.[60] The most useful source of confirmation was still the Bible.

This morning I spent reading the Bible. I read from an old book that mother had when we were children, first I read through the book of Daniel a story of vision & courage & faith ever rewarded ... The word 'Mother' was twice underlined in one place and it was as though dear mother were speaking to me from the invisible world ... All this was as my very soul, it seemed to me clear mother was watching over me, and that God had His purpose in my life ... I am sure the invisible reality is all about me here. In the silence I feel & *know* the presence of God, & loved ones gone before.[61]

In this process one sees King's inability to accept autonomy, his need for support, and his religious beliefs combined in a defence mechanism which, through the practice of spiritualism, would come increasingly to dominate his life.

The question most Canadians have asked, since knowledge of King's spiritualist activities became public, has been what influence did these messages have on his political behaviour. To a non-believer there can be only one source for the messages that King thought he received at the table, in signs and coincidences, in dreams and visions – King himself. It is clear that the contents of the messages came from King not just to him. This being so, the question Was King influenced by King's feelings on the matter? is answered obviously by yes. Therefore, to the extent that the activities were directed to seeking confirmation of decisions already reached, it was a case of self-direction and nothing more.

There was no basic inconsistency between King's intellectual doubts about this activity – 'my nature & reason revolt against "spiritualism" & all the ilk'[62] – and his continued need to experiment in the area. The psycho-dynamic approach holds that 'behaviour is neither random nor purposeless; it derives from particular needs or interests of the organism.'[63] As King got older, as his political career lay revealed in all its ambiguities, his blindness to the discrepancies between his potential and intentions and his accomplishments became harder to maintain. His obsessive concern with the record and his tendency to flesh out arguments with references to intentions are the political manifestations of this personal development. He was unconsciously and uncontrollably driven to seek the assurance of his own worth and dependability from unimpeachable sources. The only trustworthy source was himself but his estimation was valueless on its own. Only as reflected back to him from those beyond the veil could his certainty be sustained.

It contributes nothing to our understanding of King to draw a sharp line between his private world, dominated by his interest in the survival of the human spirit, and his public world of practical politics. Nor is it accurate to portray King as an individual struggling to maintain two separate levels of existence, one worldly and one other-worldly. King's concern for spiritual matters and his conscious disregard for material ends pervaded every level of his activity. He put this position most clearly in 1942 when he wrote: 'He [Hanson] went on to quote what Hutchinson said about my reading the Bible, having faith in prayer, and believing in immortal life ... Personally, I felt proud to have this declaration made in Parliament of foundation of my beliefs. I have always hoped the day may come when, in the Canadian Parliament, I might stand for ... political action being based on religious conviction.'[64] It is also inaccurate to suggest that there was 'an irresolvable tension between King's private and public world.'[65] In the context of King's neurosis it is suggested that spiritualism is best regarded as a defence mechanism directed to easing the tensions and anxieties aroused in the public world.

Politicizing the neurosis:
The first Canadian

5 ❖ In the bosom of the party

Although King's self-image emphasized statemanship and general service to mankind, he was essentially a party man. The death of Sir Wilfrid Laurier and the leadership convention that followed brought about a merging of the personal and the political in King, which was never dissolved in his lifetime. The identity confusion, which had intensified after the death of King's mother, disappeared to be replaced by the ego-enhancing work identity of Liberal leader and later prime minister. King's generative drives were diverted to the party and its followers. He also attempted to resolve the crisis of intimacy within this political context. The party was to be his surrogate family – centre of all the support and assistance that his nature craved.

DICING FOR THE MANTLE

King had anticipated that 1919 would be a turning point in his life. His new year entry in the diary began with the customary mixture of humility and optimism: 'This is to be a year of momentous decisions so far as my own life is concerned, a year of momentous decisions in the history of the world. I pray for God's guidance on my judgment for I shall need the leading spirit as never before.' His consideration of possible alternatives for the future was comparatively short-lived, for the death of Sir Wilfrid opened the road to a political career and ended speculation about any other course of action. King's reaction to his leader's death was characteristically egocentric. 'Naturally I feel an increased sense of loneliness,' he informed his brother on 21 February, 'especially as there is no one near and dear to whom I can talk over the big problems' associated with Laurier's death. King's diary entry for 18 February was more explicit regarding the nature of his concern:

This begins a new chapter in my life, a chapter of great responsibilities & I believe great opportunities. Had Sir Wilfrid lived there is no question that his guiding hand would have secured me the leadership of the Liberal Party ... In his death I lose a political father as well as a great leader. The thought uppermost in my breast is one of peace & rejoicing that I remained true to him when he was true to Liberal principles. That loyalty will secure me the leadership in the end.

The biggest problem and the source of King's greatest disappointment lay in the fact that Sir Wilfrid had not made public his preference for King as his successor. King needed the mantle of Sir Wilfrid, like that of Mackenzie, for his personal security and as a basis on which to attempt to gain the anxiety-creating role of party leader. The view that Sir Wilfrid had chosen him had practical as well as psychological consequences. King believed that there was a general antipathy within the party to those, like Graham and Fielding, who had failed Laurier 'at a time of great need ... when the popular tide was rising against him.' [1] King needed to underline the fact that he had stood at Laurier's side and what better way to do so than through Laurier's personal endorsement of his candidacy. Any doubts which King had had about contesting the 'conscription' election were now forgotten. He had been loyal, albeit reluctantly, and had suffered personal defeat as a result. Accession to the leadership would be his just reward for the earlier sacrifice.

It was inevitable that from the time he first allied himself with the Liberal cause King would visualize himself in the leadership role. It is not clear at just what stage of their relationship King convinced himself that Laurier shared this view, but it probably antedated Laurier's view by many years. The fact that Laurier knew of King's hopes for leadership and had done nothing to discourage him was in King's view evidence of Laurier's support, as was the fact that Laurier had not expressed a positive preference for anyone else. King's need to be publicly enshrined as Sir Wilfrid's heir did little to help his political judgment. Just as he had once sought to don his grandfather Mackenzie's mantle in his old riding of North York, now he tried to follow Laurier in the riding of Quebec East. Obviously the future leader of the Liberals would only be a man who had the confidence of the Quebec Liberals, but the man who wanted to be prime minister of Canada as well would need a wider appeal than this. His position could only be weakened by accepting a Quebec seat. King's actions may have been motivated by his need for absolute security. He had contested two marginal seats and been defeated twice in three attempts. To run again in North York might reflect loyalty to grandfather's memory but little more. Absolute political security for a Liberal in 1919 might appear to be a seat in Quebec.

King's political strength lay neither in long-term planning nor in steady application in pursuit of a specific goal. Rather it was his ability to capitalize on an opportunity that contributed most to his success. The Liberal convention provided just such an opportunity. Without Laurier's public endorsement, King was just another candidate. It was essential to King that he be 'the chosen one,' that his duty and mission to lead the party be clearly endorsed as the will of God and not merely the choice of men. He therefore found it necessary to 'deliberately refrain from attempting *anything*,' in the way of canvassing; he even left the country to make it absolutely clear that he was not ambitious for the office for its own sake. He was nevertheless practical enough to ensure that loyal supporters were left behind to work for his interests. 'I had been counting on Fisher to watch my interests, in case the party's wish was to have someone who had been true to Laurier.' His friends in the party were expected to undertake the kinds of tasks his father had in fact assumed during his adolescence – securing his nomination, canvassing for him, even sacrificing their own interest in the nomination if necessary. All who were not active on his behalf were either villains or knaves. He saw corruption and machinations of 'the interests' on every side but despite these handicaps believed that he won 'through God alone ... [through] being true ... to principle, undergoing great sacrifice for truth.'[2]

The Liberal party convention had brought together a gathering of the torn and tattered remnants of a badly divided, even actively feuding party. The organizers had hoped to capitalize on the loss of Sir Wilfrid Laurier so as to paper over the breach and silence the discord that had characterized the final years of his leadership. A public display of strength and common purpose was intended to reassure the contemporary electorate and hide the organizational weakness of the once mighty 'Grits.' The federal party had little strength to offer the man they endorsed. The provincial parties were represented at the convention, but their presence was not an assurance of active co-operation and support. In fact subsequent events showed that the convention had not strengthened the leader's position *vis-à-vis* the party organization when it came to electoral strategy and other matters. The status of leader could have provided a base on which King could confront his rivals and force a showdown but this was not his way. The party was his family and showdowns within the family were avoided at almost any cost. In the short term a great deal would depend on the success or failure of King's early actions, particularly his showing in the first general election he would face as leader.

King was concerned to see himself as more than a representative of the Quebec wing. As well as being the choice of the whole party, he believed he had the support of Providence: 'I have sought nothing, it has come. It has come from God. The dear loved ones know and are about, they are alive and with me … It is His work I am called to, and to it I dedicate my life.'[3] God's service, the mantle of Laurier, and the maternally blessed role of carrying on his grandfather's work were all dominant elements in the strength with which he clung to this new identity, but there were several aspects of the path to leadership that reinforced the regressive aspects of his new personal framework. His absence on neutral territory for much of the war years and the self-imposed isolation of 1918 meant that King had had only a detached contact with the political events of the period. For King, the world of 1919 was not essentially different from that of 1911, except for the great personal sacrifices he believed he had made and the losses he had suffered. Thus the leadership problems he faced were in his view those that Sir Wilfrid had faced in the earlier period and the lines of battle were the same. Violet Markham expressed astonishment that he would be contemplating a political campaign on pre-war lines, but King's position was shared by sufficient of his fellow Liberals and Canadians to make it tenable.

In practical terms, King's lack of a long apprenticeship in politics prevented his establishing his own distinctive style of leadership at the outset. He was caught up immediately in the issues of the troubled period that followed the cessation of hostilities and had little time for detailed consideration of his approach. As Laurier had been the leader of the Liberal party throughout King's adult life, it is probable that King had already accepted many of his methods and techniques as the norm long before he assumed the leadership. But this model would be dominated by King's perceptions rather than by an objective evaluation of the qualities of Laurier's leadership.

It was important to King to be right and to see the path of right, but Laurier had not always been right – quite the contrary. As with two other internalized figures – Mackenzie and Gladstone – Laurier had split the party and left the cause in dire straits. In this sense these internalized models were negative, representing a challenge rather than an ideal. The challenge would lead King back to 1911 to pick up the task from the point of error in an attempt to accomplish in the mantle of Laurier what Laurier had failed to achieve – national and party unity.

This regression was necessary because King had begun to identify himself with Laurier and Laurier's actions long before 1919,[a] and was very much influenced by his need to see himself in such a relationship. To be able to throw himself wholeheartedly into the cause of Liberalism he had to be convinced that it was the path of righteousness. If he could be the person who had directed the leader's steps, he would have no doubts. In this respect his loyalty to Laurier and his defence of Laurier's positions were a defence of himself. Laurier's general 'personal consideration and kindliness' towards his colleagues provided the straw necessary for King's brick making.[b]

It is difficult to draw a clear distinction between imitation and parallel development in the careers of these two men, who were leaders of the same party in the same country and who faced a number of similar problems. Although Laurier provided the practical example for King's leadership, he was not the only model. Because of the major differences in personality, there was not a perfect fit between the role King inherited and his personal needs. King's basic insecurity caused him to be dependent on continuity, and he consciously stressed the links between his leadership and that of Laurier, just as he had stressed his links with Mackenzie. But any imitation was based on what King believed Laurier's response would be. In practice this usually consisted of projecting his own reactions and beliefs onto Laurier.

DEFENDER OF THE FAITH

On 13 March 1922 King made his first speech in the House of Commons as prime minister. It should have been a memorable occasion full

[a] During his association with the Department of Labour King had seen himself as the instigator of the Liberal party policy on labour matters and the author of the leader's main utterances in this field. Once he had joined the ministry this belief was strengthened and expanded as he was able to exert an influence on subjects outside his portfolio. In his letters to Miss Markham during this period he had regularly reported his growing closeness to Sir Wilfrid and the influence he was having on Laurier's actions. It was a satisfying picture of an ageing leader leaning on the able young man whom he was grooming for stardom.
[b] When Laurier told John King in 1912 that he was sorry King was away, King rushed back from Europe to be with him. Nor did the sacrifice seem unrewarded. By February 1913 King had written: 'I have been in very close touch with Sir Wilfrid right along. Our friendship is developing into real intimacy.' The difficulties of the period following 1917 were forgotten once King became leader.

of praise and fine sentiment – the customs and traditions of the house almost guaranteed it. Instead, the occasion was irrevocably marred by the speech of Arthur Meighen, the leader of the opposition, who mingled a few perfunctory platitudes with a bitter attack on King and his leadership. King found little solace in Meighen's words of best wishes: 'Notwithstanding the feelings many of us have of opposition, of, indeed, antipathy, to the methods indulged in by himself and his followers, by which their so called success was achieved, we all, as Canadians, wish him long service in the life of the country.' King could not help but contrast such asperity with the magnanimity, profession of friendship, and memories of shared undergraduate days which his own speech contained.

More serious, in terms of the anxieties it aroused, was Meighen's reflection on King's probity: 'Indeed, under his aegis, Liberalism has become merely a synonym for political dishonesty.' Referring to Meighen's speech, King replied:

I was hoping that he would be perhaps a little more chastened than he appeared to be. My hon. friend has a way of speaking which at times savours considerably of bitterness, and I fear that his remarks to-night had just a shade of disappointment in them as well. There are many things he said which under other circumstances I am sure he would have expressed a little more happily. However, I do not wish to dwell upon what to him are painful recollections of the late campaign.

King consistently practised the Biblical injunction 'a soft answer turneth away wrath,' but there seems little doubt that Meighen's 'grievous words [had stirred] up anger.' King could not bring himself to express this anger openly but it nevertheless gave added intensity to his division of the political world into the forces of good and evil. In attempting to rebut Meighen's specific policy points, King outlined clearly the lines of battle.

King's perceptions of Liberalism and the role of the party in Canadian politics were the key elements of his political frame of reference. Although factors of this kind are central to an understanding of any political actor, they became crucial in King's case because of the merging of his individual identity with that of party leader. A great deal of the confusion in the popular image of Mackenzie King derives from the myth that he was an absolute pragmatist without political principles and a compromiser without parallel. Associated with this image is the complementary view that under King's leadership the Liberal party was a party of expediency, with merely an accumulation of 'Vote'-oriented policies – the complete model of brokerage politics.

It is clear, as Neatby has observed, that 'Mackenzie King was incapable of any coherent presentation of his philosophy' and that he never got 'beyond trite and meaningless platitudes' in his own attempts to declare publicly his philosophy. This does not mean that King had no principles, but it does suggest that these apparently trite platitudes were his guidelines, however inadequate they might seem to a political philosopher. King's world view was derived in large part from his referent group – the people through whose eyes he judged himself.[c] From this point King stood with both feet firmly planted in the mainstream of Gladstonian Liberalism and viewed the problems of modern Canada from this nineteenth-century stance.

This Gladstonianism was not limited to the early years of King's political career. The period in opposition in the thirties could have been a time for reassessment and for endeavours to revitalize the party. But for King it was essentially a period in which he reaffirmed his commitment to the principles that had guided his life. He regarded himself as the only surviving Gladstone Liberal, and Morley's *Life of Gladstone* was one of the volumes that King frequently turned to for inspiration.

To understand Mackenzie King's perception of the main political issues, it is necessary to grasp the essential features of this nineteenth-century ideology as he applied it to the Canadian scene. First, it involved a general acceptance of the existing political structure as long as all were able to participate. Thus King would attempt to mould the Liberals into a party in which every Canadian would feel at home and through which every Canadian could express his needs and interests. This was the practical side of his commitment to party and national unity. Essentially he was asserting that there was no need to change

---

[c] In this regard the stream of British – Gladstonian – Liberalism engulfed him from several directions. The personal and family political links of the Kings were distinctly liberal. John King had been actively involved with the Ontario party which was still strongly influenced by the liberalism of George Brown and Alexander Mackenzie. His grandfather, William Lyon Mackenzie, had been active in the tradition of Jacksonian liberalism, and in the family version of his exploits Mackenzie's actions were given a Gladstonian tinge. Intellectually King had formed close ties with Gladstone and had added emotional links through contact with Gladstone's living relatives. At the practical level, King had learned his liberalism under the guidance of Sir Wilfrid Laurier, himself an admirer of Gladstone, at least in King's version. King also maintained extensive contacts with British Liberals.

the system once the enemy – the Tories and Big Business – was vanquished. This task was so important that it was given priority over all other matters. The outlook also had heavy religious overtones. Political issues were conceptualized as a struggle against sin, and evil men and contemporary political issues could not be allowed to distract attention from the fundamental problems of life.

King expressed this belief when he told the Liberal summer conference in 1933: 'I am inclined to believe that there are great moral issues, as well as great economic issues of which account has to be taken. The problems of today are world problems, they are human problems.'[4] King shared the Presbyterianism that lay at the roots of Ontario liberalism and the concern for moral issues which it encouraged. As he had told the u.s. Commission on Industrial Relations: 'Back of all forms of organization lies character, and character is going to be the determining factor in the long run.' 'If it [power] is in the hands of men who are benevolent in their attitude towards life, and charitable in their relations, then it will be a blessing. It depends in the last analysis on the character of men.'[5] Although he rejected predestination, King shared the Calvinist view that sees life in terms of implementing God's plan for the world, and early in his career he had emphasized his belief in the need to improve the quality of men in public life. Men of his outlook, King believed, would be moved by a sense of duty to serve their fellow men, seeking neither recognition nor reward; those who achieved high public office did so to serve the end of Christian fellowship, peace, and order.

From this viewpoint the main practical issues involved in Liberal leadership were to recruit men of principle into the cause and to defeat the enemy. It was assumed that once these goals had been achieved Liberal policies of sound financing, economy in government, and removal of economic privileges would do the rest. During the time in which these changes were occurring, however, circumstances might arise where government intervention was necessary to remove existing anomalies or to prevent the growth of new ones.

Traditionally, the Liberal party had been a spokesman for the outsiders, for the minority groups seeking a place in the system. Thus, in Canada the Liberal party would continue to be the voice of provincial rights, national autonomy, and French Canada. The party was not, however, the voice of the proletariat against the world of business. Liberals were suspicious of 'big business' but , as long as businessmen were operating competitively in an open society, liberalism was not anti-business. The liberal way was the way of rugged individualism.

R.I. Kelley argues that the Gladstonian Liberal neither sought change nor resisted it. He merely ensured that necessary change was implemented through the forces of law and order and in keeping with the political heritage so that continuity was maintained between past and present. Thus Liberal reforms were presented as 'predominantly factual and specific, with copious references to historical precedent.'[6] This is a perfect description of King's speech on tariff reform in May 1924.[7]

For King the attempt to create a bridge between past and future helped to fulfil his need for personal security. His historical outlook was attacked by the editor of the *Canadian Forum* who declared in an editorial on 13 October 1921: 'Mr. King will never make progress by facing the past. Whatever opinion one may entertain as to the place of Sir Wilfrid Laurier in the history of Canada, this is not the time when electors are disposed to say their prayers to his image ... They are asking for leaders who have ideas ... who are looking to the future ... The eye raised to the image on the wall is less likely to presage victory, than the eye turned to the living present.' The warning fell on deaf ears. King certainly looked to the future but with a perspective controlled by the past. Thus he sought to solve the issues of tariffs, railways, fiscal policy, war, and social welfare by methods that had worked in the past. In so doing he helped ensure that nineteenth-century liberalism survived as a major force in Canadian public affairs long after it had ceased to be an effective factor in other parliamentary democracies.

In considering King's outlook it is difficult to over-emphasize the importance of the concept of the enemy. In North America, where aristocracy was not an important factor, the enemy was identified with certain groups in the political and business world which were designated as Tory. King's enemy was of this ancestry. In the mantle of his grandfather, he refought the battles of the Family Compact. The arrogant and power-hungry Tories of 1830 lived on in King's demonology in the British and Canadian Conservative parties – identifiable by their lust for power, their corruption, and their jingoism. In the guise of Laurier, King refought the battles with the railways and the liquor interests, the high-tariff men, and the forces of self-interest and corruption, once again identified by their allegiance to the Conservative party.

King's intensely personalized view of the Tory menace predated his assumption of the Liberal leadership. He absorbed it in part from the extremely partisan politics of his time and it had been reinforced by his own personal campaign experience in 1911 and his rationalization of his failures. He had told Violet Markham in that year:

Then came defeat – wholly unexpected – even the Conservative leaders conceded my certainty of election until within the last three days. Then money began to be distributed through the riding. Dozens of voters in doubtful polls were bought ... Joseph Seagram, the Distiller and his allies have corrupted them in the past, and this time they were assisted by all the interests that were fighting reciprocity ... had there been no bribery, had bribery been even less wholesale I would have won out.

In 1925 he was still repeating this theme: 'I really dislike to have to say it, but the evidence of corruption in the recent campaign, I believe, unparalleled in the political experience of our country ... In the case of my own constituency chances were taken which even highwaymen would have thought twice before attempting.' Again in 1926: 'The opposition, described as "independent" was in reality, "Tory"; the candidate was a tory, his speakers ... were Tories, he was supported by the Tory press and financed by tory money.'[8]

King's belief that politics was the path of duty and that his course was pre-ordained meant that when he won he took electoral success to be a recognition of his virtue. Defeat at the polls had to be rationalized in a form that did not imply lack of virtue or rejection by the people he had chosen to serve. While he tried to see these set-backs as tests by Providence, he was tempted more often to believe that Tory corruption and manipulation of the electorate were the only causes of defeat. The more King satisfied his personal anxieties with this explanation, the more he was forced to maintain this 'black' view of the Conservative party even in the face of objective evidence to the contrary. The more he could persuade others of the validity of this rationalization, the more he could be secure in his self-image. Thus, he could believe that Liberal journals were impartial although they never printed a good word about the Conservatives; if a journal supported the Tories under any circumstances, it was guilty of betraying the forces of the good.

The notion of the enemy prevented King from developing a realistic view of party conflict in Canada. The intensity of his self-image as virtuous, unselfish, non-partisan, and well-intentioned dictated that those who opposed him, particularly those who ridiculed him and questioned his motives, must serve ignoble ends. Once he equated this opposition with the forces of evil, he found it difficult to foresee a situation in which it would ever be permissible to allow the Tories to assume power. King could thus consider it a positive achievement to have kept the Tories out of office.

While this exaggerated view of the opposition had dysfunctional features, it was not necessarily a political liability. King's exaggerated image and intense loathing of the Tory enemy was shared by the main bloc of his party supporters – the Laurier Liberals and the minority in Quebec. Hostility towards a common enemy was an important factor in keeping the party together but it also meant that the distortion must be maintained. The leadership of Arthur Meighen was a key element in this animosity. As long as Meighen was considered the enemy of Quebec, there would be no drift of loyalty from the Liberals. King may not have been personally responsible for the 'remember conscription' tones of post-war elections in Quebec, but he was not opposed to the benefits that accrued.

In the west the rallying power of the common enemy was not as acceptable as in the east. Many of the individuals whose support King needed were former Liberal Unionists or Conservatives and unlikely to equate Toryism with evil *per se*. Others were responding more strongly to the appeal of radical doctrines such as socialism.

King clearly made a distinction in his own mind between socialism and social welfare. As early as 1899 he had read and recommended to others R.T. Ely's book, *The strengths and weaknesses of socialism*, which argued that the choice was between state socialism and social democracy.[9] The former King associated with public ownership and government monopoly and rejected outright:

If ... by socialism is meant the ownership by the state of certain natural or quasi natural monopolies ... then the practical politician's main consideration becomes one of the extent to which the monopoly can be better administered by the state than by private corporations.

You would have to consider the alternative advantages of a system of government control of rates ... The possible disadvantages to efficiency and production through political pressure in connection with businesses conducted by the state, also the effect of individual character and enterprise on positions secured through the state rather than through individual initiative and effort.[10]

Social democracy he interpreted as Liberalism:

Opposition to socialism or a socialist state is not to be regarded as opposition to so-called social or humanitarian legislation. Neither is it to be inferred that because humanitarian legislation is a desirable thing and because the state has gone a long way in enacting so-called social legislation ... that because one favours legislation of that kind which is not infrequently termed socialistic, one necessarily favours a socialist state.

Social legislation of the kind ... mentioned is based on the assumption that individual initiative and enterprise will continue ... These are developed under a system of private property with its rewards for service which permits individuals to take great risks with the possibility of great reward or great failure. It is thought that on the whole human society is apt to progress more where that opportunity is given.

Most of the social legislation on the statue books of different countries throughout the world today is the result of great Liberal battles ... great battles to give first place to the well being of the many, rather than to the privileges of the few.

We shall improve conditions infinitely more quickly and more effectively in the end by continuing ... a step at the time, as the opportunity presents itself ...[11]

King was also influenced in his opposition to socialism by the possible links with communism and the anti-religious tone of the latter: 'There is nothing more menacing to the happiness of mankind than the atheism which lies like a heart of iron within the folds of some of the revolutionary movements of our day.' 'Communism representing atheism must be crushed.'[12]

On practical grounds King's rejection of socialism and his caution in social welfare matters were complicated by the traditional party position on provincial rights and the belief in sound financial management which would save the tax-payers' money. In a speech to the House of Commons on 27 February 1933, King attacked socialism on the grounds of feasibility:

If what the resolution proposes were carried into effect it would involve a change in the constitution ... It would be impossible for the federal parliament without a change in the constitution, to control all the socially necessary means of production, all the natural resources of the country. It is surely well known that matters affecting property and civil rights are under the jurisdiction of the provinces; the provinces have to do with all matters affecting master and servant, employer and employee, the factory acts, the mining laws and similar matters. All of these would immediately have to be brought into the federal arena and the provinces, under our constitution, would have to be parties to the change. Is it conceivable that the various provincial administrations and the people of the different provinces will ... suddenly yield all their control over their natural assets and the powers and rights they exercise as provinces over property and civil rights in order that a federal socialistic state may be formed in Canada? ... I heard the hon. member ... say that he did not wish to argue the question whether it was the crown in right of the dominion or the crown in the right of the provinces, but if you are going to have a federal socialistic state, you must argue this question.

This was a position that King was also to espouse in relation to the Bennett government's social welfare legislation.

It can be argued that King looked upon his leadership of the Liberal party as a trust and a confirmation of his own trustworthiness. It was a responsibility not to be taken up lightly nor to be laid aside until God, speaking through the people of Canada, should so ordain. This fundamental viewpoint persisted throughout his career and is best summed up in his speech in Vancouver in 1945: 'It is for you, the people of Canada, to decide in the light of the manner in which the present administration has discharged the trust you place in its hands, whether you wish to have the affairs of our country ... carried on by the tried and trusted administration which you know.'[13] King's personal need for trust had been reinforced by the anxieties created by the unusual features of his party leadership and the unrest which dominated the country during the period of his leadership.

GATHERING THE FORCES OF GOOD

In many respects the selection of King as leader had been little more than a gesture to Sir Wilfrid's memory. Sentiment was likely to give way to harsher reality unless he proved to have the necessary practical qualities to fulfil the role. Until the leader had brought his party through an election successfully he was on probation and could take little for granted other than the fact that others would be waiting their time. Not all the Liberals or even the Laurier supporters were agreed that a reconstructed Gladstonian-type party was the best way out of the schism provoked by the war.

The unrest and division within the party were matched by the unsettled nature of the general political environment. The whole political process in Canada was in a state of flux. Liberal journalist J.W. Dafoe saw little hope in the situation, declaring: 'I think any person who holds office now or any time during the next five years is entitled to a measure of sympathy. It is going to be demanded of him that he do things that cannot be done; things that are mutually contradictory and destructive; and whatever he does he will have more critics than friends.'[14] The events of the last year of the decade did little to alter the situation. The Unionists lost some support, the Liberals and Progressives gained a little, but there was no real change. As Morton said of the 1921 election: 'Those results spelled out in parliamentary terms what the press and politics had made clear since 1919, that the main task of the national government would be the restoration of national unity. The composition of the new House made it equally clear how difficult that task would be.'[15]

The racial and sectional cleavages which Morton saw dividing the country had so disturbed traditional party loyalties that later observers concluded that the two-party system had been destroyed. It is probably more accurate to suggest that party politics in Canada was at a crossroads in 1921 and that many alternatives seemed possible as a solution to the crisis. It was by no means inevitable that national unity involved the re-establishment of a strong and united Liberal party in Canada or that Mackenzie King would be the man to achieve such a solution. Contemporary predictions, both private and public, between 1919 and 1921 suggested that the contrary was inevitable – failure and the rise of a new party and new leader. 'The position of the official Liberal party seems to me to grow more hopeless every day ... I see nothing before the Liberal party, but disintegration.'[16] As will be seen below, many prominent Liberals were actively receptive to the idea of abandoning the 'old' Liberal party. In fact, some felt that it was necessary, as well as inevitable that Canada's political parties be rearranged either on the basis of a class division or along tariff lines.

Because the focus of this study is Mackenzie King, discussion of these developments will be limited to the Liberal party; nevertheless, it is clear that the course of all three parties on the federal scene was uncertain. The Unionist coalition had collapsed and Meighen faced the future with a depleted body of Conservatives, including a group opposed to his continuation in the leadership. The dramatic electoral success of the Farmers' and Labour groups masked the existence within them of fundamental disagreements over the role and the objectives of the movements, particularly in the federal sphere. In such a situation the potential for both cleavage and consensus existed, as did the opportunity for leadership. Since there was support for so many alternatives, the way was open for an individual to gather a body of followers and to guide the party system into a new channel.

It is not ignoring the power of the followers or of the people as a whole to suggest that the development of the party system at this time owes a great deal to Mackenzie King, to his view of the party, and to the choices which he made in this crucial period. The leader of a particular group is often popularly displayed as the captive of his followers, a man with no choice but to go where the followers direct. This may be true of a situation where a man becomes the leader of an effectively functioning and united group; it cannot be the case when the followers are divided and wanting to move in contradictory directions. In such a situation, exemplified by the Liberal party in 1919, there is a maximum of flexibility available to a leader. He can impose a direction provided it already has the support of a significant element of his followers. By emphasizing certain ideals and themes already acceptable to some of the party and by gradually introducing new but related ideas, a leader can mould the party to a form more consistent with his own needs. The leader by his stance will attract new followers more closely attuned to his point of view and gradually shed those followers who are distinctly out of step with the new image. If this can be done gradually and without a public rupture, then a new party, the party of the leader, can emerge from the old party.

Once King was elected to the leadership the Liberal party became his in a way that it could never have been while Laurier remained alive. King's opportunity to serve was now tied to the fate of the party and its continued role in Canadian politics. Because of his need for absolute security and because of his precarious hold on the loyalty of his followers, personal and party maintenance became his first priority and began to preoccupy the greater part of his time and energy. Because of the intimacy of his identity with the party, his stance on the party system was ambiguous. He did not accept the view that the two-party system was finished in Canada or that class was the only basis on which future combinations could be built. His need for security and for omnipotence meant that before he could take any further decisive step he must restore the status quo as he understood it – the situation which existed in Canada prior to 1911.

Because of King's success in rebuilding the Liberal party, there is a tendency to underestimate the difficulties he faced and to forget that the path he chose was by no means the easiest or the most obvious of the alternatives. The correspondence between J.W. Dafoe and Sir Clifford Sifton provides a good background against which to see the immense problem King faced. Dafoe was full of foreboding:

Take the case of the Liberal party ... There are two or three cross currents here. There is the eastern Liberalism that in its regard for financial and manufacturing interests is not very easily distinguished from Conservatism. There is the

Quebec brand which is largely clerical in its direction and is identifiable with the bi-lingual movement, which waits in the scenes ready to come upon the stage at an opportune moment. The western liberals are not in sympathy with either form of eastern Liberalism. Their ambition is to build ... policy that will absorb all the radical elements in the west and Ontario, thus heading off the third party movement which is in sight. I do not see how these various tendencies can be merged into a single party.[17]

In King's perspective there was no question of any alternative solution – the re-emergence of a single Liberal party under his leadership was the only option compatible with his personal need. But the party did not have to be rigidly delineated; his concept of Liberalism was broad and in his own mind did not involve any obvious compromise. It was to be a return to the principles of nineteenth-century Liberalism, a reconstruction of the party of Laurier but in its 'purest' form, a forward-looking party committed to peaceful progress and necessary change. Thus he had to deal with two major tasks at the same time. He must entice back to the fold all the apostates of Liberalism wandering in the wilderness, those who called themselves Unionists as well as those who had drifted into the new Progressive movement in the west. At the same time he must retain the support of the Laurier Liberals and convince them of the need for tolerance of those who had strayed or who emphasized a different pace for Liberalism. To do this he had to ignore both the possibility of failure and the attempts to undermine his position; he had to project his ideal of Liberalism and the Liberal party in a manner positive enough to counteract the siren voice of prairie radicalism without in any way distressing his more conservative French Canadian support. Little wonder that so many saw his course as hopeless or disastrous.

King was aided in this task by his misunderstanding of the third-party movement. He had been absent from Canada during the period when prairie dissatisfaction was mounting, although this did not prevent him from believing that he understood what was involved. For King, '[the] farmer and labour movements were simply manifestations of liberalism representing an indignant response to the autocratic reactionary policy of the government ... during the war.'[18] He assumed that they would rally to a call for a 'united front against the forces of evil.' In a speech in Russell County in 1921, King declared that, 'the forces of reaction and privilege behind the Meighen government were a unit from coast to coast. Those who opposed autocracy, secrecy and wastefulness in government should heal their divisions and work together.'[19] When his appeal to the electorate and to his own followers went unheeded, he did not renounce the idea; he merely transferred his attention to the Progressives in the House of Commons. 'I was perfectly sincere when I said, and I repeat it here, that I believe many of the hon. members who belong to the Progressive Party regard themselves, if you like, as Progressive Liberals ... The word "Liberal," to my mind, has always stood and will ever stand for progress.'[20] To the extent that the Progressive movement did contain a substantial group not unsympathetic to this idea his overtures to all supporters of liberalism would be successful. But to the extent that the movement included a number of individuals who totally rejected the old party structure and favoured radical change, he would not succeed completely and would never really understand why. The deficiency in his understanding was to have more serious consequences when he later attempted to deal with the rise of the Co-operative Commonwealth Federation (CCF) in the same way as he had approached the problem of the Progressives. This misperception had the advantage, however, of strengthening his will to persevere despite the meagre success of the first venture.

His identification of the Progressives with the Liberal family meant that King expected them to show the same characteristics as the filial group. They must be prepared to trust him, to declare themselves as family members, to work with him to achieve the common objectives. This was necessitated by his view of Liberalism.

Liberalism implies a point of view which embraces not merely one class but is broad enough to include representatives of all classes who take a like attitude upon public questions. I take that position to-day and I will always take it as long as I have to do with the affairs of the government of this country. Any body of opinion in Canada which represents itself as Liberal will be entitled to a place in the councils of this country, but it must be for gentlemen themselves to say whether or not they wish to have views regarded as Liberal, or as of some other point of view.[21]

As fellow Liberals the Progressives could expect to be heard and, if the situation permitted it, to influence policy. But trust must come first; King would make no commitment in advance of trust. No bargains, no compromises, no agreements could be made with the enemy and until the Progressives were united with the Liberals they would be so regarded. The demanding and apparent half-heartedness of King's position reinforced for many Progressives their mistrust of his intentions and motives. The suspicions thus aroused limited the success of his overtures.

The task of winning the co-operation of the Progressives was not helped by the actions of many of King's Liberal followers. He was aware that his leadership was not completely secure or his approach completely acceptable to his colleagues. In fact, his selection at the convention did not greatly diminish speculation on the future of the Liberal leadership. Contemporary observers had no difficulty discerning the undercurrents. Dafoe informed Sifton:

I am told, on what I think is pretty good authority, that King is having a good deal of trouble with the Frenchmen plus Charles Murphy. It appears that he imagines he is a leader and tries to act accordingly; and that they find it necessary periodically to advise him as to his actual status.

Gouin's attitude towards King, according to the same informant, is not far removed from open contempt and defiance.[22]

King's own view of the same difficulties was more sanguine. He reported that: 'There were naturally many jealousies to overcome, and differences of one kind or another to be composed ... I believe that the result of the session was a distinct gain in the loyalty of the support which I have behind me in the House.' '[The] net result of the years work has been added confidence not only on the part of my followers ... in my position as the leader of the Liberal party.'[23] By this type of rationalization King attempted to avoid the full implications of his position. As long as the malcontents took no positive action against him and the intra-party opposition was not brought into the open, King felt he could ignore the issue. His action has been misunderstood by his contemporaries and later commentators and an entirely false image of his malleability developed on the strength of it.

His low-key response and his apparent ignorance of or indifference to the ground swell against his leadership gave added credence to rumours of Liberal decline. Even if he managed to ignore the disunity in his following, it was assumed that the disaffection evident within the party would be unpalatable to the electorate. King did not share this pessimistic view. He believed that the electorate would understand the difficulty of the situation and would give him credit for the manner in which he was going about his task. His year-end accounting to Miss Markham was phrased in terms of cautious optimism.

It was my first year of leadership of the party in the House of Commons. I must leave it to others to give to you the impression which the public gained of my efforts at leadership. So far as I am able to view them myself, I have a feeling that the effect of the work of the session was greatly to consolidate my own forces and to strengthen the goodwill of the members of the party, practically without exception, towards myself ... I have tried to be faithful in my attendance in the House, and to be vigilant in its various duties. Our men, I think, appreciated my efforts in this direction, and I believe that the result of the session was a distinct gain in the loyalty of the support I have behind me in the House.[24]

According to Dafoe, 'the facility so necessary to a successful political career [was that] of seeing things as they are and refusing to follow phantoms.'[25] King, in public and private life, continued to live in a world of his own creation. This lack of realism, which is usually considered a dysfunctional solution to personality problems, proved to be an asset in these particular circumstances. Had King been persuaded that the third-party movement was inevitable, he might have faltered in his efforts and by inaction strengthened the case for a radical realignment, which would have split the Liberal party. Instead, his fantasy of gradual progress was to give him the confidence to persist and to capitalize on these elements of his perception which were closest to reality.

In the meantime the gossip about his inadequacies gave his rivals a false sense of security, and plans to rearrange the Liberal splinters after his fall became more positive. On the right, Sir Lomer Gouin, the prominent ex-premier of Quebec, stood ready to gather in the disgruntled Quebec wing if King should lean too far towards the west. Even a moderate shift in tariffs might give Gouin enough strength to cross the floor accompanied by a number of the other Quebec Liberals. On the other flank, there was Fielding whose popularity had been demonstrated at the Liberal convention and who then appeared more acceptable to some of the Farmers than his later tariff policies might suggest. Should both of these factions gain momentum simultaneously King's future would be bleak. In 1920 and again in 1921, Dafoe and Crerar seemed to be seriously considering the possibility that King could be reduced to a subordinate position in a new party or to an associate leadership with Crerar.

It was obvious to everyone, including King, that his future and that of the party he was endeavouring to reconstruct would depend on his handling of the west. The defection of Gouin to the government might even be an asset provided it did not involve any widespread loss of support from Quebec, but the defection of his reform-minded supporters was an issue of a different stature. The ideal of party unity, which King had been advocating from the moment the conscription issue appeared, could not survive such a loss. Without a nationally based party his idea of national unity would also suffer. His personal unity would also be shattered if he were rejected by all the reforming elements and left in the dangerous position of being leader of the sectional and conservative interests of French Canada. The situation called for all his ingenuity. For him to be rejected outright by the Farmers would be a great blow to his self-image; it would raise doubts of the wisdom of his initial position. 'I have taken the view from the very start that the whole farmer movement is an expression of liberalism, and the evidence of a revived liberalism to be welcomed by all men of liberal thought and feeling.[26] On this basis King could propose a merger of the Liberal party with the Farmers' movement without any fear that he would be compromising his principles.

How did these merger offers differ from the idea of coalition? For King a merger involved the idea that the Liberal party under his leadership would retain its dominant position. It was a situation in which all men of liberal ideals would form a 'united front' against a common enemy. It would represent an alliance of mutual interests leading to the overthrow of the autocratic Tory interests and their replacement by the forces of enlightment. King described it to Violet Markham on 29 October 1920:

The leaders of the farmer movement are very sympathetic toward me ... in the House of Commons the group of farmers' representatives and our own followers worked as allies throughout the whole session. I have been seeking to make that alliance a feature of the relations of the parties in the country. I think we are not far apart, and it may be that, once the government has entered vigorously upon its protectionist campaign ... the farmers will realize that the defeat of the administration will lie in the direction of union with our forces ... at present ... the most that can be effected is to keep relations friendly between the liberal and farmer groups, so that the certainty of a coalition, either before or after a general election, may not be impeded.

In this one letter King uses three terms interchangeably – alliance, union, coalition. It can be suggested that 'union' is the interpretation which should be placed on the others. Crerar would seem to have believed that it was not a coalition of two separate parties that King sought. He had told Dafoe 'of the precautions he had had to take to discourage Mr. King in his plans looking towards a merger of the Farmer and Liberal parties.'[27]

Nor was King prepared to abandon the west to the Progressive party in the hope that some arrangement could be negotiated whereby they would form a coalition in the house. Such a position would mean in all probability that the Liberal party would be nothing more than a sectional party. It would also perpetuate the challenge to his leadership of the forces of progress in the country. Such alternatives were not possibilities that King could accept. The Farmers were a manifestation of liberalism to King only as long as they were prepared to co-operate with him and join the Liberals against the government. He wanted their support and was prepared to go as far as he honourably could to demonstrate his sincerity and genuine sympathy for their ideas. He was particularly anxious to avoid three-way electoral contests which could only favour the Conservatives, but he demanded in return for Liberal co-operation that the Farmers also refrain from contesting seats where the Liberals had a good chance of winning. Without it they must be treated as 'the other' and a threat to King and his party. He had justified his stance to Violet Markham in his letter of 29 September 1921.

I have steadily resisted all talk of further coalition between the Farmers and ourselves, maintaining, and I think rightly that what the country needed was an administration with a mind, purpose, and policy of its own not further compromise ... I have all along insisted that the whole farmers movement is a real liberal movement and that as such, it should be sympathetically viewed by the Liberals ... I have both in private and public proposed to its leader that we should openly co-operate and, if possible combine our forces in the face of the common enemy.

If in the face of such magnanimity the Farmers continued to run candidates against the Liberals then they could not expect any further tolerance. The leaders of the Farmers' movement and a large section of the supporters, however, saw in any such 'open coalition' or 'working combination' an attempt to undermine the movement and to subvert their cause – a not unreasonable interpretation of King's position.

King for his part was not going to repudiate the Quebec wing merely on the off chance that a more radical image would bring the Farmers back into the fold. The Quebec wing had given King its support and therefore had first call on his loyalty as long as the members continued to demonstrate their trust in King by not opposing his attempt to effect a reconciliation with the prairie factions. In the light of the common belief that King was easily led, vacillating, and strongly dependent on the advice of the prominent members of his party, it is interesting to note his response to Sifton's attempt to persuade him to commit himself to the idea of a formal coalition between the Liberals and the Farmers. Both Dafoe and Sifton appeared strongly in favour of the coalition idea and were inclined to interpret King's efforts to effect a merger as a move towards this accomplishment. But King's position on coalitions remained rigid. As Meighen noted: 'He preceded the election by loud denunciations of coalitions ... he depicted the extravagancies, the evils and the compromises that coalition engendered, and declared time and time again that the country was sick of coalition and that he would have nothing to do therewith.'[28] His position after the election was no different. His need for the support of the Progressives in the house in no way softened King's attitude towards a formal coalition.

The narrow focus and precise limitations of his obsessional defences allowed him to distinguish between a coalition and taking members of the Progressive party into his Liberal administration. This was not a compromise but a step nearer to his objective. As he said in his report to Miss Markham, 28 September 1922, 'I have been working steadily, of course, for an amalgamation of the Progressives and ourselves ... there is a real possibility that ... the Progressives and ourselves will be welded into one homogeneous whole.' The same letter also confirmed that Dafoe was correct in his assertion that King had no real appreciation of the popular support for the Progressives. To King they remained as he had first perceived them: 'We are, on fundamentals practically one. Indeed for the most part the Progressive Party is composed of erstwhile Liberals who would never have become Progressives had Liberal leaders in many parts of the Dominion remained faithful to their trust.[29] Here again is the repetition of the betrayal theme so common in King's personal and public rationalizations. Because the Liberals were so obviously the forces of good, their failure had to be attributed to such causes as personal weaknesses. King's refusal to compromise, to recognize the obvious practical advantages of a coalition, was based on a refusal to admit that there was any real cleavage. A coalition would only perpetuate an unnatural division and subvert the course of the natural reunion that was his primary objective.

The election of 1921, although it brought King to office, did not

substantially alter the task of managing the party. Despite the apparent
rebuff from the Progressives King had continued to believe that his
method was meeting with success. But his expression of satisfaction
with his progress was coupled with recollections of the trauma of his
years in the 'wilderness.' This association suggests that King had not
completely succeeded in suppressing awareness of the continued
threat to his plans and his identity. He took refuge in his self-image as
the man of destiny who could cope with the problems of the times.[30]
King had gone into the election full of hope that he would achieve the
impossible, that despite inroads on his anticipated support by the
Farmers he could be returned to office. His confidence was based on an
optimistic appraisal of the Liberal Unionists' attitude. King accurately
predicted that the government would be reduced to fifty seats but he
had not anticipated the great upsurge of Progressive support. The
result meant that he was still on probation, still attempting to solve the
same problems, but now he had the additional burden of running the
country as the head of a minority government.

The changes that occurred added to both his strength and his weakness. The most important element in his favour was the decision of the
Progressive party's leaders not to assume the role of the official opposition. It is doubtful if King's policy of overtures and attrition would
have succeeded had the Progressives not placed themselves outside
the main lines of conflict. Despite his need for voting support in the
house King refused to make the substantial concessions that might
have won the Progressives to active co-operation with the Liberals.
King's first loyalty was to his own. The interests of those within the
family would not be sacrificed; his progressive thinking would be
demonstrated by giving prominence to the more liberal-minded within
the party. While King continued to court the leading Progressives his
practical overtures were circumscribed by his determination to do
nothing which would create divisions within his party.

By 1925 King had felt that his patience and his steadfast devotion to
duty had been rewarded. He had faced the electorate certain that he
had achieved his primary objective. He asserted confidently:

I believe the Liberal party stands today more united than it had been at any
time since the Reciprocity campaign of 1911. The disruptive influences of that
contest, and the still more disruptive influences of the War-Time Election of
1917, have spent their power, and I think I have been able to heal many
wounds & scars by asserting at the outset the rights of Liberals to an indepen-

dent judgment on great national issues, and by making my position clear in disclosing no ill-will but a fair & impartial attitude towards all who at anytime have differed with me in opinion.[31]

The election results were a great disappointment. The Progressives had lost support but the Conservatives rather than the Liberals had benefitted in terms of seats. The set-back did not appear consciously to affect King's view of the problem or shake his faith in his approach. He continued to believe he could have the Progressives' support in the house without having to make any compromises. He optimistically told a colleague: 'I think the election has put an end to the Progressive party ... Meanwhile, however, unless the citadel is to be surrendered to the enemy, we shall have to seek and obtain the co-operation of such Progressive members as have been returned to the Commons.'[32] In the same tone he assured Violet Markham that 'the government is framing its own programme and has done so without fear or favour in any direction.'[33] His belief in a time and place for everything would allow him to bring forward those policies likely to be favoured by the Progressives without fear that such behaviour involved a compromise.

One can see here the essence of King's cognitive problem. He had to reconcile the belief that the danger from a third party had been overcome with the practical fact that he was in a worse position in the house than he had been prior to the election. Since the Liberals had lost six seats, including King's own, and now held fifteen seats fewer than the Conservatives, his duty to struggle with the forces of evil was clear but his feelings of contempt for the leader of the opposition may have indicated his fear of losing the leadership at Meighen's hand. Since the December 1925 election had brought King perilously close to loss of office, he may well have feared that any change of responsibilities at this time might produce a drive to end his leadership of the party and with it his personal identity. One mechanism for reducing this dissonance was to 'cleave to the right' – to see virtue in his own responses and villainy as motivating all who opposed him. But although he entered the fight for survival with vigour, he derived little pleasure from it. He described the coming session to a friend in revealing terms: 'Now I feel as though the walls of the prison house were beginning again to close around me.'[34]

The 1926 session was a period of great potential anxiety for King because of his lack of control over the issues to be faced. The customs scandal and the censure motion brought matters to a head. Faced with Lord Byng's refusal to take advice King reacted with surprising vigour and aggression to put an end to an intolerable situation. The subsequent ego-defensive behaviour needed to justify his actions in the King-Byng crisis increased his inner tensions, and the cover mechanisms – fatigue and nervousness – revealed his inner doubts. The apparent vindication of his action in the crisis should have put an end to his tensions and the fatigue and nervousness. They continued, however, even though King appeared to have achieved his main objective – the reuniting of the Liberal party – with the admission of the Liberal-Progressive leader Robert Forke into the cabinet in 1926. King's need to reassert the facts constantly, and his uncertainty about his own future after his party's defeat in 1930 is revealing. He described to his friend Violet Markham both his options and his reasons for refusing to resign.

It is curious the sort of feeling I have come to have about politics. I would gladly drop the whole business all together and devote the rest of my life to the study of spiritual problems ... [The] years of office, and years of struggle before, left me but little opportunity to go down deeply into anything. I have covered a lot of surface, but it is depth not surface, that I desire to seek.

Perhaps some of the feeling I have is due to fatigue – a fatigue that is greater at times than I had thought it would be. I still tire quickly when certain 'complexes' get started. Mr. Rockefeller Jr. made me a splendid offer some weeks ago to devote a couple of years to the study of the work of foreign missions in India, China and Japan ... I really would have enjoyed a task of the kind. It would be a fascinating study with all expenses paid and salaries and allowances equal to that I received as Prime Minister, and every facility afforded for inquiry and for meeting people in all walks of life. Had I been defeated, as well as my party, I would, I believe, have accepted the offer, but I have, of course, declined it. It is just as well to keep this quite confidential but I have felt I would like you to know of it, especially as it seems to present just the kind of opportunity needed to realize much of what you have in mind as in the currents of thought which are becoming increasingly important in our day.[35]

To explain King's responses as merely ambitious is to ignore his feelings of despondency and his distaste for so many of the tasks of leadership. To retire in 1930 might have been an admission of defeat but his victory in 1935 intensified, if anything, the 'strain' syndrome.

King's feelings of depression and resentment continued until late 1939. A revealing insight into some of the antecedents of the tensions is given in Violet Markham's letter to John Buchan following her visit to Canada:

But as he admits himself he is very tired & on domestic matters I don't feel his mind has any resilience. I couldn't get him to discuss any domestic question – railways, provincial relations, unemployment. He just shied away from my enquiries & I could get nothing out of him. He raised himself with me the question of his retirement; spoke of his great mental fatigue & realisation that he couldn't go on indefinitely. He was anxious about the election ... If the moment were propitious he would be glad to retire but when is the moment ever propitious? Or the right successor obvious?[36]

The question of why, in the face of such obvious strain and distress, did King cling to political office for so long will be considered in the epilogue of this study.

6 ❖ Knights of the Round Table

The Arthurian legends were more than just a story to Mackenzie King. They represented an ideal which he sought to recreate in twentieth-century Canada. As early as 1899 he had expressed 'the desire to be such a knight' and longed for a group of like-minded, chivalrous men in whose company he could 'fight the good fight' and put the world to right. Many young men have dreams of attempting great deeds of valour at some time in their lives but the dream soon fades in the face of the practical demands of life. Not so with King. His romantic dream did not fade as he was caught up in his career as a party politician and political leader. It pervaded, with strongly religious overtones, his whole political outlook and in particular his approach to personal relations.

The main parameters of these ideal associations reflect, as might be expected, King's need for affection and reassurance. The more King failed to establish supportive intimate relations in his personal life, the more he was driven to impose this need on his public life. Thus King had a strong personal preference for being surrounded by men with whom he had personal empathy. Fortunately for his political career he did not allow this preference to dominate his behaviour in such important political tasks as cabinet making or civil service appointments. That the ideal was a long-term goal rather than an immediate necessity was a tribute to the effectiveness of his defences and to the supportive qualities of those personal relations that he did establish.

King was prepared to work with less than congenial colleagues if he had to, particularly if they had qualities such as competence or representativeness which he needed. But this acceptance of political necessity did not end his endeavours to create the ideal relationship. King devoted considerable attention and energy to the task of attracting into all levels of Canadian government men formed in his self-image. These were the finer type of men, conscientious in their desire to serve their fellow man, loyal and willing to devote themselves unstintingly to the causes King espoused. Such men demonstrated their superior qualities through trust in King's insight and judgment, through acceptance of his perception of the issues, and through willingness to shoulder the tedious burdens that surrounded him. It was at this level that King focused his hopes of being part of an order of knights. And it was at this level that he was most disappointed – the qualities that made these new recruits so desirable ensured that they could never maintain the position that King required of them.

Clearly, King responded more readily to those who appeared to value him personally, and his need for this overt appreciation was insatiable. It was not enough to thank King once for a gift or courtesy – there was no end to the praise and support that he expected from his political associates. To a considerable extent his receptivity to ideas and opinions was coloured by the attitude of the person expressing it towards King. Even after he became an established, international figure King was inordinately pleased by the attention he received from other prominent men. He interpreted the formal courtesies that were his due as head of the Canadian government as signs of personal appreciation. But what he particularly treasured were any informalities or intimacies in these contacts which could be interpreted as a sign that he was getting preferential treatment, that he was different, that this relationship was more personal than official. In the expression of this need he showed little discrimination. He was as flattered by such responses from Hitler and Mussolini as he was from Roosevelt or King George. It was the reaction that was important not the source. He was of course meticulous to a fault in his own behaviour in similar circumstances. His notes of thanks were fulsome in the extreme and he was prepared to 'run himself ragged' over the details of formal visits to Canada.

In his relations with his staff King was more capricious than in his responses to world leaders. These men were squires or body servants rather than candidates to knighthood and it was in these interactions that the marked contrast between his capacity to demand and to give affection was clearly revealed. Here any tendency to put personal needs and wishes before those of the prime minister or any non-compliance with his whims and wishes was interpreted as lack of affection and often aroused a degree of 'rage' completely disproportionate to the original misdemeanour. King expected his subordinates to interpret their position literally even to subordinating their views of the nature of their responsibilities and duties to his. Traditional lines of job demarcation meant nothing to him. The function of his subordinates was to serve him in any capacity that he chose, for only thus could they demonstrate the personal nature of the service. King preferred personal devotion to institutional or role loyalty, and where possible he demanded it. And the same time he insisted that his staff use their initiative and not bother him with the petty details of his political responsibilities. For his staff, therefore, empathy with or an intuitive insight into King's priorities and intentions was an essential qualification for a successful working relationship.

THE KING'S MAN

King's attempt to personalize the institutional dimensions of his political role was all pervasive even extending as far as his relations with the governor general. Although this interaction is not the most important in which a prime minister is involved in contemporary politics, it is one of the most interesting to study in terms of King's behaviour, for it demonstrated most effectively the degree to which King's personal needs impinged on his political actions. To a certain extent the problems of staffing, party organization, and cabinet formation would have been the concern of any Canadian prime minister during this period; the same cannot be said of the energy and concern that King expended on matters related to the formal executive. Even as early as 1921 the role of the governor general had become such that most contemporary commentators would have considered the relationship of marginal importance. The fact that King became actively concerned with this question and was prepared to devote a considerable amount of time to its clarification meant that it assumed an importance it might not otherwise have had. In King's mind the issue was closely related to the whole question of Canada's ties with Britain.

King's attitude towards the governor general was a complex one which had developed and hardened over time. In assuming the Liberal leadership and the premiership of Canada, King had reached the peak of his aspirations. He appeared to have no ambitions for honours or status outside Canada, seeking from abroad only that additional lustre that came from heightened recognition of Canada and his leadership. At the same time he was disconcerted to find that as prime minister of Canada he did not stand alone at the pinnacle of power and as the monarch's first servant; at least in formal terms he must always be overshadowed by the governor general. King's affection for royalty and the sovereign over the seas was strong; his feelings towards the sovereign's representative in Canada were less straightforward.

King's expectations of the relationship had been coloured by his experiences with earlier incumbents and his own personal needs. The development of his acquaintance with Lord and Lady Aberdeen, the tolerant interest shown in him by Lord Minto and the Duke of Devonshire, and the active patronage of Lord Grey had predisposed King to view the governor general in a favourable light. With the death of Sir Wilfrid Laurier, King had been deprived of his political counsellor and personal friend, and the governor general might well fulfil this role. The relationship with Lord Byng, however, revealed the ambiguity of King's outlook. His extreme partisanship and fear of Tory machinations predisposed him to suspect the worst, even of close associates, in moments of tension and disagreement. When these doubts were intensified by identification with his Mackenzie heritage, the disharmony assumed crisis proportions.[1] The apparently successful resolution of the King-Byng crisis did not end King's ambiguity towards governors general. The relationship was most complex during the term of John Buchan, Lord Tweedsmuir; therefore, this relationship can be examined in some detail.

King's preference for congenial relationships in public life and the anxiety which any obvious lack of harmony provoked strongly influenced his attitude towards appointments. Just when King thought of John Buchan as a possible governor general is not clear, but it is evident that without King's persistence Buchan would not have been considered for the post. To a man as concerned with omens and coincidences as King was, the links between Buchan and the vice-regal post may have seemed extraordinary.[2] Nevertheless, it was as friend and companion that King first expressed his growing admiration for Buchan following the latter's visit to Ottawa in 1924: 'I can honestly say that I know no man whose companionship I would rather be privileged to share, to me he is truly a man after God's own heart, so full of all the qualities most to be admired and so utterly devoid of any flaw of character.'[3] The inconclusive election of 1925 and the differences of opinion with Lord Byng which followed in 1926 strengthened King's conviction that the selection of the next governor general should not be left to the whim of the Tory government. It was a simple step to link the need to find the right successor to Lord Byng and King's desire for the companionship of a man who was sympathetic to his aims and aspirations. In a letter (2 December 1925) in which he discussed the election and his reason for staying in office, King told Miss Markham of his thoughts and appealed to her for confirmation of his wisdom and for practical aid in achieving his end.

Once or twice I have wondered whether, in the event of the Government being continued in office, it might not be possible to have Buchan succeed Lord Byng in the Governor Generalship of our Dominion ... In dealing with the problems with which we are faced, I should find the association with a man like Buchan an ideal one, and I do think it is of the greatest importance that there should be the utmost sympathy and confidence between the Prime Minister and whoever may come to Canada from Britain. Perhaps I am adopting an unconventional method of suggesting, in a letter of this character, who the successor of the Governor General should be. On the other hand knowing how close in friendship you are to both John and Mrs. Buchan I have felt that perhaps you, better than anyone else, could tell me how they would be adapted to view a suggestion of this kind.

There were a number of factors which contributed to King's enthusiasm for Buchan. In the first place, Buchan was not titled and was a personal friend, and both of these factors would help reduce the distance between the prime minister and the sovereign's representative. As King's personal choice, Buchan would be in a sense King's protégé, a situation which would reverse the dependent relationship which King had had with Lord Grey and other governors general. As a man of noble character and parliamentary experience, Buchan would be less likely to misunderstand either King's motives or the proper course to be followed. In this way he could fulfil King's need for a non-partisan judge on whom he could depend for confirmation. He would thus be a person with whom King could discuss his difficulties and his problems, and because of his lack of family and reluctance to form close ties with any of his colleagues King was particularly isolated and in need of support.

It was one thing for King to express a preference for Buchan, but it was an entirely different matter to transform this preference into an actuality since the nomination of the governor general was not within the providence of the Canadian government. The existing conventions reduced the Canadian government to the passive role of approving the names on a list submitted to it, and King did not find this situation congenial. As always, however, he was prepared to accept temporarily the letter of the arrangement, but this did not mean he accepted the spirit. Miss Markham was entrusted with the task of ascertaining if Buchan was willing to serve and of explaining King's position to him. Buchan carefully refused to make any endeavour on his own behalf, although he was not unwilling to accept such an appointment. Consequently, Miss Markham was also given the task of putting King's views indirectly to the British government.[4] To enlist the aid of a private individual to conduct delicate negotiations between the Canadian and the British governments on a matter of royal prerogative was certainly an unusual step, but it was not uncharacteristic of King. This indirect approach through personal channels had advantages. It maintained the illusion of constitutional propriety, without restricting King's freedom to manoeuver. Also, where no official overture had been made no failure or compromise was involved.

King's need for control over the alternatives could be catered to by the parallel development of several alternatives. In this way the solution reached could always be interpreted as the one he had sought. At the same time as King was indirectly canvassing for Buchan in England, he was making the acquaintance of the Willingdons in Ottawa and convincing himself that their appointment would be satisfactory. But King's approval of Lord Willingdon did not mean that he had given up his wish to have Buchan as adviser and companion, and his belief in the desirability of his appointment remained. Any further step must await the clarification of Canada's role in vice-regal appointments. It was not King's way to trouble smooth waters – such a change must wait on a suitable occasion.

King continued to correspond with Buchan over the years and responded enthusiastically to Buchan's sympathetic understanding of his difficulties and expressions of personal concern. When rumours of a possible vice-regal appointment reached the Buchans in July 1934, however, they were less than keen; they had been through this situation before and this time the outcome appeared even further beyond King's control. Although the responsibility for advising the sovereign on the appointment was now firmly in the hands of the Canadian government, King was in opposition and there was no precedent for consulting the leader of the opposition on such matters.

To King, the rush to make an appointment before it was constitutionally necessary seemed to indicate a Tory plot. Just as the Meighen government had sought to improve its position in the dying days of its term of office so now R.B. Bennett appeared to be trying to make an arrangement which would favour Tory interests. King, confident of his party's victory in the next election, felt that he had a right to this appointment. This equation of the problem with the earlier conflicts enabled him to move with confidence since he already had a formula of proven success – a constitutional crisis. The 1935 episode has not received as much attention as the 1926 incident because it lacked a spectacular issue, but, as J.R. Mallory noted, if King had carried through his proposal to seek the removal of any governor general whose appointment Mr Bennett might recommend, 'the consequences would have been a number of awkward constitutional issues.' It was left to the next governor general, Bessborough, to find a way out of the impasse which Mallory characterized as 'bring[ing] about agreement between the two party leaders,' but which appears to be more accurately described as King getting all he demanded.[5] If compromises were made they were made by Bennett and by the crown. Mackenzie King's description of the incident implies that the initiative was his and this seems the most accurate view.

I may tell you privately, to permit of the Bessborough's getting back to England this fall, Bennett was obliged, not only to confer with me about a successor, the appointment was to be made before a general election, but to have someone who would be acceptable to me. He let me make my own nomination, and I suggested the names of Buchan and Spender. There was others mentioned by him, but he accepted Buchan, saying that he regarded mention of his name as an inspiration ... It was fortunate we were able to agree on Buchan. Had we not been able to agree on someone, we would probably have had another Governor General issue, had Bennett himself attempted an appointment before the general elections were over seeing that Bessborough's term is not up until next year.[6]

In every positive sense, John Buchan appeared to King as '*my*' governor general. The appointment was a culmination of King's determination, steadfastness, patience, and courage. It created what King regarded as an ideal relationship, one King had been seeking throughout his career. He set out his expectations in a letter to Buchan on 19 July 1935: 'I shall have you at my side as a counsellor and friend, and shall be holding toward yourself a similar position. I shall feel indeed that our paths have been brought together through the guidance of Providence, and, under His guidance. I believe we should be able to do together very much for this country and for the Empire of which it is a part. No years could possibly be more important than those which are immediately ahead.' Yet, from the beginning the relationship was built on a weak foundation. King persisted in his tendency to endow all his friends with exaggerated virtues and with characteristics which reflected his own hopes and sentiments. Consequently, he was inevitably disappointed when the relationships were less idyllic in practice than he had anticipated.

If Buchan was to stand at his side in a personal and a public capacity, it was important that there should be no misunderstanding as to their relative status. King made it clear to Buchan on 29 July that he was maintaining the stance he had taken in the King-Byng crisis: 'the appointment of the governor general, *like all else*, is exercisable upon the advice of ministers ... neither the Sovereign, nor the Ministry, can escape this responsibility – the one of accepting, and the other of tendering advice.' In this relationship only one man could lead and this must be King. Buchan seemed to be prepared to accept this definition of their public relationship.

The first challenge related to the question of Buchan's accepting a title. King was enthusiastic about the possibility of a commoner as governor general. Once more Miss Markham had been called upon to make his view known to Buchan, who was urged at least to postpone taking a peerage until his return from Canada. The appeal was made in the name of the Canadian people, but it is possible that the action also involved King's resentment of his formal superior, an earlier manifestation of the sentiments he was to express in 1940 regarding not being the first Canadian. Buchan, who appears to have favoured a peerage, was able to avoid the issue when the crown took a firm stand on the matter. King accepted the royal view although he denied its validity, reasserting his claim that the crown could only act on the advice of the responsible ministry. As if to have the last word he pointedly addressed the new governor general in his welcoming speech as John Buchan.[7]

King had sought in Buchan that combination of patron, friend, and assistant that characterized his model and his need. It was almost as if he anticipated a return to the carefree days of his youth when together with Harper he had wandered through the Gatineau Hills and discussed the finer things of life. He had envisaged evenings of companionship and earnest talks, weekends at Kingsmere, and long country walks. When he welcomed the governor general to Canada as plain John Buchan, he was signalling that it was the friend rather than the official or rather the friend in the official that he needed. These expectations were unrealistic; even if Buchan had shared King's outlook (which he did not), he had a family and a role which would make great demands on his time and resources.

No one could have tried harder than Buchan to make the relationship work. He appeared to have a genuine admiration for much that King had done and agreed with his basic view of the role of the governor general. He was prepared to take every opportunity to keep the waters smooth. He was ready to adopt the supportive role and offer appreciation, praise, and encouragement, including small but extremely important gestures such as dedicating his book *Augustus* to King. He was willing to take on many quasi-political chores for King including providing notes and memos for speeches, vetting prospective candidates for lieutenant governorships, sounding out foreign heads of state on policy issues. He allowed King to veto and amend his public speeches on informal occasions in order to avoid controversy. He appeared prepared to co-operate in any direction that the prime minister wished within this range. At the same time, he was not prepared to nullify the governor generalship to the point of becoming 'invisible' nor to become a cipher. He had a fitting sense of his own importance and maintained a voluminous correspondence with men of political substance in England. Although these connections allowed King to use Buchan as an avenue for informal approaches, they might also underline the difference between the two men and accentuate an incipient rivalry. The governor general may have appeared to King as more convivial, more popular, more attention-catching than he was and therefore unconsciously a potential rival and enemy. In situations such as the visit to the United States of the governor general or the visit to Quebec of the president of the United States, this 'fame' could be a source of considerable ambiguity in terms of appropriate reactions from King. To understand the process we must revert for a moment to King's expectations.

A great deal of King's favourable perception of Buchan was based on a supposed identity of interests. This was revealed in practical actions such as King's endeavours to have Buchan attend St Andrew's Presbyterian Church, King's place of worship, rather than the Anglican Cathedral and the assumption that Buchan would share King's stand for 'old Presbyterianism' against church union. Coincidences such as the death of Buchan's mother on the anniversary of the death of King's mother had great significance in themselves. King's interpretation of the meaning can be seen in his letter to Buchan on 17 December 1936.

Over many years, I have cherished the hope that the day might come when you and I might be found working together in the relationship which we at present enjoy. It was a large hope but I never doubted that some day it would be fulfilled. It has been fulfilled at the most critical of times not only in your life and in mine but in the affairs of the world. To the Providence that has made our friendship and companionship a part of His will, and has guided and directed our paths till they have crossed to be shared as one, I cannot be too humbly and profoundly grateful.

Again, there is uneasiness in the repetition of the appeal for frankness noted in earlier correspondence. It is possible that King continued actively to fear a repetition of the type of misunderstanding that had marred the relationship with Lord Byng.

Because Buchan was both supportive and threatening it was difficult for King to make an unambiguous judgment concerning the situation. One can note over time that response which Heeney so aptly described as 'an infuriating blend of disappointment and tired patience,' in the sequence that follows.[8] King's reaction reflects the failure of his efforts to rationalize his disappointment with the relationship:

I feel quite sure that from now on my relations with all at Govt. House will be the happiest possible; – a relationship of old & close friends, with many human interests, as well as political duties, which it is possible to share in common.

Our relations are much less strained than they were, but I still feel less at home at Govt. House than almost anywhere else. I find the President of the u.s. a hundred times easier to talk to and get along with than the Gov. Gen. of my own country.[9]

Miss Markham's letter to Buchan on 20 August 1939, following her visit to Canada, conveys a clear picture of the way the relationship had developed:

He spoke of you in warmest terms as the best Governor General he has ever worked with – that you have been perfect throughout. Do you realize his deep personal affection for you? When you came to Canada all his sentiments & emotions were keyed up to the highest point about you. His second house at Kingsmere was enlarged & beautified & rooms added for the express purpose of occupation by yourself. He dreamt of long walks & talks with you in the woods & among those distressing ruins. I hope I am not indiscreet in saying this ... but I think there has been a shade of disappointment in his mind that he has found you more of the Governor & less of the personal friend than perhaps he had hoped – that he feels your state has kept you a little apart.

It can be inferred that a common characteristic of all King's personal-political relationships was revealed in this example. The demands that all be intermingled and shared, 'a relationship of old and close friends, with many human interests, as well as political duties ... to share in common,' put an impossible strain on the recipient and ensured that almost inevitably disappointment would follow.[10]

The experience of 1926 and 1935 meant that when faced with any subsequent challenge to his view of the relationship between Canada and her sovereign, King would react in the manner validated by earlier successes. The third, and least known, constitutional crisis arose over an apparently trivial point of ceremony concerning the royal visit of 1939. The incident is important because it absorbed so much of the time and energy of the prime minister and related officials at a period of almost overwhelming international tension.

Despite his suspicions of British aristocracy and his genuine distaste for honours and distinctions in the dominions, King was neither anti-British nor anti-monarchy. In fact he took a child-like delight in the visit and concerned himself with the most minor details of its organization to the detriment of other business. The visit would be a triumphant occasion for him; the grandson of the rebel would greet the reigning British sovereign on Canadian soil as first minister of the senior dominion. But George vi had expressed a desire for Lord Tweedsmuir to meet the sovereign at Quebec to hand over his stewardship. This request disconcerted Mackenzie King who had no wish to share the great occasion. Tweedsmuir recognized the importance of this occasion to King and agreed to wait in Ottawa. Buckingham Palace did not favour this expedient: 'I am certainly nervous about what people will say if the Governor General does not appear at Quebec ... I do hope that the Prime Minister will not think that we are being deliberately obstructive and trying to lower his status. Which of course is the last thing we should want to do.'[11] As is obvious from the correspondence which follows King was not prepared to accept this situation.

The matter is, I am afraid, more delicate than it appears ... When my Prime Minister came back ... from his holidays, he raised at once the question of my meeting Their Majesties at Quebec ... When I informed the Prime Minister of your view I discovered that he now took the matter very seriously, and in an entirely different way. He thought there was a point of constitutional importance involved, and that the Prime Minister, the elected representative of the people, should be the first person in Canada to greet Their Majesties.[12]

Palace officials continued to oppose the arrangement, placing King in the position of having to insist on his viewpoint, which he did in a letter to Lord Tweedsmuir on 24 February 1939.

As a result, Your Excellency may regard the following as expressing the considered view of the government ... As the solution which appears to us to be not only in accord with the forms and spirit of the constitution but also that best fitted to contribute to the symbolic values of the occasion, we consider that the first words spoken to the King in recognition of his having in person entered his realm of Canada, whether they be words of advice or report, or words of greeting and welcome on behalf of his Canadian people and government, should be spoken by the person who happens, for the time being, by the will of the people, under due operation of the constitution, to be the principal servant of the Crown of Canada, and His Majesty's principal Canadian adviser.

King's revised position contained very significant echoes of the King-Byng crisis and 1935 incident. In the light of the sovereign's fear of controversy it was inevitable that King would get his own way.

Tweedsmuir's death in 1940 brought the relationship to an end but not the response. King continued to make capricious demands on subsequent governors general and to think in terms of a constitutional crisis when his view was challenged. As a transference response to unsolved personal problems it could have no end.

SQUIRES TO THE BODY POLITIC

The party conference of 1919 had conferred on King the titular status of leader; it remained to be seen whether he would be able to activate the role in practice. Politically speaking King was young, inexperienced, insecure, and surrounded by associates only too willing to usurp the reins of power if his grip should slacken. It has already been suggested that King submerged his personal identity into an incorporative party identity as demonstrated in the statement 'when I say "I" I mean of course the party.' In such circumstances he might be expected also to transfer to the party scene the anxieties and defences of his personal development.

No matter what his personal inclinations were, it was inevitable that King's first concern as party leader must be the winning of the next election. It was an essential step not merely for the survival of the party but also in terms of his own survival as leader. It is possible that King's early experience reinforced his uncertainty and tensions in election campaigns. Although his belief in Tory machinations as the root cause of Liberal party defeats was satisfying, it could not allay his fears of the next encounter. He had argued strongly that organization was the key to electoral success, and this theme was to remain a consistent feature of his approach. At the same time, the personal factors which made elections a source of tension precluded effective action on his part to deal with the problem.

There were two important dimensions to extra-parliamentary leadership – co-ordinating election activity and financing the campaign.

King was reluctant to get personally involved in these activities on moral and practical grounds but was equally reluctant to give any subordinate complete charge. The solution preferred was to find men who would act as an extension of King, seeing the issues through his eyes and acting as he would have done in the same situation. These men would be encouraged to act independently as long as their actions were in accord with these criteria; they would be an order of party squires to support the governing order in cabinet.

The issue which received King's close personal attention was that of the financial resources of the office of leader. The friends and supporters who had dealt with the practicalities of his candidacy were reminded that their continued support was essential to the venture. In fact, King was rather peeved by the need to take the initiative in this regard. He preferred his friends to anticipate his needs and meet them spontaneously. King realized that because he was not a member of parliament he could not receive the salary of the leader of the opposition and was immediately concerned that he should not in any way deplete his capital.

I wrote Mr. Fisher a long letter, referring to the position I find myself in, in getting beyond my income considerably in running along, making outlays on incidental party expenses. I am determined to see that my capital remains intact come what may. One never knows what the future may bring and it is my only security against all its vast uncertainties. I am prepared to give all my time and all my income on the capital I have, but more than this I am unwilling to do without a protest.[13]

Discussions were held with Sydney Fisher and Arthur Hardy, and as a result the latter agreed 'to meet [King's secretary F.A.] McGregor's expenses, till the next session opened & whatever else was required in the way of staff.' Fisher was left with the task of organizing a party fund from which the leader's expenses could be met. King was not altogether satisfied with the outcome of this endeavour. A month later he wrote:

I had lunch with Mr. Fisher. I felt some what exasperated when I spoke about making payments of disbursements on account of the party and found no willing expression on Fisher's part to see that this was reimbursed. He has been collecting money for the purpose of my office, and money has been collected from members to assist, and yet he puts me in the position of having to ask and seemingly beg for it. I told him pretty plainly that I was giving all my time and service for nothing ... I think he felt a little taken back when I spoke out.

King repeatedly referred to Fisher as mean and 'too old maidish' when he failed to anticipate King's financial needs; although these were characteristics that he himself shared, he did not recognize the attributes in himself. He was more receptive to Hardy's open-handedness, terming his cheque for $1,000 'very thoughtful and generous.'[14]

The problem of finance was just part of the burden that the leadership placed on King. Although McGregor had been retained to provide assistance, King found himself increasingly unable to cope with the work load. Once again his friends rallied around and Andrew Haydon was appointed to assume some of the party responsibilities. In the person of Haydon, King had the type of support he craved. An undemanding, loyal, and hard-working individual who was not unduly worried by specific boundaries of responsibility, Haydon was just the type of associate King preferred and was rewarded by an appointment to the Senate in 1924. The key to Haydon's success lay in the fact 'that he never presumed to be more than an advisor.' Thus he did not constitute a rival or a threat to King, at least not until the Beauharnois scandal in the summer of 1931. On this occasion King preferred to sacrifice Haydon rather than 'accept responsibility' for his actions. At the time of Haydon's appointment King had been careful to keep aloof from the financial arrangements, stating 'I expressly asked to be kept out of all financial interests and obligations.' Although he was anxious to work in harmony and to avoid any positive conflict, he was prepared to be ruthless when necessary even if these actions took a heavy unconscious toll in terms of the energy necessary to justify his behaviour.[15]

To get round his difficulties King thought it necessary to reorganize the party and turned to Britain for a model. A permanent central office – the National Liberal Federation – could 'make more formal the separation between the party leader and party finances.'[16] It would, however, give undue prominence and formal status to someone else within the family, and the situation did not augur well for Vincent Massey, who was appointed to head the new body and who in many respects was perceived as a rival and a threat. Still the plan had the essential elements of success and King wrote enthusiastically to Violet Markham about it on 28 January 1933: 'You will be pleased to know that Vincent and Alice Massey have thrown themselves wholeheartedly into the work of party organization ... It is something I have striven to effect ever since I became leader of the party, but until Massey put his shoulder to the wheel in earnest, and lent his quite exceptional organizational abilities, as well as financial aid to the project, it was impossible to bring it about.' But while King welcomed Massey's shoulder to the wheel he clung to the illusion that it was he rather than Massey who was pushing and steering.

It was possible that the wealthy, dynamic Massey raised feelings of inferiority in King and at the same time unconsciously reminded King of his own thrusting impatience when waiting for Laurier to step aside. King had been instrumental in getting Massey into Liberal politics and Massey had had to be promised a portfolio before he had been prepared to run. Massey, defeated in the 1925 election, had sought a by-election seat with the same ardour as King in 1911. Failing to find one he had taken up, at King's instigation, an appointment in the United States. Massey's desire for 'an adequate opportunity for useful work' echoed King's earlier sentiments. In 1930 Massey returned to Canadian politics. It is possible that King saw a parallel with 1917 and suspected Massey out of his own guilt about the earlier situation. It can be no more than a plausible hypothesis but it does help account for the latent hostility which King expressed towards Massey and his disproportionate suspicions of the latter's motives.

As long as Massey was prepared to limit himself to a supportive role King could be magnanimous: 'I found both Vincent and Alice most sympathetic and understanding concerning myself, and quite prepared to admit that my judgment on some of the matters over which we had differed in the past ... was best. Vincent also agreed that from now on the National Liberal Federation would be used primarily for organizational purposes. He told me he would give special attention to its work.'[17] But it was difficult for a man of Massey's background to give King the type of subservient service that he required. King could tolerate only one focal point in his relationships – himself – and could feel strong empathy only with those who reflected this concern. King's comments on Massey in his diary took on an increasingly derogatory tone. 'Vincent and Alice Massey came at 3 ... They were both "crawling out" – saving their faces by not telling the truth ... He cannot do other than want to manage everything.' 'He talked of his own health, but had not a considerate word about myself. Is purely selfish and self-seeking & I find it difficult to be patient with him.'[18] It was difficult to draw the fine line between freeing King from his burdens and infringing on his personal responsibilities. The abrasive element in the relationship had become particularly strong after the Port Hope Conference and during 1933 and 1934. Campaign organization was one of the areas which King felt to be a burden, a responsibility of which he wished to be relieved. He recorded his outlook in his diary on 4 November 1933:

Most important letters were to Vincent Massey and the ex-Liberal Ministers ... giving them to understand I did not intend to do their work for them in S. Oxford. That it was for them to organize and to speak in the campaign ... It was a sort of ultimatum to the lot to get busy and disclose whether they are deserving of any recognition should the party be returned to power. I regard it as cheek that they should meet & resolve (with Massey) that I should open the campaign, putting it up to me again. It is amazing that every time there is a contest, I am looked to to bear the brunt of it, to get the candidates into the field, do the speaking, supply the ideas, for a lot of lazy men who are using the party to serve their own ends, not using their lives and influence to further its great purposes.

By 10 April 1934 the tension had increased and King's diary comments about Massey were more openly critical: 'I knew he was lying & opened out straight on him ... [said] I had enough on my hands just now without having to meet opposition of our members to his mistaken utterances ... He is so inconsistent and selfish – just a slave driver used to his wealth & "Efficiency" etc. riding rough shod over others.' The immediate cause of this outburst was Massey's desire to shoulder the burden of the election by undertaking a speaking tour in the west despite King's wish that he should restrict himself to organizational work behind the scenes. To King, Massey's efficiency was an error since it put pressure on him which he resented. King would go as far as to describe an invitation to visit the Masseys as an attempt to 'corral' him, to restrict his freedom and he declared forcefully: 'I must never again let myself be "driven" by any one. I feel a resentment beyond words at the manner in which Massey had crowded me in the last year or two. I shall always feel that not a little of my ill health has been due to the "pressure" he has exerted & sought to exert upon me at times ... it has been a grievous annoyance.'[19]

Much of King's sensitivity to pressure from behind was due to persistent rumours about his health and the possibility of a new leader. King had noted the talk in his diary (1 September 1934): 'I have been not a little annoyed at the number of reports that have come to me lately and which continue to be circulated about my health that I am very ill, etc. ... It is of course mostly Tory propaganda, a desire to weaken my hand – & that of the party.' These tensions, associated with doubts about the future, served to strengthen King's concern about financial matters and a further discussion paralleling that of 1919 was necessary: 'Vincent and I had breakfast together in the sunroom during which time I spoke to him of the fund Arthur Hardy is getting together to cover disbursements of the office. I pointed out how I had allowed all contributions to go to the Federation instead of coming to my office ... I expected some one – the Federation Exec. – wd. at least see to travelling expenses of my Secretary etc. & outlays for telegrams.'[20]

Massey was completely confused by the intricacies of his relationship with the leader by 1935. Massey later described the relationship as follows:

On October 5, 1935, I saw Mackenzie King aboard his private car in order to report to the Leader, as chairman of the party organization, and to receive whatever instructions he cared to give me. I hadn't seen him for several weeks. My visit that morning was most unwelcome and gave rise to a conversation that was far from pleasant, and the atmosphere was not sweetened by the fact that King's valet had wakened him on my arrival. I was accused of invading his privacy on numerous occasions, even to the point of affecting his health; of making suggestions which were unacceptable; of being generally wrong in my views and not stressing sufficiently in the campaign publicity his own qualities as leader; as being moved in my work in the campaign by self interest. After Mackenzie King's outburst on this occasion, I felt it better that we should not meet again for a while, and I didn't see him until after the election in October.[21]

But nothing Massey could do would end the awkwardness of the relationship. After electoral victory had reconfirmed King's leadership of the nation, he continued to resent Massey and to criticize his actions even when Massey moved to London as Canadian high commissioner.

King's reluctance to relinquish personal control in situations which he identified as crucial and his desire to delegate the work component of his various responsibilities affected his attempts to establish an adequate support staff. The inadequacies of the existing arrangements and his need for personal and secretarial assistance were recurring themes in his correspondence. But a great deal of the burden was of King's own making. Along with the premiership he had retained the presidency of the privy council and the portfolio of external affairs. Only the latter office was served by a staff of any size. King made little attempt to differentiate between the duties associated with each office or to clearly demarcate the responsibilities of those who served him in any capacity.

The role of his staff members was complicated by King's inability to distinguish between personal responsibilities and professional or public responsibilities. Harper and McGregor had been companions and friends as well as associates and subordinates. The dual role was difficult to fulfil. King's insecurity and low self-esteem meant that staff members must be supportive and undemanding; they must be willing to assume those duties he considered a burden but careful not to infringe in those areas which King considered his personal prerogative. King's extensive personal correspondence added an extra dimension to the problem of secretarial help. He explained to Violet Markham the situation which existed at the time he assumed office in 1921:

From Dec the sixth when the results of my election were made known ... my time was busily occupied ... Letters to the number of many thousands came in upon me, and I was wholly unprepared to cope with any of them ... As Prime Minister, a wholly new set of responsibilities were thrust upon them [the two secretaries he had had as leader of the opposition] as well as upon me. I had to go into an office filled with clerks of whom I knew nothing, and many of whom were known to be closely allied with the late Administration.[22]

The situation had not improved when he wrote again on 19 July 1923.

I have not yet reached the point where I have been able to delegate to others much of the work of my office, or, perhaps I should say, offices ...What, however, I find it wholly impossible to cope with is the volume of correspondence which comes to me from all sides. My secretaries do the best they can with the major portion of it, & I distribute to Ministers as much as I can: but I am left, notwithstanding, with a host of communications to which I have to give personal attention.

King received advice from several sources on how to deal with this problem and resolved to try to do something about it, but his obsessive defences limited his capacity to respond.

It was not until 1927 that King attempted to make any major change in his staff arrangements when he offered a post described rather vaguely as 'Executive Assistant to the Prime Minister' to J. Burgon Bickersteth. King apparently had in mind something similar to Sir Maurice Hankey's role in the British government, but he also anticipated that Bickersteth would actually take over the responsibility for organizing the office, thus relieving King of the burden. It is indicative of King's ambiguous attitude towards the British connection that he would choose an Englishman for this post and encourage him to consult Hankey and the British deputy secretary, Tom Jones, on the matter. As a result of this consultation Bickersteth presented a memorandum to King outlining British theory but he refused the post. As he told Jones: 'I feel certain I am right in not going to Ottawa – at any rate at the present juncture ... If the Memorandum and talks with Hankey (if as I hope, he visits us) make him alter his conception of the whole proposal, then the situation might be different.'[23] It is clear, however, that Bickersteth had correctly interpreted King's wishes. What King was seeking was a combination secretary, assistant, friend, and fellow spirit, not an impartial public servant. The refusal allowed him to postpone further action on the appointment. When John Buchan took up the post of governor general in 1936 King revived the idea and approached him for help in the matter. Tweedsmuir approached Bickersteth who provided him with a copy of the original memorandum and commented: 'The failure of our public men in Canada to surround themselves with really able assistants is notorious. It would almost seem as if the P.M. & Cabinet Ministers were suspicious of brains in this capacity. Norman Rogers became a sort of super-secretary to Mr. King in 1927 or early in 1928 but it did not work & Rogers left partly, it is true, because of his health but more, I think, because King did not know how to use him.'[24] It is probably more accurate to say that King had his own unique view of how such assistants should be used, and in the short term no help was better than the wrong person in the job.

King continued to decry the lack of organization but did nothing concrete about it. His letter to Violet Markham on 17 March 1937 outlined the issues as he saw them. 'Of course, I know my secretarial help, both at the Office & at Laurier House, is far from what it should be. My difficulty is to find the kind of person who can serve as Deputy Minister & organize my office for me. That I simply am unable to do myself & at the same time do what is expected of me in the House of Commons and in public appearances outside.' Three months earlier he had lunched with a young lawyer, Arnold Heeney, and noted in his diary, 'I have a good mind to bring him into my own office.'[25] An important indication of King's time-scale and perspective can be seen in the fact that at a time of continued domestic uncertainty and widespread international unrest he was prepared to devoted six months to settling the staff situation.

The procrastination ended the following year when Heeney accepted the post of principal secretary to the prime minister. In turning to Heeney, Mackenzie King was following what can be regarded as his basic pattern in personal relations. Throughout his career he endeavoured to recruit into the public service 'the better kind of man.' In Heeney's case it was the virtues of the father as much as the son which led to the post. In his memoirs Heeney notes the common outlook on Christianity and socialism which had led Mackenzie King to make friends with Canon Heeney in 1934 and the close friendship that followed. There appear to be strong echoes of the Kings' visit to Mr Mulock in the incident described by Heeney. 'In July 1938 my father and I spent an afternoon and evening at Kingsmere. After dinner King asked me to expand on my interest in the public service [discussed the previous year].' This visit had been followed up, as in King's own case, by the offer of a newly created civil service post and the suggestion that this could be considered a stepping stone to the cabinet, as it had been in King's case and that of others. Heeney found he was expected to 'be with him, travel with him, and so forth.' 'My responsibilities over the busy month [during the Royal visit] were extensive but undefined, and they bore little resemblance to what had been discussed the previous summer. I became in fact a sort of handyman at the disposition of the Prime Minister.'[26] While this was obviously King's personal choice, he tended to explain it as if it were a circumstance beyond his control.

You will be glad to know that I have been able to secure, as a principal secretary, a friend whom I have had in mind for that office for some years past. His presence has made a great difference in my life. Unfortunately, since his association with my office, his time has had to be devoted almost exclusively to matters pertaining to the Royal visit and, like my own time, has been taken away in large part from the work of Parliament.[27]

The major problem that the appointment had produced was the difficulty of reconciling the divergent views held by the incumbent and the premier. Heeney wrote subsequently:

To Mackenzie King it would have been the natural order of things for me to share in all his activities, and to progress from his office – whatever my style and title – into direct participation in political life under his auspices. My idea, on the other hand, was to create and set to work a new and permanent mechanism which would rationalize and accelerate the business of government at the cabinet level. Because of this difference, I proved a disappointment to King after the first year of our connection.[28]

The difficulty was that King saw no real ambiguity between his role in party politics and his function as premier; therefore Heeney's action in attempting to draw a rigid line between the two responsibilities was not acceptable. It conflicted with King's self-image as a statesman rather than a politician; it threatened the ego defence mechanism which had been developed to cope with his own political preferment while a public servant; and it threatened the integrated public-private identity which King has assumed during his adult life. The anxiety reinforced King's natural reluctance to take any precipitous step. To a man who had taken so long over the apparently simple matter of choosing the right appointee, any delay in beginning the reorganization was merely part of the natural process of waiting for the right moment. That moment appeared to come with the outbreak of war, when as a result of the great increase in business to be dealt with, King was forced to accept a change.

King constantly expressed feelings of disappointment with the men he selected to serve him, but could never accept that his demands were unrealistic. His general response can be seen in a diary entry of 28 September 1937. 'Was amazed when I saw quarters Pickering & his staff have ... away beyond anything I have ... The entire staff [were] ... having tea at 4 o'clock, when I went to find Pickering – they actually had the audacity to ask me if I would ... join them. I confess my staff knows more about looking after itself, than I do, & does so 100% more than after its work ... It irritates me beyond words.'

In the cases discussed so far King had the opportunity to establish the structures and to recruit personnel to meet his own needs and ideas. These situations, however, were endowed with a high degree of flexibility. His techniques of personnel management might be less successful where prior rights and commitments already existed. Just such a situation existed in his department and in cabinet.

The leading member of the Department of External Affairs in 1922 was Loring C. Christie, a man whose reputation and influence far exceeded his official position as legal adviser. But Christie had been a protégé of Sir Robert Borden and had been actively and publicly associated with the two Conservative prime ministers under whom he had served. These associations would arouse King's suspicions but, at the same time, King had his non-partisan self-image to maintain. To move against Christie would be to behave in a manner incompatible with this important belief. But it was equally impossible for him to rely on a man whom he could not trust. Christie subsequently described the occasion when he inadvertently confirmed this belief. He told Borden of his first official meeting with King: 'Long afterward I recalled that at our original interview he [King] had talked about his political creed at great length, contrasting it with Mr. Meighen's and so on, and that at one or two appropriate pauses I had either been silent or had sought to talk about the Department.'[29] Christie was only half right, however, when he concluded 'it was simply a crude invitation to declare myself his faithful slave.'[30] King did not require his subordinates to be slaves; on the contrary he preferred active and responsible colleagues, but he did require faithfulness from those who had his confidence. The problem was solved by the application of the technique which Lester Pearson later described as 'subtle separation. Separation planned to make it look like self-determination.'[31]

Christie's willingness to carry out a policy contrary to his personal beliefs was never put to the test. His position was probably not improved by the efforts of friends such as J.A. Stevenson, nor his association with leading British imperialists. King however continued to assert his confidence in Christie and even after Christie's resignation King invited him to act as an adviser at the 1926 Imperial Conference. John Munro has suggested that King changed his attitude in 1935 when Christie re-entered the department.[32] In this regard it is necessary to emphasize that while Christie still had his Tory connections he had shed his commitment to the imperial ideal in the meantime and that it was Christie and not King who had changed his stance. Further, with O.D. Skelton firmly in charge, it was unlikely that Christie's Tory leanings would have much effect on department activity. King could thus avail himself of Christie's expert services and reassert his impartiality without in any way endangering Liberal policy.

It is informative to compare King's relations with Christie to his relations with O.D. Skelton, as examples of King's leadership style. In contrast to Christie, Skelton had unimpeachable credentials. As Stacey has noted, Skelton 'was Laurier's biographer and his devoted and partisan admirer.'[33] Such associations were important to King. But more important was the fact that Skelton had revealed that he had the right ideas in a speech before the Canadian Club in Ottawa. Stacey describes this speech as 'a slashing attack on the whole concept of a unified Empire foreign policy formulated by consultation between governments and executed through the British Foreign Office.'[34] Skelton had also shown the willingness to relieve King of irksome duties and to meet King's wishes that was an important qualification for trust. Here was a man on whom King could rely for whole-hearted support, and when the opportunity arose Skelton was appointed undersecretary of state (1925). As Skelton's views were more isolationist and nationalist than King's, his appointment allowed King to see his own more moderate stance as an admirable compromise.

The closeness of his relationship with the prime minister and the agreement they reached on policy matters did not protect Skelton from castigation at the hands of his political superior. As much as he tried,

King was never able to achieve the complete accord that he sought in his working relationships. He could consciously recognize that without Skelton in the Department of External Affairs life would be more difficult for him. His diary entry of 9 October 1937 records his reaction to Skelton's illness:

I went over to see Skelton who has been in bed for three weeks ... What would happen to the External Affairs without Skelton I hardly know, I am hoping a rest may bring him back as I believe it will but he will have to go very carefully from now on. He has attempted far far too much, is over conscientious in all things. He should have remained away a month or two ... How I wish I could find such a man for the Prime Minister's office. I spoke to him of Macdonald, & of Heeney. I shall have to continue to search. Henry & Pickering never have grown as they should. I have tried to 'contract out.'

Skelton's conscientiousness had been described in less complimentary terms on 4 February 1937. Following a dispute over the high commissioner's staff in London King wrote: 'Very wearisome – especially as Skelton keeps all these things in his own hands. I know he tries to do the fair & just thing, but in many things his outlook is difficult, and he is most persistent in holding to his own point of view.' In the same entry King reacted to Skelton's opposition to King's taking a newsman with him on his trip abroad in a petulant and self-pitying way: 'It is the old story. – I work for others – others get what they want & need & I cannot get a helping hand ... "Skelton" is apt to be penny wise pound foolish in this way & to apply the same to me – yet he has a great staff of his own.' And any lowering of standards could be explained in terms of taint, as it was on 11 February 1937. 'I can notice that the five years' association with Bennett has made Skelton less sensitive to these dangers, and more inclined to protect officials, etc., than he would have been five years ago. No Prime Minister, however, ever had a better counsellor than Skelton is.' King's response reveals an important aspect of his criteria of service. Undoubtedly he could have had his own way over the London appointment and the journalist had he been prepared to insist, but this was not his style. King wished to be surrounded by others who would anticipate his needs and comfort and care for him without being asked. In fact he sought in his companions and associates the complementary ideal self and thus was always disappointed with the reality. Nevertheless Skelton was one of the men who came reasonably close to fulfilling King's requirments. Christie and Skelton were both considered outstanding civil servants. Both became closely associated with prime ministers who shared their political outlook, and this relationship must be considered the key factor in the influence they asserted.

THE SEARCH FOR KNIGHTLY COMPANIONS

Unlike an American president, the prime minister of Canada is unable to surround himself with men of his own choosing, especially in the field of cabinet selection. The task of bringing together a loyal, competent, and representative cabinet is one of the most crucial that any government leader faces. It is especially difficult for a young, relatively inexperienced man, selected to lead a badly bruised, divided party. His ability to work with the older, more experienced, often hostile members of the team and to recruit other able men is very important to his success as well as to his inner security. King's reluctance to act without support made the composition of his cabinet a dominant element in subsequent policy direction. King's long period in office makes it impossible to do justice here to the whole gamut of cabinets which he selected during his career. Instead attention will focus on the way he was able to adjust his personal preferences to the political reality and to balance his long-term objectives with a short-term acceptance of the status quo.

Just as the Liberal party could appear as a surrogate family, so would the collegiate nature of cabinet encourage King's belief that it could be a partnership from which he could derive strength and support while zealously maintaining his own life space. He had publicly declared his faith in team effort rather than individual leadership in a speech to the House of Commons in 1922.

I look upon these questions of Government, not as questions to be decided by any one man, but as matters requiring the most mature and careful consideration which it is possible for men of many points of view, assembled together, to give to them ... I shall ever look to the able men who are associated with me for guidance and direction which I need in regard to these all important public questions.[35]

From King's point of view, the particular advantage to this arrangement was that it took responsibilites off his shoulders. Consequently he allowed a great deal of freedom and opportunity to the individual ministers. The degree of responsibility permitted each minister was an important factor in King's leadership success, as was his willingness to be advised by his colleagues in areas where he felt he lacked personal expertise.

Although King outwardly treated all members of the 'political' family with the same courtesy and attention, it is possible to distinguish between those he worked with out of necessity and those who would fit into the category of like-minded men. In particular King's infinite patience in working with the men he inherited had a negative effect on his wish to recruit the more moderate, reforming elements into his team. Throughout the early period of his administration King consistently made overtures to the more moderate members of the Progressive party and to reformers such as E.C. Drury, J.S. Woodsworth, and Agnes Macphail. While these individuals stood outside the Liberal party, they could not be allowed to have a major influence on policy decisions; only if they abandoned their independent position and came in under the wing of his leadership could they expect to be part of the decision-making unit. They, however, were suspicious of old party politics and accepted the prevailing myths of King's ineffectiveness and subordination to the old guard and consequently refused his overtures, thus making it difficult for King to increase the reforming element in his government. The whole process of negotiation involved a self-fulfilling prophecy. The left-wingers suspected King of being lukewarm about reform and by refusing to join him ensured that his government would be more conservative than reformist.

The failure to recruit the leading Progressives does not mean that King was completely unsuccessful in his attempt to enlist cabinet colleagues committed to moderate reform. His first need, however, was to remove his main opponents in such a way as to cause the least disruption to his party and himself. His technique involved a combination of superficial harmony beneath which he manœuvered, usually successfully, for voluntary withdrawal. The technique had its advantages and its costs. In the case of Sir Lomer Gouin the effort was commensurate with the achievement. In the case of Charles Murphy, however, it involved an amount of tension and involvement quite incompatible with the need for Murphy in the team.

Murphy was one of the few remaining Laurier Liberals in Ontario, he had been the driving force behind the decision to select the new leader at a national convention, and he had carried much of the burden for this successful party gathering. He appeared to rate highly on all three ministerial qualities. He was an experienced politician, an energetic organizer and campaigner, with close links to the Irish Catholic vote. He had had departmental experience in the Laurier administration, had held his seat in the House of Commons throughout the period in opposition, and would have an important claim to be part of Ontario's voice in the cabinet. Above all he had been devoted to Laurier and active in ensuring that those who had been loyal to Laurier in 1911 and 1917 would reap their just reward.

Murphy, however, had no personal empathy with King's outlook and no real sympathy with King as an individual or leader. Murphy was an outspoken and controversial figure, fanatical in his causes and loyalties, rigidly opposed to most of King's plans to reunite the party and the government. These qualities were not enough to ensure that his virtues were overlooked, but they did ensure that he could not work harmoniously with his new leader. It was never King's policy to meet opposition head-on if it could be avoided, so it was inevitable that Murphy would be in the cabinet. The diary of 1919 contained numerous entries indicating a complete lack of rapport between the two men:

Expected Charles Murphy but he failed to turn up, fear he may be difficult to manage, thro' wishing to run everything.

A very difficult man to get on with. Means well but is afflicted with a suspicious Irish nature, fault finding to a degree. I do not know just where he is at in what he has in view.

Murphy, too, was a bit on the rampage, not having been the first to be consulted, he evidently wants to 'boss the show.' He is a thorn in the flesh to whoever has to do with him.[36]

The pattern developed during these early weeks of the relationship established the course of their interaction until Murphy's retirement. King continued to turn the other cheek while recording his increased resentment and dissatisfaction in his diary. Murphy continued to resist King's policy and to become increasingly outspoken and publicly critical of his leader. It was only a matter of time before the two men parted company and the one goal behind King's patience was to ensure that Murphy's departure would have no repercussions on him personally or on the party. By refusing to confront Murphy openly, to enter into any direct conflict with him, King kept his team intact although it meant five years of personal anguish before he promoted him to the Senate. King summed up his position on the whole situation on the occasion of Murphy's funeral:

It is fortunate I should be here – away from Ottawa at this time. It spares me from saying – not saying anything: from attending and not attending the funeral. Poor Charles, I have never wronged him in thought or word or deed, though he has done his utmost to destroy me. I have always felt it was his misfortune due to a species of insanity; he will know that he was mistaken and wrong, he will know too that my heart cherishes no ill feeling toward him.'[37]

Sir Lomer Gouin posed for King a greater but more rational problem. Premier of Quebec for fifteen years and with close ties with the Montreal business interests, Gouin was an influential figure among eastern protectionists and a force to be reckoned with in the prevailing political climate. King could not afford to disregard overtures made on Gouin's behalf nor could he allow Gouin to take a prominent role inside the government. Either alternative constituted a direct threat to his leadership. The bargaining over Gouin's position in the government was the first test of strength between the two men. King opened with his lowest offer – leadership of the Senate without portfolio. Gouin counter-proposed justice or presidency of the privy council – the former an important portfolio, the latter a direct challenge to the leader himself. King was prepared to consider railways or justice if he had to. Gouin was prepared to be disappointed over the privy council if King would agree to take two other strong Montreal protectionists into the cabinet as well as himself. King gave way on Rodolphe Lemieux but held out against Walter Mitchell even when Gouin continued to press on Mitchell's behalf. Gouin finally agreed to justice and one protectionist colleague. Neither man had achieved his original objective but King could not believe that no real concessions had been made.[38] His original proposal had been wishful thinking rather than realistic, and Lemieux would probably have had a post under any circumstances. The final decision to give Gouin the portfolio desired by Ernest Lapointe was no real weakness and, in revealing the willingness of Lapointe to give him the support he needed, had additional merit in King's eyes.

Many contemporary commentators felt that Gouin had emerged the stronger from this initial clash of wills but subsequent events were to show that this was not so. The traditions of cabinet solidarity ensured that Gouin would be forced to work behind the scenes in opposition to the leader, and such activity would increase King's mistrust of his colleague and his determination to ease him out of the government. As long as Gouin was prepared to support his leader publicly he was gradually dissipating his strength. King could underline his own magnanimous attitude by appointing Gouin to positions with prestige but without power; for example, Gouin led the Canadian delegation to the League of Nations and was one of the Canadian delegates to the Imperial Conference. Gouin's intransigence on tariffs could only strengthen the image of King as a low-tariff man and the justice portfolio offered Gouin no secure base on which to build up a rival faction. By subtly increasing Lapointe's power and prestige King further undermined Gouin's standing with the Quebec wing of the party. Gouin's importance was gradually reduced until it was only a matter of time before he withdrew from the government altogether. His resignation in 1924 reflected his complete political impotence. He had not been able to hold the government to a high-tariff position, and his ties with the high-tariff opposition had been undermined by his service with the Liberal government. There was no longer a middle ground on tariff that Gouin could span – the tortoise had won yet another race.

The pattern applied to Murphy and Gouin characterized the relations between King and all colleagues not of his own choosing; it reflected the technique he developed in his family for achieving his own ends while appearing to accept the decisions of others. It imposed a great deal of personal strain on a leader who preferred harmony and abhorred discord, but as a technique of cabinet leadership it has seldom been bettered. It should be noted in regard to this approach to interpersonal relations that King's technique was neither completely passive nor entirely negative. At the same time as he was patiently easing the dissonant elements out of the cabinet King was actively recruiting new men to fill the gap. The ranks of the new men would include those who were acceptable because they would strengthen the team even if they were not personally congenial. King was not unwilling to make sacrifices of this kind for great benefits. However, he was not always able to hide his resentment of behaviour that was out of step with his own. Men who would fit into the group of those to whom King was never really close but who contributed to the effectiveness of his administration include J.L. Ilsley, C.D. Howe, C.G. Power, Angus Macdonald, and J.L. Ralston.

The group who could be seen as kindred spirits was less extensive, which perhaps explains partially his attempt to find substitutes elsewhere. A man such as Norman Rogers could be perceived as reflecting King's self-image. James Gardiner, on the other hand, was acceptable because he was prepared to follow King's lead and carry his burdens. It was in this group that he found his regional lieutenants – men who shared the responsibilities for organizing the party without challenging his leadership.

The most important of the new men had already been in the house for sixteen years when King became prime minister for the first time. The relationship between King and his Quebec lieutenant – Ernest Lapointe – was probably the most important in King's political career but requires little in the way of analysis. As with Joan Patteson in King's private life, Ernest Lapointe embodied in the political sphere all the practical qualities that King needed in a colleague. The most important of his virtues was his willingness to subordinate his personal preferences to King's view of political necessity. This characteristic was most clearly demonstrated by Lapointe's willingness to accept the marine and fisheries portfolio when he preferred justice in 1921 and to accept justice when he wanted external affairs in 1935. It mattered little to King that he had promised Lapointe his choice of portfolios on the earlier occasion. Lapointe was required to demonstrate that King's promotion of him to a position of prominence in the government was justified. This he could do by accepting King's decision regarding political necessities.

As with many self-centred men King was inclined to be parsimonious when it came to recording his satisfaction with his colleagues. The high value that he put on Lapointe's active support in cabinet, caucus, and the House of Commons must be inferred from such diary entries as: 'Lapointe ... made a strong appeal against the agreement,' (that is, in support of King's position), 'Lapointe ... followed strongly endorsing my position.'[39]

In return for this sacrifice of self and for his loyal support, Lapointe was accorded a unique authority in French Canadian affairs. In this role Lapointe was expected to assume the responsibility for the welfare of the party in Quebec and in return was granted the right to be consulted on all issues of a sensitive nature in this context. This mandate depended a great deal on Lapointe's capacity to be right on Quebec matters, for King showed little tolerance of failure in others. Even so, King did not abdicate the entire responsibility. Although he professed to have no expert knowledge of French Canadian matters, he did have great faith in his general political acumen and his knowledge of what was acceptable to men of good will. The situation seldom reached a confrontation for each man was more than willing to meet the other half-way. In matters pertaining to Lapointe's own portfolios, on the other hand, King was less likely to heed his colleague's opinion if it conflicted with his own judgment; an example is the disallowance of Alberta legislation in 1937.

It is perhaps necessary to emphasize that this was essentially a working relationship. Lapointe was not one of King's kindred spirits. He gave King no cause for suspicion of his loyalty or motives and he did not challenge King in any of those areas which King identified as his own. He made no demands on King over and above those necessary in the cause of national unity and political success. In these respects he was an ideal colleague. King could work with him because of the absence of personal conflict, and the absence of this personal element ensured that the relationship would be far less stormy than those discussed above.

7 Consensus not compromise

The view of King as a great compromiser is a popular one which needs to be re-explored in the light of the foregoing analysis of his personal conflicts and defences. It will be suggested below that consensus is a more accurate description of King's approach to practical policy making and that consensus differs significantly from opportunism. It will be suggested also that consistency rather than vacillation or mere expediency characterized King's attitude to policy making. These two themes will be traced in selected areas of domestic and foreign policy. The tariff question and the problem of relations with Britain have been selected as issues with which any Canadian prime minister would have had to deal. King's approach to industrial relations and the Hitler episode reflected more the individual dimension of King's policy making.

One can discern in all four areas repetition and continuity. King's attitude to appeasement, for example, was clearly expressed as early as 1 November 1899 when in a letter to his parents from London, England, he said: 'it seems to me that before war comes something else might have been done. I cannot imagine even the Boers being unreasonable if every effort possible had been made to conciliate them.' Forty years later he would put these ideas into practice in regard to Hitler.

A similar commitment and consistency can be seen in the policies in the 1920s and 1930s regarding tariffs and the mother country. Although each decade required different solutions, there was no reversal of aims or objectives. It can be suggested that the extent to which the decision-makers' image diverges from reality will decide the success or failure of policy. Where this perceptual error is shared by the followers, however, such a divergence may not have drastic political consequences. King's image of the Tories as enemies at home and as a threat to Canadian autonomy abroad may have been distorted but it did not produce failure. He projected onto this group the blame for the defeat of 1911 which sent himself and the Liberal party into the political wilderness. He blamed them for the racial strife of the first conscription crisis and condemned them as centralizers and imperialists who threatened both Canadian unity and world peace. The fact that many Liberals shared these views ensured that King's subsequent actions, based on these perceptions, were popular and widely accounted successful. On the other hand, King's image of Hitler and his misperception of the intentions of the German government, although accepted at the time, eventually contributed to the failure of his hopes for a peaceful solution to the European crisis in 1939.

WITH CHART AND COMPASS

King's personal approach to policy making was summed up in his acceptance speech at the leadership convention and described in terms of the chart and compass analogy:

If more [guidance] is needed, that more is to be found in the platform which has been laid down by this Convention. That platform ... is the chart on which is plotted the course desired by the people of the country, as expressed through the voice of the Liberals assembled here.

I shall rely upon the counsel of those who are outstanding in the ranks of the party, the Liberal members of the Senate, the Liberals in the House of Commons, the leaders of the party in the several provinces, the representative men who are gathered here ... in this way I shall find a compass which will point the direction that ought to be taken.[1]

For anyone else a statement made on a formal occasion in a heightened emotional atmosphere might be dismissed as mere rhetoric, thoughts for the moment which would have no influence on subsequent activity, but not for Mackenzie King. He reiterated his pledge in the House of Commons, 13 March 1922, when in answering Meighen's accusations of opportunism he said: 'That was the position I took on the occasion of being honoured with the leadership of the party ... That is the position I took during the recent campaign, and that is the position which I take at the present time.'

It would be a mistake to see this as a willingness to subordinate his judgment to that of the party. Rather it should be seen as his willingness to stand on a base which closely reflected his own leanings. He had been a member of the National Liberal Advisory Committee which had worked on policy matters prior to the convention and had told Violet Markham in a letter (10 December 1919) that the platform followed closely the lines he had discussed with her during his visit to England. Further, he had retained for himself the right to check the course with the compass of public opinion. This would allow him to plot the various tacks and adjustments necessitated by weather conditions. Although both the crew and the passengers would participate, King was the captain of the ship of state and must stay at the helm listening to the voice of Providence.

During his first session as prime minister, King made repeated references to the need for judgment and timing. On 24 March 1922, in the course of defending the failure of his government to introduce early legislation to implement several campaign promises, he declared: 'The Leader of the Opposition seemed to forget that there are times and places for all things, and that a course which one moment may be the most advisable may not be the best at another time.' Since the time perspective of the obsessive personality is uniquely his own, it is not surprising that many critics found the twenty-five-year span before he implemented some of these promises to be an inordinate delay in reaching the destination.

The slow pace at which King tackled the problems of policy implementation was partly a response to his ideological stance but was also a direct result of the absolute priority which King gave to the question of party and national unity. King had accepted unity as an ideal and a practical necessity and this commitment had been reinforced by his precarious minority and the fractious nature of his support during the first administration. He had concluded his speech of 13 March 1922 with the observation: 'We have a great country, but we can only keep it great as we have all parts united and contented. That ... above all else will be the aim of the present administration, to see that every shade of opinion, other than that to which we are diametrically opposed, every shade of Liberal and Progressive thought is duly considered in the shaping of the policies of the Government and in the carrying out of these policies.' It remained a dominant theme throughout King's life and has become so widely accepted that it has dominated thinking on Canadian politics. This uniformity of acceptance disguises the fact that it was a self-fulfilling prophecy. King hesitated to act because it might destroy the fragile unity of the nation, but by failing to act forcefully he ensured that the elements of cleavage were never fully confronted. From King's perspective such a response was justified in terms of his own fragile identity and his low tolerance for dissonance. King tended to react to continued conflict in an impulsive, aggressive manner quite incompatible with his self-image and customary style. Justifying such impetuousness absorbed a great deal of his creative effort, brought on bouts of excessive fatigue and melancholy, and further restricted his capacity to act.

The platform drawn up by the Liberal party was King's political capital. It was proof that his intentions were honourable and progressive, and it provided him with the security to enter the turmoil of public debate. Throughout his life King had shown an unwillingness to use his capital in any way that would deplete his reserves. If his government during the first administration were to squander these resources recklessly on spectacular legislative changes, might he not endanger his whole political future and the security of the party and the nation? The returns that could be expected from such a program were unknowable, but the dangers were clearly visible from such earlier actions as Laurier's attempt to introduce reciprocity in 1911. Throughout his career King looked for guarantees of success before he would venture into unknown waters. Note, for example, his words in the House of Commons on 27 February 1933 when opposing policy of the CCF: 'Assuming ... that such a thing were possible. Would conditions thereafter be any better than they are now? ... have we any guarantee that if the state were controlling everthing conditions would not be infinitely worse?' Such a stance was not likely to produce spectacular or innovative legislative programs.

For King, the right way to handle capital was to hoard it. He had advised his brother Max that it was better to leave money lying in the bank without interest than invest in anything doubtful. He counselled himself and others not to take any chances with capital and had consistently handled his own investments in terms of low interest and security rather than seek the higher gains of speculative investment. The same characteristics dominated his approach to policy implementation. Policy ideals should only be implemented when clear gains could be guaranteed, gains in terms of increased political and public support or lasting and substantial improvements for the people he served. King had stated his position to the House of Commons on 27 March 1922: 'A government has to be very careful before announcing any policy, to view the end from the beginning, and not to raise hopes in the minds of men and women unless they see a possibility of these hopes being realized.'

The action of the Judicial Committee of the Privy Council in declaring the Industrial Disputes Investigation Act *ultra vires* the federal government in 1925 would further confirm the need for a cautious approach. King would see little point in implementing impressive policies with much flourish and enthusiasm if they were subsequently to be disallowed. This was not the way of genuine reform and real concern for the welfare of the people. This was the way of the mountebank and the political opportunist. One must consider how much King's caution in implementing social welfare programs and his behaviour regarding the Bennett government's 'new deal' legislation can be attributed to his awareness of the 'federal' fact and his unwillingness to risk his capital in ventures doomed to failure at the hands of the judiciary.

King's approach to policy reform paralleled his approach to savings – small but cumulative increases to reach lasting improvement. Success was achieved by cautious incrementalism, and the success of his techniques can clearly be seen in King's approach to the tariff question. The main lines of the Liberal party's tariff policy had been laid down by Laurier but endorsed by King and the 1919 Liberal convention. King had been intimately involved in the reciprocity débâcle of 1911 and was strongly influenced by his interpretation of the cause of the defeat. He had personally believed in the policy, 'I never doubted the wisdom of Reciprocity on economic or national grounds,' but felt that Laurier had erred in risking his policy capital when the return was uncertain, 'I felt that the government was taking a great risk in proposing any change whilst the people were contented.'[2] King had felt that the need for caution was obvious in a situation where emotional factors would be involved.

King readily accepted the commitment to 'lower tariffs' in principle and the declaration against protection made at the party convention. Those who believed in this intent were expected to join him and to share the expenses/risks of implementing the policy change involved in a return to low tariffs. King's main responsibility was to control the pace of the change so as not to risk the investment. Because many of the low-tariff group refused to join directly in the cause with him, the pace of the change was slower than it might otherwise have been, but it was change nevertheless. The 1919 platform had advocated a revenue tariff and closer economic relations with the United States and this was the direction in which the King government moved. The 1921 budget introduced a number of reductions and this tendency was maintained until 1924 when the removal of his high-tariff minister of finance and several prominent protectionists made the task easier.

King's intention and the principles on which his tariff policy was based were set out in detail in his reply to the leader of the opposition during the 1924 budget debate. It was a message of continuity: 'those are the principles for which the Liberal party has fought during the years which have passed and for which it will continue to fight during the years which are to come.'[3] This commitment continued to dominate King's behaviour long after public interest in the tariff question had declined. King had put a great deal of time and effort into ensuring the success of this investment, and he was reluctant to abandon it merely because it was no longer returning an obvious dividend. He persevered with it even into the early 1930s when low tariff no longer had popular appeal and saw his effort as vindicated in the signing of trade agreements with the United Kingdom in 1937 and the United States in 1938. King never wavered in his commitment nor changed his perception of the issue. As late as 1937 he was still expressing fears that tariff questions would provoke political defeat. His diary entry for 18 November 1937 reveals the extent to which the whole issue had been personalized:

This afternoon's proceedings were anxious ones, but I was able to carry the matter through without controversy. I confess I feel, however, a very heavy load ahead. I dislike controversies on tariff matters more than any single thing concerning with Government, the pressure of selfish interests etc., etc. However, it is clear that whether I like it or not I am to be the very vortex of the whole discussion. Perhaps that is what I was borne into these times to endure. If I can throw off fatigue sufficiently to have my mind rested, I shall have no fears; unless I do, I dread very much the consequences of the strain once Parliament re-assembles.

THE PEACEMAKING MODEL

It is difficult to understand much of King's activity in the policy field without an understanding of the great value he placed on peace and the role of peacemaker. It is a commonplace of Canadian politics that King rated highly the role of conciliator, but in a sense it is easier to grasp the meaning that King gave the role by equating it with peacemaker. The essential dimensions of King as a peacemaker must be sought in his inner conflicts and in his early experiences in the industrial relations field. King saw the wider problems, such as international issues, through a lens ground in his experiences as a labour conciliator and polished by his personal needs.

In a personality containing as many tensions and ambiguities as that of Mackenzie King, inner peace was a 'precious commodity.' King's diary is full of laments over the struggle that characterized his daily existence, of his longing to abandon public life for the 'peaceful haven' of the cloistered existence of a life of scholarship. His property at Kingsmere was to become a retreat from politics, and he zealously guarded his moments of 'withdrawal and tranquility.' While this 'perpetual' longing for peace did not dominate him to the extent of forcing his withdrawal from public life nor blunt his enjoyment of the occasional 'confrontation,' it was a predominant feature of his personal existence.

For further insight into his approach it is necessary to return briefly to the King family and to examine the way in which the notions of partnership and conciliation had been worked out in that milieu. 'Partnership is essentially a matter of status,' King was to write. 'It does not involve identity or similarity of function on the part of partners, or equality of either service or rewards; but it does imply equality as respects the right of representation in the determination of policy on matters of common interest.'[4] In this statement lies the key to understanding a great deal of King's political behaviour. It also reflects the basic condition of the King family. Each member had equal status in any gathering to determine the common good, but some contributed more in terms of service and reaped more of the rewards. What it had involved in practice in these situations was that the common interest was the interest of the dominant figure – first Isabel King and later Willie. In the political context it meant that although all participated equally there was one who knew already what the answer should be and who acted to bring them to this truth. Thus King himself was never merely one of the partners; he was instead the benevolent all-seeing 'father' above the conflict, the one who was able to bring peace and harmony in place of turmoil.

From the same source it is possible to trace the basic method of King's approach to peacemaking. There was little upheaval or violent conflict in the King family. Battles of will were fought covertly beneath the veneer of harmony and accord. Gains were made by taking opportunities when they offered and by quiet persistence. The apparently successful message of his own life could be the answer for everyone: 'It [change] must be brought about in an evolutionary manner, here a little, there a little, line upon line, precept upon precept, all working toward the consummation of one ideal.'[5] Because of the fragility of his personality and the need for extensive defence mechanisms to maintain his self-image, King had a low tolerance for controversy and unrest. Consequently he gave high priority to achieving peace and to quiet negotiations over noisy confrontations. At the same time he was concerned to make concrete gains for those he served. Success was to be measured in any small positive concessions which allowed peace with honour. Even a return to the status quo was a gain if the original situation had deteriorated to an even more unsatisfactory level.

This personal orientation was reinforced by a conscious rejection of the concept of class conflict in favour of a belief that workers and management were not inevitably antagonistic. King's notion of the working man and the field of social reform was a romanticized one, better suited to a world of moderate craft unions than to the realities of industrial unionism as practised in the mining and railway industries. Like many people in the early years of this century, King tended to associate militant unionism with foreign influences and anarchism. When King put himself forward as the spokesman of working men, he had in mind the 'sensible kind' of working man.[6] This distinction he continued to make throughout the period and during his work as a labour conciliator in the next decade. It was a view consistent with his overall view of labour and labour policies. It was the grounds on which he took his stand on labour issues and which he continued to affirm even as his social message became increasingly outmoded by the growth of socialism and industrial unionism. The development of this technique of peacemaking is most easily seen in an early example of King in action.

The outbreak of trouble at Valleyfield, Quebec, in October 1900 provided an opportunity for such activity. The dominant role that King pursued in this event was a matter of his own choice, but his sympathy for the working man could not mean that he would take their part unquestioningly in any dispute. The issues would be judged on their merits and any solution would be along the lines that King thought best. As he wrote to his family on 4 November 1900: '[I] had a talk with some of the men, in order to get their point of view ... I drove then to the meeting and by putting leading questions to the meeting got the men to accept the plan of settlement I deemed wisest, and to make it appear to them as if it were their own proposal.' This is the key point to be understood in regard to King as a conciliator. The settlement was the plan that he deemed wisest; it was not a compromise worked out either by the disputants or to please the disputants.

Because patterns of behaviour and responses receive reinforcement from success, one must expect that this incident in which King first acted as an industrial conciliator would become the model for other responses. The situation was probably the first real test of King's work identity. It has already been noted that King had a low tolerance for discord and dissension. Although he was capable of becoming emotionally involved in a situation and of acting impetuously, such responses drained him of emotional and physical energy and increased the tensions associated with memories of William Lyon Mackenzie. His impulsiveness was in conflict with his need for reassurance and his desire to be seen as trustworthy. If he could achieve a solution it would be confirmation of his worth.

King's concern for partnerships for peace also emerged in his approach to industrial relations legislation. His Industrial Disputes Investigation Act placed the major emphasis on industrial peace. When recommending that the legislation be put before parliament, King stressed that its aim would be 'promoting in the interests of the people the cause of industrial peace.' Not, of course, peace at any price, but peace nevertheless: 'Now men do not strike or lock out for the fun of it. They do that because they feel that, in the last resort that is their means of obtaining justice. We contend that under our measures we afford them a better means of obtaining justice than a strike or lockout.'[7] In practice he was inclined to see the word justice as synonymous with peace. With this principle firmly entrenched King established his division of both employers and workers into categories of good and bad, thus integrating the concept of the enemy into this area as well. Those who accepted the opportunity afforded by the act to settle their differences were unquestionably the former.

King's enthusiasm for peaceful solutions was tempered by the prolonged time scale in which he viewed the struggle, an outlook reflected in the following statement. 'While much good can be accomplished by wise legislation, the labour problem, so-called, is incapable of final solution, and that it will be with us as long as human nature remains what it is, and present civilization endures.'[8] This pessimistic outlook was coloured by his own experiences and it in turn coloured his approach to labour issues. It was a lifetime task that he saw ahead of him, needing consistent dedication not spectacular, short-term successes. This outlook was not conducive to radical change. When in 1943 he claimed to be implementing the philosophy of *Industry and humanity* and that of the Liberal platform of 1919, he was remaining true to his timetable.

FRIEND OR FOE: BRITAIN AND CANADA

It was natural, given the world war, that the association of industrial and international conflict had a prominent place in King's book, *Industry and humanity*, published in 1918. It has been suggested above that personal factors induced an element of permanence into what might have been merely a contemporary issue on which to hang an idea. Once King had argued publicly the case for the association, it would assume a permanent place in his outlook: 'Industrial and international relations are the warp and woof of modern world intercourse. They constitute the obverse and reverse of a world problem of human relations in which political and industrial considerations are inseparably intertwined.'[9] It was part of the record and to a man of principle it was important that the record be seen as honoured. It also provided an important element of continuity when as prime minister he was more concerned with the international context than the industrial scene. His fundamental viewpoint was equally valid in either sphere: 'The transition from fear to faith is being wrought out slowly in international and industrial affairs. Wherever it has progressed, an attitude of militancy has given way to one of co-operation. The transition has been accompanied by changes in outer form and organization, but the indwelling spirit has been its one sustaining reality. Where the spirit fails, the whole fabric becomes dismantled.' International problems, like industrial issues, would have to wait the passage of time since 'their ultimate solution ... awaited the inspiration of a universally accepted faith in human brotherhood.'[10]

Peace was an essential component of King's attitude to alliances, international responsibilities, and defence policies, yet it is seldom given prominence in studies of these aspects. There is an obvious paradox to be resolved in the fact that the prime minister who successfully led Canada through five years of war was, in the words of one of his biographers, 'unequivocally against war.'[11] King's earliest statements on the subject were associated with the Boer War as can be seen in the diary entry for 4 March 1900: 'The Love of God and War cannot be reconciled by any philosophy under Heaven, it is to fetter men's intellects and to insult them to ask them to accept it.' But in King's case being against war was not to be equated with 'pacifism.' It was necessary to resist the forces of evil and if necessary this resistance might involve the resort to arms, but it was only in this defensive context that war could be justified. Once justified, however, there could be no holding back. As Dawson noted, 'like many of his contemporaries ...

King admitted that once the decisive commitment had been made, there was no choice but to see the war through to the end.'[12] Such a viewpoint made mandatory both the careful scrutiny of proposed commitments and positive action to achieve peace.

His equating of international and industrial problems included the view that they had a common cause and could be dealt with by the same methods. McGregor notes: 'He [King] thought of the causes of unrest in industry and international relations as basically the same. To achieve peace in either area the application of reason rather than force was vital, with reliance always on an educated public opinion and the development of a spirit of goodwill.'[13] The onset of World War I strengthened his convictions. The fact that age and family responsibilities limited his active involvement probably encouraged him to think more of the post-war period and the role that he might play there. He wrote to Lord Grey (21 October 1914) of the hope that 'surely, surely out of it will come a recognition on the part of the world that international relations hereafter must be based on contract and not on organized power and destruction.' It is also possible that anxiety over public reaction to his wartime activities, perhaps even guilt, would strengthen the tendency to see industrial problems as facets of international issues and vice versa. These personal feelings, if they did exist, would be reinforced by the deep religious convictions that he held and their emphasis on Christ as the Prince of Peace.

I cannot bear to speak of the war. I cannot accustom my mind to take thought of it. It seems such madness in a world where we believed the spirit of Christ was to be found among men. I have had all along, and oddly enough have expressed several times the two views you put forward in your letter – that it may be the price of a great world peace, and that a deeply religious movement will surely follow upon a saddened and repentant world. I shall consecrate myself to the task with the deeper earnestness because of the great belief in peace – whether industrial or international – which this terrible war helps to instill. We must take up the cause of the master with a new zeal and a firmer conviction that the path he sought to bring to men is the only way of happiness for mankind.[14]

From this perspective the major policy objective of King's foreign policy must be seen as peacekeeping – not as a pragmatic response to divisions in Canada (in the Liberal party or in caucus), not because of timidity or isolationism, but as the cause to which he dedicated his life.

King's belief in an active commitment to peace as a means of imperial defence, an idea that strengthened his support for Chamberlain and appeasement thirty years later, was outlined to his friend Lord Stanhope on 23 July 1909:

I think you will find that Canada is prepared to do her part in Imperial Defence, but I believe that security can be in part obtained by promoting the safeguards of peace as well as anticipating possibilities of war which arouse a war enthusiasm. I sometimes fear the latter is being done too much in Europe just now ... If we can sign pledges of mutual friendship we will be building on a safer foundation than by arming against each other.

The letter also contained a spirited defence of Laurier's position and the problems he faced:

I cannot but feel that you do Sir Wilfrid Laurier an injustice in regarding him as an opportunist. He understands the problems of self government within the Empire as few men before him or living today have done, and his support from the people comes from the fact. We have had no man in Canada who has done as much ... to make the people one nation. If he hesitates to go the length that some desire, it is because he does not wish disruption and believes that a united progressive Canada is a more valuable asset to the Empire, and will be so throughout time, than a Canada divided in opinion, or professing an obligation it is not in a position to meet.

One need only substitute the name Mackenzie King for Laurier in this statement to have in King's own words a justification and defence of his policies in the critical period 1935–9.

In the general defence of the Liberal policy that King advanced in several dozen letters written during a period of five years, certain points became noteworthy by virtue of their emphasis and the monotonous repetition with which they were stated. Most prominent was King's adoption of the role of spokesman for the Liberal party. In this posture he maintained inflexibly that the Liberal policy was unquestionably right and he refused even to consider that there was any logic in the alternative viewpoints, in particular the Conservative position. Furthermore he absolutely refused to consider the possibility that he was being partisan in his outlook. As there was merit only in the position held by the Liberal party, those who opposed Liberal policy were either villains, motivated by selfish interests, or dupes, who opposed it through ignorance.

The prime candidates for the role of villain were obviously Borden and the Conservative government, the 'jingoistic press,' particularly the Round Table, and the English imperialists. Regarding the dupes, King appeared to feel, as he had argued so strongly in regard to his industrial disputes and anti-combines legislation, that they would support the Liberal viewpoint if only they had the truth put before them. He wrote in this vein to Violet Markham on 3 June 1912: 'I wish the people in England understood this question. If I could afford it I would feel there was no greater service I could render the Empire than to explain the situation as I see it to some of England's leading men.' Twelve months later, when the European situation was even more threatening, he still believed that the people in England who opposed the Liberal party's actions did so only through ignorance of the real issues. King continued to believe that the centralizers could still endanger the empire and Canadian unity and disturb the peace.

The Liberal convention of 1919 gave him a policy that matched his own outlook; his only outstanding need was for subordinates ready to carry this policy into effect. Once again King was able to reap the rewards of a shared perception of the enemy. The convention had considered a resolution which read: 'Resolved that we are strongly opposed to centralized Imperial control and that no organic change in the Canadian Constitution in regard to the relation of Canada to the Empire ought to come into effect until, after being passed by Parliament, it has been ratified by vote of the Canadian people on a referendum.' The speeches of the various delegates on this proposal reflected the view that to these Canadians imperial federalism was not a mythical beast but a real and present danger. Their fear seems to have been based equally on suspicion of Tory motives and extrapolation from a proposal being discussed in Britain concerning local parliaments for England, Scotland, Wales, and Ireland.[15]

The various speakers also made it clear to the new leader what they believed the Liberal outlook was:

It may be neatly summed up in the phrases 'Imperial Unity and local autonomy.' In this country we firmly believe in the British connection; we believe also that the strongest and the best way to maintain that British connection which we want to see endure is by the maintenance of the fullest measure of local autonomy on the part of the self-governing Dominions of the Empire ... let us maintain not only the traditions of liberalism but the avowed policy ... of the Liberal party – the policy enumerated by our late lamented leader ... Imperial unity, British connection, and ... the fullest local autonomy. The maintenance of this principle is the best means of maintaining that British connection which we prize and of contributing to the happiness and well-being of the Empire as a whole.

This prescription, defending the traditional stance against the forces of evil, was one which King readily took as his own. In this sense it was a positive commitment to a defensive stance, to maintaining the status quo as an ideal against those who sought to change it for the worse.

Subsequent historical research has suggested that the apostles of imperial unity were not as influential in British government circles as Canadian Liberals believed. Therefore it can be accepted that there was an element of irrationality in this fear of British motives. The Tory imperialist provided a convenient target for colonial anxieties, but although the centralists may not have been influential, they were certainly prominent and highly vocal. The fact that any scheme for imperial federation was completely impractical, given the conditions of transport and communication, did not reduce the implications of the anxieties aroused nor the influences of the defences involved to resist these anxieties.

In the light of King's ever-present concern for national unity, the expression of Quebec feeling on the subject of external relations was also important. Speaking to the autonomy resolution at the Liberal convention, Rodolphe Lemieux explained the sentiment of the average French Canadian as follows:

We are British subjects, happy and proud to be so ... We treasure our British institutions which we will keep safe and sacred for our descendants.

When the Mother Country and the British Empire are on trial, they can depend on the support from both the colonies and the dominions. You do not require ... a written instrument, to rouse the feelings of free Canadians in support of the British flag whenever the flag is in danger.

We, as Canadians, we, as reformers, are historically opposed to any policy of centralization. We, as Canadians, will manage our own affairs, and when the Mother Country is on her trial she need not call for her friends; she knows that wherever floats the British flag she has friends who are ready to sacrifice their all in order to secure the triumph of civilization and liberty.[16]

King's behaviour during the subsequent twenty years suggests that he was committed to this view as the proper policy for Canada with the same rigid determinism that characterized other aspects of his political position. Compromises were possible and consensus was desirable, but always within the lines of this traditional policy position formulated for him at the Liberal convention.

In order to see this pattern of consistency clearly revealed it is necessary to consider the first major foreign policy decision which King made after taking office. The Chanak incident confronted King

with a situation in which he was forced to make an immediate response under public pressure in terms of his prior assumptions about
the imperial relationship. 'It was all, King suspected ... an imperialist
device to test out centralization versus autonomy as regard European
wars.'[17] And this perception was to dominate all King's subsequent
actions.

It is essential to attempt to establish the degree to which this perception was dictated by King's personality needs rather than by the actual
facts of the situation. Hall suggests that this response can be explained
completely in terms of personality traits.

The analogy of the readjustment which coming of age involves for the individual was more than a mere analogy in the case of the Dominions. They were
coming of age as nations, loosening their ties with the Mother Country,
moving out from the family to take their places in the world.

A change of this magnitude was bound to cause bewilderment and question-
ing ... This bewilderment was natural enough. Many ... had their doubts about
the whole business. But the doubts did not usually take the form of suspicions
of the motives of the Mother Country.

Such suspicions, on the other hand, are characteristic of 'a personality
with obsessive mechanisms' and therefore, for Hall, there was no need
to look further than King's unconscious defences.[18] Such an observation has only a limited validity. As noted above, King's personality
development was influenced by obsessional traits, but before Hall's
conclusions can be useful it is necessary to know what aroused these
obsessional defences and to what extent the suspicions were justified
by evidence. It is possible that there was a link between King's suspicions of the government of the Mother Country and unconscious
feelings about the motives of his own parents and other authoritarian
figures in his life, for example, Mulock and Laurier. There was certainly centralized control in the King family and in the upper echelons of
the Liberal party even if it was not overtly expressed in either group. It
is possible that unconsciously King drew a parallel between the indirect manipulation which characterized the *modus operandi* of these
two personal associations and the approach used by the British government.

Certainly events at the Imperial Conference of 1923 encouraged his
suspicions. Lord Curzon at the Foreign Office fulfilled all King's fears
that Jingoists still dominated British policy making. At the conference
King immediately took exception to Curzon's use of the phrase 'Impe-

rial Cabinet,' he strongly urged publication of correspondence related to Chanak, presumably to assure the Canadian public that there were no 'secret diplomacy agreements,' and he insisted that the formal conference resolutions reflect his outlook.

The apparent achievement of his objective did not quiet his fears because the spirit of Imperialism lived as a hydra. Defeated at one point it would spring up in another. The price of success was eternal vigilance. Thus, the development of the Dominion Office and the move to establish a regular meeting of high commissioners, which British neo-imperialists like L.S. Amery advocated as an alternative means of consultation, met with the same opposition as Lord Curzon's more spirited policy. Amery describes King as follows:

I readily took up a suggestion of Mr. Peter Larkin's, the Canadian High Commissioner, that I should be 'at home' one morning every week for all the High Commissioners. This .. gave me an opportunity of telling them collectively of ... affairs in which they were generally interested ... Unfortunately when Mackenzie King heard of this ... he at once suspected a sinister design on my part of gradually working towards some sort of Imperial policy council situated in London ... Larkin had to come and tell me, very apologetically, that he was not allowed to see me except by himself.'[19]

King may have been unduly suspicious on this occasion, but on the other hand, given the tendency of British politicians to behave in a manner that can best be characterized in historian A.P. Thornton's telling phrase as 'the habit of authority,' King's suspicion cannot be considered completely groundless. King's long acquaintance and correspondence with Amery meant that he was aware of Amery's earlier views and therefore predisposed to see Amery's more moderate stance as a veneer. Because of the rigid consistency with which King held to his own earlier positions, it was logical that he would assume others acted similarly. Therefore, although it is possible to characterize King's view of the danger as a misperception derived from dysfunctional elements of his personal defences, it is not possible to argue that they led to a failure in foreign policy. There was sufficient overlap between the personal image and the reality for a practicable solution to be reached.

The history of the commonwealth is full of metaphors and analogies which portray the imperial-commonwealth connection as a family relationship. It can be suggested that the imagery of the family provides a clue to deciphering much of King's behaviour towards the association. He had described to his friend Stanhope his reaction to demands from the group: 'I am willing to lay down my life for the group, if that act is left to me, and I can feel that my life is essential to the common welfare but I must be conscious of an individual existence as well as a collective responsibility and that the one is intimately related to the other.'[20] Translated into terms of national autonomy *vis-à-vis* imperial unity, King's remarks make his behaviour in the inter-war years much more explicable. If the imperial-commonwealth relationship is compared to his general reaction to his own family, King's alternation between devoted enthusiasm to individuals and rigid adherence to principles, which so bewildered British politicians, becomes comprehensible. The reluctance to have demands made on him, his inability to give except in situations where the return for the investment was obvious, the need for support and approval, the desire to prove himself superior and independent without risking the security of family approval – all bedevilled his relations with the British government and ensured that he would often be misunderstood. He demanded on behalf of his nation the freedom of action and autonomy that he had not been able to demand for himself.

In the family analogy also lies the clue to King's perception of the practical meaning of autonomy – a semi-dependent autonomy but not a compromise worked out to placate the dissident within Canada. It was to King the goal for which to strive and an achievement to be defended. Thus, in regard to his policies, the inter-war years fall into two periods, the 1920s in which he struggled to establish through specific events the natural development of autonomy, with the Balfour Declaration of 1926 and the Statute of Westminster representing the 'key to the door,' and the 1930s in which the autonomy was jealously guarded, with King's support of Chamberlain over Munich and the response to war being the climax to the struggle. Within these two general periods, however, there were tensions, challenges, and regressions, just as there had been in his own personal development. In troubled phases the impetuous rebellious pattern of behaviour emerged and became dominant.

It should be noted that the policy of non-involvement which he subsequently chose as the main element of Canadian policy was not isolationism for its own sake but a belief that domestic matters were important and that the growth of a strong unified Canada was a major contribution to world peace. He believed that a Canada intent on her own business would constitute a better basis for any future role in international conciliation. This position was expressed most clearly in a speech made in 1938: 'The true Canadian task was to build up a genuine democracy at home, to promote sound social relationships, and to develop a tolerance and readiness to work together with the other members of the Commonwealth and friendly relations with other countries.'[21] The lesson of the past was that foreign entanglements led to situations in which the decision-maker had maximum obligations and minimum freedom of choice or control over developments, a situation particularly anxiety provoking for a personality dominated by obsessional features. King thus felt most secure following two courses of action. The first emphasized total voidance of any prior commitment as a matter of principle and resort to parliamentary supremacy as a doctrine of sharing the consequences.

He stood then upon a rock of principle. From that rock he was not to be moved either by the cajolings of imperialists or in subsequent years by the plight of the League of Nations. King was under no misapprehensions about the wider implications of his stand. The principle he had enunciated was one that could be ... applied as effectively against international as against imperial commitments or obligations.[22]

The second course involved a consistent effort to develop a bank of good will in Canada among those likely to be opposed to foreign involvement, so that if such responses could not be avoided they could be effected with a minimum of disaffection.

These twin forces continued to dominate King's outlook in the second half of the 1930s when he faced his greatest challenge and achieved his greatest personal satisfaction. On 7 October 1940 he wrote to Violet Markham: 'I am sure [you will] agree that no Prime Minister ever had his position more completely vindicated ... I shall always feel that if I had achieved nothing else in my political life than ... to make possible an all but unanimous decision by Parliament to enter the war, that that in itself would have more than justified my course of the proceeding twenty years.'

This achievement had not been won at the cost of his early principles. His stand at the conference of 1937 had not differed essentially from his earlier position. He had found ample evidence to maintain his suspicion of British Tories and officials. During the consultations over the governor generalship in 1934 he had been incensed by the peremptory tone of messages from the British secretary of state for the dominions, declaring 'they will never come to think of us in Canada as other than theirs, and a subordinate lot.'[23] The same official was responsible for another diary outburst eighteen months later when he issued a statement to the press regarding general defence policy. King observed: 'This is about the third or fourth time that I have had the unpleasant duty of saying in our Parl't that some statement made by a British minister in relation to Imperial Defence was not a true statement. It came up once in a difference with Ramsay McDonald ... it came up again, if I recollect aright, with Curzon ... '[24]

King felt the need for eternal vigilance to keep Canada 'free of entanglements.' His suspicions of 'Downing Street domination' had only been allayed in that area – appeasement – where the British government was advocating King's own views. He could endorse a united Commonwealth policy on international affairs because it was his own policy and would involve no prior commitment or threats to Canadian autonomy. His response in subsequent events, in the field of defence and in air training, indicates that King had not sacrificed his priorities in accepting a common policy on appeasement. To offer conciliation while actively preparing for war was not King's method. His preparation was of a more subtle variety, as he told Violet Markham on 11 January 1940: 'While I had hoped all along that war might be averted, I never the less felt ... that it might come, and all that I have said or done, or declined to say or do, for at least the last two or three years, has had that possibility in mind.' National and party unity and Canadian autonomy constituted the main avenues of King's defence preparations. His obsessive concern with the past ensured that a divided nation and party would constitute the greatest threat – and the first priority. If Mackenzie King was to achieve his deep-seated, probably unconscious, aim to succeed where Laurier had failed, this stance was justified. Mansergh has noted that 'Mackenzie King ... had at the very fibre of his being a Gladstonian feel for "the policies of virtuous passion." The "virtuous passion" which he felt was ... for Canada and against imperialism.'[25]

FRIEND OR FIEND: KING AND HITLER

King's visit to Hitler in 1937 was probably the most controversial of all his actions in external relations, yet it was also the action most characteristic of his personal style. He had shown great faith in the efficacy of face-to-face contact in industrial conflict, and his association of industrial and international disputes would ensure that his thoughts would turn in this direction as the European situation became more threatening. His impulsive interview with Mussolini in 1928 had set a precedent which could be followed. King had taken the opportunity while in England in 1936 to propose such private negotiations to Prime

Minister Baldwin, and the following year he discussed the desirability of such meetings of heads of states with Franklin Roosevelt.[26]

King's early enthusiasm for summit diplomacy, later to become an important facet of international relations, was in part derived from his perception of the European situation. On 15 June 1936 he had observed in his diary that: 'The European situation as it is today has nothing to compare with it at any time. No man can have to do with public affairs without feeling the necessity of coming to grips with it first hand.' In one sense the European situation offered a perfect example of a problem which he felt uniquely qualified to resolve – the building of confidence through the 'personal individual effort ... [of] men of different countries.'[27] He hoped that his talents as an intermediary could lead others to seek his aid. At the beginning of the year he had noted: 'I would be happy beyond words were I called on to intervene in the European situation. It would be the greatest joy of my life – but it seems too great a mission to expect.'[28]

His belief that through intervention he could avert war had a national as well as a personal component. He sought to make Canada's voice heard in 'a situation which threatens to engulf her in a world war and which, by being heard, might prevent such an appalling possibility.'[29] His confidence was derived from a simplistic view of both the European crisis and Hitler: a situation viewed in terms of juvenile personal associations and a projection onto the German leader of his own hopes and desires. His decision is best considered in his own words:

I had been born in Berlin in Canada, in a county which had several communities of German names, and had represented that county in Parliament. Had also lived one winter in Berlin and felt I knew the best sides of the German people ... if I were talking to Hitler I could reassure him what was costing him friends was the fear which he was creating against other countries. That there was not so far as Canada, for example, and other parts of the Empire were concerned, any thought of continued enmity toward Germany but a desire to have friendly relations all around.

On talking the matter over with Skelton, he still feels very strongly that it would be resented in Canada; that it would only be flattering Hitler by having him feel that some more persons were coming to him; that he was so much of an anglo-maniac, that nothing could influence him. That his speech three months ago that he was following his star of destiny just as a somnambulist walks in his sleep, showed how completely mystical he was, and unwilling to view anything to influence him in any way from different sides.

My own feeling is that I made Canada's position vis-à-vis Europe and Great Britain, very plain, that to go to Germany might undo a little of the solid position in which I had already placed matters by creating doubts and suspicions as to what underlay the visit of Germany. It might also seem to obligate us to side with the British, should war come later. The Jingo press of Canada might misconstrue it all. My feeling, therefore, is that while I feel I could do some good and might do a great deal at this juncture, unless something should come up before I go away which would give a real reason for going, it might be better not to take the risk involved ... [30]

The following year he reconsidered this verdict when in the course of discussions with the German ambassador the possibility of an interview with Hitler arose. King accepted the invitation and with the approval of Chamberlain made the trip to Berlin.

The outcome of the visit was predetermined by two personal factors. King had throughout his life demonstrated a tendency to be very impressed by and enthusiastic about new situations. His enthusiasm often later gave way to misgivings and disappointment, but King made only one visit to Berlin. In the light of his determination to avoid overseas entanglements and his belief that peace was still a viable alternative, King was already strongly predisposed to see Hitler in a favourable light. It has already been observed that an individual's commitment to a particular course of action creates unconscious barriers to information that threatens this belief. Hitler did not fit into the category of enemy as long as he was willing to listen to King and to appear to accept King's interpretation of the issues.

The structure of the interview only reinforced this predisposition. A great deal of the diary record of the encounter focuses on the physical surroundings and appearance of Goering and Hitler, and the whole entry reflects King's personal satisfaction in the formal courtesy and laudatory tones of such diplomatic occasions. He did not hesitate to read personal approval into the slightest gestures, observing that 'Hitler nodded his head as much as to say that he understood,' and 'he would turn and look at me sideways and would smile in a knowing way as much as to say you understand what I mean.'[31] There was none of the lack of courtesy, the personal invective, the criticism of the opponent that King associated with the enemy.

To a man obsessed with signs and divine guidance there were many auguries of God's purpose. His Bible reading the day of the meeting was by chance just that chapter that he had read to his mother prior to her death. His day was filled with meetings and symbols associated with 'witnesses' and parallels. He could believe that 'it would seem to be the day for which I was born – Berlin 1874.' Nor did King have any difficulty with the German leader, and noted: 'while he was talking ... I confess I felt he was using exactly the same argument as I had used in the Canadian Parliament last session.'[32]

In his summary King stressed Hitler's mysticism, his deeply religious nature, his humble origins, and the fact that he was 'a teetotaller, and also a vegetarian, unmarried, abstemious in all his habits and ways.' These were the characteristics of the virtuous not of the enemy, as was the need for 'quiet and nature to help him think out the problems of his country.' A man who had so much in common with Mackenzie King, who could look 'most direct at me in our talks together,' who 'never once became the least bit restless during the talk,' could not be other than 'eminently wise.'[33]

King saw and heard only those things that he needed to see: 'a genuine patriot,' a 'simple peasant,' a man 'with whom it should be possible to work with a good deal of trust and confidence,' and was completely duped.[34] Once he returned to Canada he did not find it difficult to find further evidence to reinforce his original misperception:

I felt I wanted to read to Joan something re Hitler, to talk of his life. I had cut out recently articles concerning him. I am convinced he is a spiritualist – that he has a vision to which he is being true – His going to his parents' grave at the time of his great victory – or rather achievement – the annexation of Austria was most significant – I read aloud from Gunther's Inside Europe, concerning his early life – his devotion to his mother – that Mother's spirit is I am certain his guide and no one who does not understand this relationship – the worship of the highest purity in a mother can understand the power to be derived there from – or the guidance. I believe the world will yet come to see a very great man – mystic in Hitler. His simple origin & being true to it in his life – not caring for pomp – or titles, etc., clothes – but reality – His dictatorship is a means to an end – needed perhaps to make the Germans conscious of themselves – much I cannot abide in Nazism – the regimentation – cruelty – oppression of Jews – attitude towards religion etc., but Hitler ... the peasant – will rank some day with Joan of Arc among the deliverers of his people, & if he is only careful may yet be the deliverer of Europe. It is no mere chance that I have met him, & von Ribbentrop & Goering & the others I did – it is part of a mission I believe ... 'Divine Commission Fulfilled' says Hitler etc. The world scoffs at these. They are given in ridicule – but they are I believe true – He is a pilgrim – his love of music – of Wagner Opera – his habits abstinence, purity, vegetarian, etc., all evidence of the mystic who is conscious of his mission & lives to it. Strange this bringing together of Hitler & Bunyan, both I believe are meant to guide me at this time to the purpose of my life – which I believe to be to help men to know the secret of the path to peace, in industrial & international relationships – If I can only live to that they will know I have been with Him that end will be achieved. I pray God I may so live that men see that I have been with him.[35]

It is important not to downgrade the influence of King's meeting with Hitler merely because subsequent events proved King's perceptions of the man to be so wrong. Despite his attempts to transcend the limits of his finite existence King was no more omniscient than any other mortal; rather his personal defence made him even more liable to misinterpretation than others. Nevertheless, it is possible to agree with Nicholas Mansergh that this misperception of Hitler's intent made little difference to King's actions: 'essentially it was the situation in Canada, not the situation in Europe that determined his approach.'[36] And he was able to confront Hitler with Canada's intentions. This does not detract from the emphasis which King placed on this personal impression and which could have affected his sense of the imminence of danger. He steadfastly held to the belief that his view of Hitler was the correct one. He told Tweedsmuir the following year: 'I shall be interested in knowing whether it is not agreed [by Chamberlain and Halifax] that my little visit to Berlin, a year ago, was not helping to inspire a little more in the way of confidence ... I think you will agree that what I told you of different attitudes and probable developments was not wide of the mark.'[37] A few months later King observed: 'I believe, however, that it will be found in the end that Hitler is for peace, unless unduly provoked.'[38]

King could respond enthusiastically to Munich because he believed he had been instrumental in it. In many ways it seemed that Chamberlain was a substitute for King himself. Throughout 1937 King had dwelt in his private record on his capacity as a conciliator in a world where such a need was clearly visible. In October, in the course of interpreting one of his visions he had written:

I am sure all this struggle is to help me in the field of international relations. It is to enable me to speak with conviction on the application of the Principles that make for Peace being a condition of mind and heart, in the nation as the individual, resulting from application of right principles bringing into being right policies in the former & right conduct in the latter – till we all 'become of one mind,' from 'being like minded' – This seems to me to be the process of spiritual evolution, from *being like minded to Christ thro' him, becoming one with God*. In this way the soul preserves its individuality and identity, and finds both preserved as they lose themselves in God, unless we lose our lives, we cannot find them. Instead of a multitude of souls, we become one soul with the One soul.[39]

He wondered about the possibility of leading a mission to Japan and told Tweedsmuir: 'How grateful I am that Chamberlain went to see Hitler! You may recall how strongly I urged these personal contacts. While it is not yet clear that war will be avoided, it is altogether certain that but for Chamberlain's meeting with Hitler we all should have been in the throes of a world war today.'[40] As Violet Markham sadly observed to Tweedsmuir, 'Hitler I fear pulled a good bit of wool over our friend Rex's eyes.'[41]

King's responses, however distasteful to some Canadians today, were perfectly consistent with his general beliefs. King was an appeaser by conviction rather than as an expedient, and his actions need to be judged in the context of Martin Gilbert's position: 'Appeasement, both as an attitude of mind and as a policy, was not a silly or treacherous idea in the minds of stubborn, gullible men, but a noble idea, rooted in Christianity, courage and commonsense.'[42] It was a policy in which, through patient and conciliatory reactions, men would be given an opportunity to declare themselves with the forces of good or those of evil. King had repeated in a public broadcast in 1936 the views he had expressed in *Industry and humanity*.

Fundamentally, the world struggle of today is one between the contending forces of good and evil. It is a part of the never-ending conflict between the forces activating those who, by their thoughts of others, and their unselfish acts, are seeking to further 'the law of Peace, Work and Health,' and the forces actuating those who, by their greed and selfish ambitions, are furthering 'the law of Blood and Death.'[43]

In times of stress King was inclined to consider some of his British allies among the latter rather than the former. King's tendency to see old threats and dangers would be accentuated by suggestions such as the proposal for an imperial war conference or cabinet. In 1936 he had been preparing himself for possible conflict by 'going pretty carefully through Lloyd George's "War Memories" ... I owe it to the country and to my work to anticipate ... the matters to be given consideration "prior to or in the event of war".'[44] Inevitably in times of stress King was dominated by the tensions of the past as much as by the problems of the present, but because he had surrounded himself with able men this perceptual difficulty did not seriously affect his capacity to lead.

The war with all its serious complications was at the same time a great triumph for King. His success in bringing a united Canada into the war has been described as 'one of the outstanding achievements of Commonwealth statesmanship.'[45]

Epilogue

In 1939, at an age at which most men are compulsorily retired, Mackenzie King faced the greatest challenge of his career – a European war. He was also facing the final decade of his life, a time when life takes on a slower rhythm, a time for handing burdens and responsibilities to a younger generation, a time for reflection and leisure. It might have been expected that at last King would be able to get his papers in order and begin the memoirs which were to ensure that history would have the true picture of his career. In practice there was no break in the old rhythm. King had merely entered another cycle in which the now well-established techniques and interactions were once again called forth in defence of the same principles and in pursuit of the same enemy. Wartime leadership was a completely new experience for King, but instead of making him apprehensive about the responsibilities, the situation seemed to bring him a new lease on life. 'You will be interested in knowing,' he wrote to a friend, 'that the war, far from having added a weight to my mind and frame, seems to have taken an enormous burden off both.'[1] To understand this response we need to consider the affective dimension of King's approach to leadership.

King had never been a 'happy warrior' in politics. Public office was a solemn duty and the road to the top had been a 'pilgrim's progress rather than a joyful undertaking.' King had pursued this course with fervent determination not to neglect his duties and to carry the burden to the end. It is interesting that this negative affect seemed to increase as his hold on office became more secure. In the 1920s, when his government was in a minority and his grasp on the leadership weak, King expressed feelings of strain and fatigue, but they were balanced by optimism and a sense of achievement. He could always justify the fatigue and nervousness that revealed his inner tensions by rational explanations – 'a strenuous campaign,' 'a demanding Imperial

Conference.'² Despondency in 1930 at the moment of defeat would have been understandable, but it was the electoral victory in 1935 that seemed to intensify the 'strain-burden' syndrome. Two years later King consulted his doctors and reported 'they all agreed ... that I gave evidence of more than exceptional fatigue, and that it would take some little time for me to throw it off.'³ In February he had written, 'I have managed to get through the first fortnight of a new session, a period which I always dread more than any other.'⁴ But it was not a happy year, nor was the one that followed. Certainly this was a period in which domestic problems and the international situation made the prime minister's task particularly difficult. However, if the anxiety and depressed feelings had been merely a rational response to the great tensions of the 1930s, King's response to the war itself was irrational. It should also be noted that King's depression returned in the post-war period. In January 1947 he wrote: 'a renewal of the dread of the approaching session [of parliament].'⁵

King's own interpretation of his response is pertinent but not completely convincing: 'I can now see that I have been living under a burden of dread much more real to myself than others could possibly have known.' Later he was to expand on this statement: 'I am fully convinced that the explanation lies in the fact that I have been carrying so long the misrepresentation of my real motive and purpose.' What was the source of 'the new strength which seemed to be given me once war itself was declared'? Certainly he had had the great satisfaction of being able to bring an undivided Canada into the war at Britain's side but it was also the death knell to all his hopes that 'somehow, the appalling possibilities of another European conflict would, in themselves prove sufficient to avert another war ... [that] some way of escape would have been found.' King could face the challenge with confidence because he had the experience of the past to guide him. He had formulated his position on crucial issues such as expeditionary forces, conscription, and preservation of national unity in the earlier contest – World War I. One avenue of defence against fear of the unknown is to see the present as a replica of the past and to act accordingly. Such a mechanism could remove King's anxieties about the future and give him the necessary omniscience that would enable him to feel in control of the situation.⁶

With the war brought to a successful, though not completely triumphant conclusion it was logical that King's thoughts would turn to retirement and the problem of his successor. It was difficult for King to take this step because leaving his political roles involved divesting himself of his defensive identities. Could he have feared that without these public identities he would lose his sense of self? Throughout his career, and particularly during the conscription crisis, King had used the threat of resignation as a technique for controlling his colleagues. They may well have been justified in not taking his statements regarding his intention to retire too seriously. These post-war expressions of intent were often presented in the context of a harangue on the inadequacies of his followers and could easily be interpreted as an order to step into line. In the course of a caucus discussion on the need for party organization, King declared 'that unless members themselves and ministers and others could find a way of bringing into being a really effective organization, I would ask them to allow me to retire from the leadership.' The cabinet was faced with the same ultimatum the next day. King stressed the organization theme in 1948 as strongly as he had advocated it during his earlier career. But there is no sign that he actually considered the possibility that the lack of organization was directly attributable to his actions.

Although King was concerned with the choice of his successor and had continued his policy of recruiting promising young men into the government, he had not given as much attention to the future of the party as might have been expected. He continued to look back rather than forward. For the party he identified a need 'to get back to the old Liberal principles of economy, reduction of taxation, anti-militarism, etc.' For himself, he was unable to accept that it was too late to attempt to start again and to explore other routes. After a successful impromptu speech in the house he decided that 'it is the method I should have adopted from the very beginning of my public career.' And he went on to observe, 'it is only now at the end of my public career that I am really beginning to do some of the things I should have followed throughout.' The Korean crisis provided him with yet another situation which he could interpret in terms of past experience. He even made the Freudian slip of suggesting that Canada should stand firm 'even if we have to get out of the League.' The old League of Nations, the organization with which he was familiar, was more real to him than the newly launched United Nations.[7]

His lack of active concern for the future of the party was not matched by an equal indifference towards his own future. King's main concern continued to be himself, no matter how he tried to rationalize his reactions in terms of wider issues. He was not unnaturally upset when the Niagara Falls Bridge Commission proposed to hang a carillon on Canadian soil dedicated to 'our nation's leaders Churchill and

Roosevelt.' But he would not admit to personal motives when he argued:

If the Liberals of Canada now permit these bells to be put in position ... without making a nation-wide protest, it will be a strange sort of thing indeed and a pretty serious reflection on members of a party who have a leader who has carried six general elections out of seven ... It would be a black blot on my escutcheon of chivalry so far as Canada is concerned if a record of that kind is permitted to exist ... A reflection on the Canadian people as a whole ... I said that I didn't want my name on any memorial of the kind ... So far as I was concerned, I was quite content to leave my service to Canada ... to the keeping of the people in future generations.[8]

In his old age King continued to be selfish in the demands he made on his friends. When Violet Markham made a trip to North America the venue chosen for their meeting was arranged to suit his convenience. His reluctance to make the effort to go to New York was presented in terms of the 'better chance for a real talk together' that Ottawa would present. Even then his response was half-hearted. After her visit he wrote, 'I cannot but feel a little sad, however, to think of how completely your time was given over to my affairs. I should have liked to have arranged to have you meet a few friends, and to have "taken you about" a bit.' These were honest sentiments but King's neurotic self-concern had prevented him from turning the wish into the deed as it had so many times before. Other friends like John D. Rockefeller also continued in their supportive role. In August 1949 King spent a fortnight with Rockefeller at his summer home and recaptured the idyllic relationship of his youth: 'we have spent our hours together in walks ... reading aloud to each other ... '[9]

King had never accepted the idea that 'one's life is one's own responsibility.' Throughout his life he had looked to others to guide the hand that steered the ship of state. He continued in his final years his detailed record of 'remarkable coincidences' and to interpret the various signs as evidence of 'God's leading.' He continued to fantasize about his love for his parents and grandfather and his desire to serve their ends in his life, a process which involved both a negation of self and a denial of responsibility.[10]

One apparently rational aspect of King's concern about retirement relates to finance. It is not unnatural for an ageing man with no close family to be concerned about his future and his capacity to provide for his needs until the end. For a man who two years later was to leave an estate of three-quarters of a million dollars, however, the reaction must be characterized as excessive. King was still concerned with depleting his capital and sought alternatives whereby he could continue to provide for his needs out of income. He considered the possibility of staying on as president of the privy council after retiring from the leadership, because it 'would enable me to have still an additional income which I will need.'[11] His letters to his friend Violet Markham painted a harrowing picture:

As I give up my salary as Prime Minister, my indemnity as a member of Parliament, the government allowance for a car, free transportation on the railways of the country, the use of the frank etc., I shall be giving up a great deal, indeed *all* that has left me without concern for the where-with-all of existence ... and I shall be without pension or remuneration of any kind. This will mean of course that I shall have to live on my capital, supplementing it with such income as I might find it possible to make, through writing, or by other means.[12]

He also talked of possible earnings from speaking engagements or special missions. King had cried poverty for so long that even as intimate a friend as Miss Markham was deceived. 'There has never been any mystery that you are a poor man without private means,' she wrote. 'I know how indifferent you have been all your life to money.' As she had in 1909 Miss Markham prepared to come to the assistance of her old friend. She may even have interpreted the statement 'I feel that if, meanwhile, [financial] embarrassment should become apparent, the wherewithal will come from somewhere to enable me to finish out my days without experiencing the ills of penury' as a hint. In October 1948 she made arrangements to send money to him despite currency restrictions in England. The significant thing is that King did nothing to deter her. Further, when she faced the bigger problem of trying to obtain dollars for her trip to Canada to visit him, King offered no help at all.[13]

Violet Markham's ignorance of King's true financial state could be put down to the fact that she had had little personal contact with King during the middle years of his life, but the same cannot be said of Joan Patteson, who was equally ignorant of the true state of affairs. 'No one suspected such an estate,' she told Violet Markham after King's death. 'I can't see how he did not know what his own personal wealth was ...' The rational explanations emphasize the hardship suffered by his grandfather and his family; such memories could have influenced his need to save but do not explain the need for secrecy. Clearly, King's need for capital had become as neurotic as his need for affection. He had the same insatiable desire to accumulate and the same restricted capacity to disperse money as love and affection. His actions in these areas were two aspects of the same syndrome. It is interesting that Joan Patteson described King's reaction when she jokingly asked if he were a millionaire as 'he was afraid,' and 'he looked terrified.' King knew that he had come by the money honestly, that there was no taint of graft or corruption attached to it. He had not felt concerned in 1947 when he told St Laurent of gifts he had received from party friends; in fact, he stated categorically, 'I did not feel embarrassment on that score, nor had I been embarrassed in any way by what had been done.' The long-drawn-out process of drawing up his will and the associated process of writing his memoirs were difficult and traumatic, for they might force King to face reality and shatter the dream world in which he existed. As late as March 1950 he was still concerned to keep intact the money that Mr Larkin had assembled for him on taking office as prime minister.[14]

When King contemplated retirement it was not in terms of a voluntary surrender of responsibilities; rather it was a conditional withdrawal. Bouts of ill health, trouble with colleagues, the emergence of controversial political issues could all give rise to thoughts of retiring, but they were always qualified thoughts: 'On no consideration, should I consider going beyond either of these dates, unless ... ' 'I really felt I must not try another election .. [but] if I felt equal to travelling about ... etc., it would be another matter.' 'On no consideration will I think of remaining in office to the end of another year ... There is, however, a natural feeling that one might, if ... strong enough, wish to stay on ... ' Even after he had finally taken the plunge he found it hard to let go and talked of his intention to be regular in his attendance in the house. This reluctance could probably be explained in terms of the financial loss involved in not drawing his member's indemnity.

Retirement brought him even less joy than political responsibility had. In August he told Violet Markham, 'I have found the complete disassociation with public life much more of a loss than I had expected ... [retirement] has not brought the sense of rest and recreation which I thought it would ... the recent Liberal victory ... has caused me to wish I might have continued on until this particular battle was over.' He could not settle to his memoirs and instead occupied himself with the disposal of his property after his death. It would be left to someone else to erect the memorial to his life of service that he so earnestly wished.[15]

The neurotic dimension of King's personality has been stressed in this study; it is therefore necessary to emphasize in conclusion that the neurotic reaction is not incapacitating. One of the features that emerges from a study of Mackenzie King is the degree to which an individual can suffer from psychic tensions and still function effectively in an insecure environment. Success was one of the main factors which helped to alleviate King's doubts and uncertainties. His neurotic rituals indicate to an observer the existence of inner resistance to distasteful memories and unsolved problems, but as long as King was successful he could lose himself in 'busy work' and avoid any real self-examination. The rigidity of his reaction provided him with the strength to persist in his chosen course in the face of fierce opposition. The obsessional defences, usually dismissed as bizarre personal idiosyncrasies, were instrumental in his responses and a crucial dimension of his personal development, and an understanding of them contributes to a more accurate perception of the longest, if not the most spectacular, career in Canadian national leadership.

Notes

INTRODUCTION

1 Nicholas Mansergh, *The Commonwealth experience* (London 1969), 17.
2 William Christian and Colin Campbell, *Political parties and ideologies in Canada* (Toronto 1974), 2.
3 Erik H. Erikson, *Childhood and society* (Middlesex, Eng. 1965); *Insight and responsibility* (New York 1964); *Identity, youth, and crisis* (New York 1968); *Identity and the life cycle* (New York 1959); *Young man Luther* (New York 1968); *Gandhi's truth* (New York 1969).
4 F.I. Greenstein, *Personality and politics* (Chicago 1969), 65.
5 J.E. Esberey, 'Personality and politics: a study of William Lyon Mackenzie King' (unpublished PH D thesis, University of Toronto 1974).
6 Karen Horney, *The neurotic personality of our times* (New York 1937); *Neurosis and human growth* (New York 1950); *Our inner conflict* (New York 1945). Helen Deutsch, *Neurosis and character types* (New York 1965). O. Fenichel, *The psychoanalytical theory of neurosis* (New York 1945). G. Mahl, *Psychological conflict and defense* (New York 1971). D. Shapiro, *Neurotic styles* (New York 1965).
7 The main source of primary material on King is the W.L. Mackenzie King collection in the Public Archives of Canada (PAC). There are extensive references to King in other collections in this repository. Among published sources one would note: R. MacGregor Dawson, *William Lyon Mackenzie King, a political biography, 1874–1923* (Toronto 1958); H. Blair Neatby, *William Lyon Mackenzie King, 1924–1932* (Toronto 1963); *William Lyon Mackenzie King, 1932–1939* (Toronto 1976). F.A. McGregor, *The fall & rise of Mackenzie King* (Toronto 1962). J.W. Pickersgill and D.F. Forster, eds, *The Mackenzie King record*, 4 vols (Toronto 1968–70). Earlier volumes of interest include: H.S. Ferns and B. Ostry, *The age of Mackenzie King* (Toronto 1955); H.R. Hardy, *Mackenzie King of Canada* (Toronto 1949); Andrew Haydon, *Mackenzie King and the Liberal party* (Toronto 1930); Bruce Hutchinson, *The incredible Canadian* (Toronto 1952); O.E. McGillicuddy, *The making of a premier* (Toronto 1922); Norman Rogers, *Mackenzie King* (Toronto 1935). University of

Toronto published a microfiche edition of King's diaries in two parts, 1893–1931 in 1974 and 1932–47 in 1980.

8 J.L. Granatstein, *Canada's war: the politics of the Mackenzie King government 1939–1945* (Toronto 1975), v.

9 C.P. Stacey, *A very double life, the private world of Mackenzie King* (Toronto 1976), 11.

10 Diary, 1 Jan. 1902.

CHAPTER ONE

1 Diary, 29 July 1897, 2 Sept. 1901, 4 Sept. 1896, 19 June 1899, 2 Jan. 1898, 22 June, 19 July, 5 Aug. 1897.

2 Diary, 29 July 1899, 8 Apr. 1901, 15 July 1899.

3 Diary, 25 Apr., 3 Mar. 1899.

4 Diary, 26 June, 24 June 1899.

5 Isabel King to WLMK, n.d. 1900, 16 Sept. 1900.

6 Diary, 18 Dec. 1896.

7 Diary, 3 Jan. 1898.

8 David McClelland, *Power, the inner experience* (New York 1975), 15.

9 Ibid, 186.

10 Diary, 22 Oct., 30 Oct. 1893, 20 Jan. 1894.

11 Diary, 7 Sept., 9 Oct., 11 Oct., 16 Oct., 15 Oct., 16 Nov., 22 Nov. 1893.

12 Diary, 1 Jan., 5 Feb., 10 Jan., 23 Jan. 1894.

13 Diary, 30 Nov., 21 Nov. 1893, 21 Sept. 1894.

14 Diary, 26 Oct. 1893.

15 Diary, 5 Jan. 1894.

16 Dawson, *King*, 43.

17 Diary, 26 Feb. 1898.

18 Diary, 8 Oct., 3 Feb. 1894.

19 Diary, 10 Oct., 1 Dec. 1893, 20 June 1894.

20 Diary, 8 Oct. 1894.

21 Diary, 27 Dec., 29 Dec. 1893, 29 Oct., 27 Dec., 29 Dec., 4 Feb. 1893.

22 Diary, 7 Sept., 9 Oct., 23 Nov., 12–14 Sept., 11–14 Nov. 1893.

23 Diary, 11 Jan. 1894.

24 Diary, 6 Feb., 8 Feb., 5 June, 4 Oct. 1894.

25 Stacey, *Very double life*, 44.

26 Diary, 2 Oct. 1894.

27 Diary, 7 Oct. 1894.

28 Diary, 11 Oct., 14 Oct. 1894.

29 Diary, 24 Nov., 23 Dec., 28 Oct. 1894.

30 Diary, 29 Nov. 1894.

31 Diary, 17 Dec. 1896, 10 Dec., 24 Nov. 1894.

32 Diary, 13 June, 28 Apr., 12 May 1894.

33 Diary, 14 Sept. 1893, 19 June 1894, 15 Jan. 1898.

34 Diary, 31 Dec., 6 Sept. 1893.

35 Steven Marcus, *The other Victorians* (London 1970), 19.

36 Ibid.
37 Diary, 6 Dec. 1896.
38 Diary, 26 Oct. 1893, 2 Feb., 19 Feb. 1894, 5 Dec. 1893, 12 Jan. 1894, 21–23 Apr. 1897, 19 Nov. 1896, 30 Oct. 1897.
39 Diary, 21 Oct., 10 Oct., 5 Oct. 1901, 30 Oct., 31 Oct. 1897, 19–24 Nov., 22 Nov. 1896.
40 Michael Olmstead, *The small group* (New York 1959), 49.
41 Diary, 2 June 1899; Isabel King to WLMK, 8 Sept. 1895.
42 Diary, 22 June 1895.
43 WLMK to H. Albert Harper, 24 July 1895 (Harper papers, PAC).
44 Diary, 6 May 1896.
45 Diary, 14 June 1896.
46 Ibid.
47 Isabel King to WLMK, 18 Oct. 1896, 14 Jan. 1897.
48 Isabel King to WLMK, 6 Apr. 1898.
49 Ibid.
50 Isabel King to WLMK, 9 Apr. 1898; John King to WLMK, 9 Apr. 1898.
51 Isabel King to WLMK, 6 Apr., 9 Apr. 1898.
52 Isabel King to WLMK, 8 May 1898.
53 WLMK to John King, 29 Sept. 1897.
54 Diary, 7 May, 1 May 1899.
55 Diary, 3 Jan. 1898, 1 May, 6 May, 9 Apr. 1899.

CHAPTER TWO

1 K. Horney, *Neurosis and human growth* (New York 1970), 36.
2 Isabel King to WLMK, 2 July 1900.
3 WLMK to family, 10 July 1900.
4 Diary, 3 June 1902, 21 Feb. 1904, 1 Mar. 1902.
5 Diary, 27 Aug. 1895.
6 Diary, 27 Aug., 4 Sept., 7 Sept. 1895.
7 Diary, 7 Sept. 1895.
8 Diary, 23 May, 12 June, 5 July 1897.
9 Diary, 24 Aug. 1896, 25 Feb. 1898.
10 Diary, 29 Mar., 30 Mar. 1898.
11 Diary, 16 Apr. 1898.
12 Diary, 17 Apr., 19 Apr. 1898.
13 Diary, 20 Apr. 1898.
14 Diary, 21 Apr. 1898.
15 Diary, 25 Apr. , 24 Apr., 28 Apr., 5 May 1898.
16 Diary, 17 May 1898.
17 Diary, 18 July, 6 Jan., 1 Mar., 8 Jan., 7 Jan. 1899.
18 Diary, 20 Apr. 1898.
19 Diary, 6 Feb. 1901.
20 Diary, 13 Nov. 1904, 4 Feb. 1911.
21 Diary, 21 Oct. 1901.

22 Diary, 2 Jan. 1902.
23 Diary, 2 Mar. 1902.
24 Diary, 20 Feb. 1902.
25 Diary, 18 Feb., 17 Feb., 18 Feb., 3 Mar., 4 Mar., 10 Mar. 1902.
26 Diary, 9 July, 10 July 1902.
27 Diary, 11 July 1902.
28 Diary, 11 July 1902.
29 Diary, 21 Sept. 1902.
30 Diary, 22 Sept., 27 Sept., 29 Sept. 1902, 23 Apr. 1903.
31 Diary, 5 Aug. 1917.
32 Diary, 10 Aug. 1917.
33 Diary, 27 Aug. 1917.
34 Theodore Reik, *Listening with the third ear* (New York 1948), 67.
35 Dawson, *King*, 176.
36 Ibid.
37 Diary, 23 Feb. 1894; WLMK to Harper, 28 June 1895.
38 WLMK to Harper, 28 July 1895, 1 Sept., 27 Sept. 1895.
39 Harper to WLMK, 10 Nov., 16 July 1901.
40 Ferns and Ostry, *Age of King*, 57.
41 Diary, 8 Jan., 11 Jan. 1902.

CHAPTER THREE

1 U.S. Senate, Commission on Industrial Relations, *Report*, vol. IX (Washington 1915), 8831.
2 WLMK to Violet Markham, 25 Mar. 1912.
3 WLMK to Violet Markham, 3 June 1912.
4 Ibid.
5 Violet Markham to WLMK, 23 Aug. 1912.
6 WLMK to Violet Markham, 5 Nov. 1908.
7 WLMK to Violet Markham, 14 Oct. 1912.
8 Reik, *Listening*, 180.
9 McGregor, *Fall & rise*, 95.
10 WLMK to Violet Markham, 1 Jan. 1911.
11 Violet Markham, *Friendship's harvest* (London 1959), 143; *Return passage* (London 1953), 83.
12 Markham, *Harvest*, 143.
13 Violet Markham to WLMK 4 June 1909.
14 Violet Markham to WLMK, 16 Aug. 1907, 22 Dec. 1908.
15 WLMK to Violet Markham, 20 Sept., 5 Nov. 1908, 17 Dec. 1909.
16 Violet Markham to WLMK, 4 June 1909; WLMK to Violet Markham, 15 Dec. 1911.
17 WLMK to Violet Markham, 6 Feb. 1911.
18 WLMK to Violet Markham, 14 July 1912.

19 Violet Markham to WLMK, 18 Dec. 1914; WLMK to Violet Markham, 14 Aug. 1914.
20 WLMK to Violet Markham, 15 Feb. 1915; Violet Markham to WLMK, 29 July 1912.
21 McGregor, *Fall & rise*, 131.
22 WLMK to Violet Markham, 11 Oct. 1915.
23 R.B. Fosdick, *John D. Rockefeller, Jr., a portrait* (New York 1956), 30–96, 154.
24 U.S. Senate, *Report*, 8831.
25 McGregor, *Fall & rise*, 190.
26 Diary, 14 Jan. 1915.
27 McGregar, *Fall & rise*, 193.
28 Ibid., 218.
29 WLMK to Violet Markham, 3 July 1913.
30 WLMK to Dr Thistle, 18 Feb. 1915.
31 WLMK to Violet Markham, 3 May 1915.
32 WLMK to Violet Markham, 3 May 1915.
33 Diary, 14–17 May 1915.
34 Diary, 14 July 1915.
35 Diary 9–16 Oct. 1915.
36 Diary, 22 June 1916.
37 Diary, 10 Dec., 13 Oct., 22 Oct., 16 Oct. 1916.
38 Diary, 29 Dec. 1916.
39 Diary, 1 Jan., 3 Jan. 1917.
40 Diary, 4 Jan. 1917.
41 Diary, 22 Jan., 20 Jan. 1917.
42 Diary, 26 Jan. 1917.
43 Diary, 4 Feb., 5 Feb. 1917.
44 Diary, 12 Mar., 13 Mar., 14 Mar., 19–23 Mar., 27 Mar. 1917.
45 Diary, 9 Apr., 10 Apr. 1917.
46 Jennie King to WLMK, 20 Oct. 1917.
47 Diary, 2 Dec. 1917.
48 WLMK to Isabel King, 14 Dec. 1917.
49 McGregar, *Fall & rise*, 298.

CHAPTER FOUR

1 Diary, 5 Sept. 1936.
2 Diary, 18 Mar. 1936, 16 Aug. 1937.
3 Diary, 16 Aug. 1937.
4 Diary, 27 Oct. 1916.
5 Diary, 1 Nov. 1916.
6 Diary, 9 Feb. 1918, 24 Mar. 1919.
7 Diary, 24 Feb., 22 Feb., 25 Feb. 1918.
8 Diary, 4 Mar., 16 Apr., 17 Apr. 1918.

9 Diary, 16 Apr. 1918.
10 Diary, 21 Apr. 1918.
11 Diary, 1–14 Jan. 1919.
12 Ibid.
13 Isabel King to WLMK, 6 Apr. 1898.
14 D. Tait to WLMK, 26 Nov. 1889.
15 Neatby, *Lonely heights*, 204.
16 G. Allport, *The individual and his religion* (New York 1950), 67.
17 Diary, 7 Nov., 10 Nov. 1893, 15 Jan. 1894.
18 Diary, 26 Jan. 1917.
19 Diary, 26 Mar. 1899.
20 Violet Markham to WLMK, 2 Sept. 1912.
21 Diary, 17 Dec. 1918.
22 Ibid.
23 WLMK to Violet Markham, 28 Aug., 14 Oct. 1912.
24 WLMK to Violet Markham, 11 Oct. 1911, 10 Jan. 1909, 12 Apr. 1913.
25 WLMK to Violet Markham, 6 Feb. 1912.
26 R. Cook, review in *Toronto Star*, 30 Nov. 1968; C.P. Stacey, review in *International Journal* 17 (Spring 1962): 162.
27 P. Teilhard de Chardin, *Le Milieu divin* (London 1964), 50, 54, 32.
28 WLMK to Violet Markham, 28 Aug. 1912.
29 Hutchinson, *Incredible Canadian*, 163.
30 Dawson, *King* 22, 82.
31 Diary, 13 May 1896.
32 Diary, 5 Aug. 1897, 2 Jan. 1899.
33 Diary, 29 July 1899.
34 WLMK to family, 30 Sept. 1897.
35 Dawson, *King*, 179.
36 Diary, 8 Aug., 9 Aug. 1901.
37 Diary, 18 Oct. 1916.
38 Diary, 1 Dec., 2 Dec. 1916.
39 WLMK to Max King, 22 Jan. 1918.
40 WLMK to Max King, 4 Feb. 1918.
41 WLMK to Max King, 28 Jan. 1918.
42 Max King to WLMK, 4 Apr. 1918.
43 WLMK to Max King, 12 Feb. 1918; Max King to WLMK, , 20 Feb. 1918.
44 Max King to WLMK, 20 Feb. 1918, WLMK to Max King, 25 Feb. 1918.
45 WLMK to Max King, 25 Mar. 1918.
46 Max King to WLMK, 4 Apr. 1918.
47 Diary, 11 Mar. 1899.
48 Diary, 10 Apr. 1899.
49 WLMK to Violet Markham, 29 Nov. 1912.
50 McClelland, *Power*, 209.
51 Diary, 27 June 1918.
52 Diary, 25 Aug. 1933.

53 Diary, 23 Feb. 1896.
54 Diary, 11 Jan. 1931.
55 Diary, 23 Feb. 1932.
56 Diary, 4 Sept., 31 Dec. 1919.
57 Diary, 27 July 1933, 24 Aug. 1936, 31 Aug. 1933, 5 Sept. 1934.
58 Diary, 12 May 1934, 2 Aug. 1933, 5 May 1934, 7 Sept. 1934.
59 Diary, 28 Aug. 1936.
60 Diary, 2 Sept., 3 Sept., 28 July, 13 May, 3 June, 14 July 1934.
61 Diary, 21 July 1934.
62 Diary, 30 Oct. 1925.
63 Leon Salzman, *The obsessive personality* (New York 1968), 6.
64 Pickersgill and Forster, eds, *King record*, I, 356.
65 R. Whitaker, 'Mackenzie King in the dominion of the dead,' *Canadian Forum* LV, no. 658 (Feb. 1976).

CHAPTER FIVE

1 Diary, 18–22 Feb. 1919.
2 Diary, 5–9 Aug. 1919.
3 WLMK to Violet Markham, 10 Dec. 1919.
4 W.L.M. King, 'The practice of Liberalism,' *First Liberal Summer Conference*, Port Hope, September 1933.
5 U.S. Senate *Report*, 8809.
6 R.I. Kelley, *The transatlantic persuasion* (New York 1969), 97.
7 W.L.M. King, 'The Liberal party and the tariff,' a speech delivered during the debate on the budget in the House of Commons, 15 May 1924.
8 WLMK to Violet Markham, 11 Oct. 1911, 2 Dec. 1925, 28 Feb. 1926.
9 R.T. Ely, *The strengths and weaknesses of socialism* (Boston 1892), vi.
10 WLMK to Needlands, 15 Feb. 1913.
11 Canada, House of Commons, *Debates*, 27 Feb. 1933, 2498.
12 WLMK to Violet Markham, 14 Dec. 1930.
13 W.L.M. King, *Canada and the war: victory, reconstruction and peace* (Ottawa 1945), 8.
14 J.W. Dafoe to Sir Clifford Sifton, 21 July 1919 (Dafoe papers, PAC).
15 W.L. Morton, *The kingdom of Canada* (Toronto 1969), 439.
16 Dafoe to Sifton, 21 July 1919.
17 Dafoe to Sifton, 22 Jan. 1920.
18 Dawson, *King*, 317.
19 *Globe* (Toronto), 26 Oct. 1921.
20 Canada, House of Commons, *Debates*, 13 Mar. 1922, 48.
21 Ibid.
22 Dafoe to Sifton, 3 Apr. 1920.
23 WLMK to Violet Markham, 29 Dec. 1920.
24 Ibid.
25 Dafoe to Sifton, 10 Nov. 1920.

26 WLMK to Violet Markham, 29 Oct. 1920.
27 Dafoe to Sifton, 2 May 1921.
28 Canada, House of Commons, *Debates*, 13 Mar. 1922.
29 WLMK to Violet Markham, 29 Sept. 1922.
30 WLMK to Violet Markham, 12 Oct. 1922; *Canadian Forum*, Dec. 1921, 454.
31 WLMK to Violet Markham, 15 Oct. 1925.
32 WLMK to P.C. Larkin, 2 Dec. 1925.
33 WLMK to Violet Markham, 2 Dec. 1925.
34 WLMK to P.C. Larkin, 2 Dec. 1925.
35 WLMK to Violet Markham, 14 Dec. 1930.
36 Violet Markham to John Buchan, 30 Aug. 1939.

CHAPTER SIX

1 J.E. Esberey, 'Personality and politics: a new look at the King-Byng dispute,' *Canadian Journal of Political Science* VI (1973).
2 King had been introduced to Buchan by his friend Violet Markham who had herself been introduced to King twenty years before by a former governor general, Lord Grey. The meeting with Buchan was at Chatsworth where the host, the Duke of Devonshire, was a former governor general of Canada. Buchan had even written a biography of another former governor general, Lord Minto, and was a close friend of Lord Byng.
3 WLMK to Violet Markham, 24 Sept. 1924.
4 Violet Markham to J. Buchan, 20 Dec. 1925; Susie Buchan to Violet Markham, June 1926; Violet Markham to Devonshire, 31 Mar. 1926 (Buchan papers (BP), Queen's University Archives).
5 J.R. Mallory, 'The appointment of the governor general,' *Canadian Journal of Economics and Political Science* XXVI (1960): 57.
6 WLMK to Violet Markham, 23 Apr. 1935.
7 WLMK to Violet Markham 23 Apr. 1935; J.A. Smith, *John Buchan* (London 1965), 440; WLMK to Buchan, 19 July 1935; WLMK to Violet Markham, 13 July, 23 Aug. 1935; Smith, *Buchan*, 375.
8 Arnold Heeney, *The things that are Caesar's* ... (Toronto 1972), 57.
9 WLMK to Violet Markham, 31 Dec. 1937, 3 Jan. 1939.
10 WLMK to Violet Markham, 31 Dec. 1937.
11 Alexander Hardinge to Tweedsmuir, 8 Feb. 1939 (BP).
12 Tweedsmuir to Hardinge, 10 Jan. 1939 (BP).
13 Diary, 25 Nov. 1919.
14 Diary, 11 Sept., 24 Nov., 10 Dec., 16 Dec. 1919.
15 Neatby, *Lonely heights*, 331; Diary, 12 Dec. 1919.
16 Neatby, *Lonely heights*, 385.
17 Diary, 5 Aug. 1934.
18 Diary, 28 Feb., 20 Jan. 1934.
19 Diary, 29 May, 12 July 1934.
20 Diary, 1 Dec. 1934.

21 Vincent Massey, *What's past is prologue* (Toronto 1963), 222.
22 WLMK to Violet Markham, 29 Sept. 1922.
23 Thomas Jones, *White Hall diary*, vol. II (London 1969), 108.
24 J.B. Bickersteth to J. Buchan, 4 Jan. 1936 (BP).
25 Diary, 10 Dec. 1936.
26 Heeney, *Things that are Caesar's*, 38, 42, 51.
27 WLMK to Violet Markham, 1 May 1939.
28 Heeney, *Things that are Caesar's*, 57.
29 Quoted in Alex I. Inglis, 'Loring C. Christie and the imperial idea, 1919–1926,' *Journal of Canadian Studies* VII, 2 (May 1972): 20.
30 Ibid.
31 Lester B. Pearson, 'Reflections on inter-war Canadian foreign policy,' *Journal of Canadian Studies* VII, 2 (May 1972): 37.
32 John Munro, 'Loring Christie and Canadian external relations, 1935–1939,' *Journal of Canadian Studies* VII, 2 (May 1972): 28.
33 C.P. Stacey, 'Laurier, King and External Affairs,' in J.S. Moir, ed, *Character and circumstance: essays in honour of Donald Grant Creighton* (Toronto 1970), 86.
34 C.P. Stacey, 'From Meighen to King: the reversal of Canadian external policies, 1921–1923,' Royal Society of Canada, *Transactions and Proceedings*, 4th series, VII (1969): 237.
35 Canada, House of Commons, *Debates*, 13 Mar. 1922.
36 Diary, 18 Aug., 6 Oct., 10 Dec. 1919.
37 Diary, 24 Nov. 1935.
38 F.W. Gibson, *Cabinet formation and bicultural relations* (Ottawa 1970), 63–104.
39 Diary, 13 Oct., 14 Oct. 1932.

CHAPTER SEVEN

1 Liberal Federation of Canada, *The story of the convention and report of its proceedings* (Ottawa 1919), 199–200.
2 WLMK to Violet Markham, 11 Oct. 1911.
3 W.L.M. King, *The Liberal party and the tariff* (Ottawa 1924), 22.
4 W.L.M. King, 'The four parties to industry,' Address before the Empire Club of Canada, Toronto, 13 Mar. 1919, 20.
5 Ibid.
6 Diary, 13 May 1903.
7 W.L.M. King, 'The Canadian method of preventing strikes and lockouts,' Address delivered at the Fourth Annual Dinner of the Railway Business Association, New York, 19 Dec. 1912, 7.
8 Ferns and Ostry, *Age of King*, 63.
9 W.L.M. King, *Industry and humanity* (Toronto 1918), 290.
10 Ibid., xv.
11 Dawson, *King*, 89.
12 Ibid., 90.

13 McGregor, *Fall & rise*, 79.
14 WLMK to Violet Markham, 14 Aug. 1914.
15 *Convention story*, 65–9.
16 Ibid., 69–71.
17 Mansergh, *Commonwealth experience*, 219.
18 H. Duncan Hall, *Commonwealth: a history of the British Commonwealth of Nations* (London 1971), 342–4.
19 L.S. Amery, *My political life*, vol. 2 (London 1953), 377.
20 WLMK to Stanhope, 29 May 1910.
21 Gibson, *Cabinet formation*, 16.
22 Mansergh, *Commonwealth experience*, 220.
23 Diary, 11 Oct. 1934.
24 Diary, 10 Mar. 1936.
25 Mansergh, *Commonwealth experience*, 384.
26 Diary, 5 Mar. 1937.
27 WLMK to Buchan, 8 Sept. 1936 (BP).
28 Diary, 5 Jan. 1936.
29 Diary, 15 Jan. 1936.
30 Diary, 1 Oct. 1936.
31 Diary, 29 June 1937.
32 Ibid.
33 Ibid.
34 WLMK to Anthony Eden, 6 July 1937.
35 Diary, 17 Mar. 1938.
36 Mansergh, *Commonwealth experience*, 382.
37 WLMK to Buchan, 23 July 1938 (BP).
38 WLMK to Buchan, 6 Sept. 1938 (BP).
39 Diary, 18 Oct. 1937.
40 WLMK to Buchan, 20 Sept. 1938 (BP).
41 Violet Markham to Buchan, 20 Aug. 1939 (BP).
42 Martin Gilbert, *The roots of appeasement* (London 1966), 3.
43 J. Eayrs, *In defence of Canada: appeasement and rearmament* (Toronto 1965), xi.
44 WLMK to Buchan, 24 Aug. 1936 (BP).
45 Mansergh, *Commonwealth experience*, 284.

EPILOGUE

1 WLMK to Violet Markham, 11 Jan. 1940.
2 WLMK to Violet Markham, 20 July 1928.
3 WLMK to Violet Markham, 17 Mar. 1937.
4 WLMK to Violet Markham, 1 Feb. 1937.
5 Pickersgill and Forster, eds, *King Record*, IV, 11.
6 WLMK to Violet Markham, 11 Jan., 7 Oct. 1940.
7 Pickersgill and Forster, eds, *King record*, IV, 6, 15, 16, 136.
8 Ibid., 37, 39.
9 WLMK to Violet Markham, 29 Sept., 10 Oct., 14 Aug. 1949.

10 Erikson, *Life cycle*, 98; WLMK to Violet Markham, 6 Sept. 1949.
11 Pickersgill and Forster, eds, *King record*, IV, 59.
12 WLMK to Violet Markham, 21 Feb. 1948.
13 Violet Markham to WLMK, 29 Feb. 1948; WLMK to Violet Markham, 21 Feb. 1948.
14 J. Patteson to Violet Markham, 10 Apr. 1950; Pickersgill and Forster, eds; *King record*, IV, 61; WLMK to Violet Markham, 4 Mar. 1950.
15 Pickersgill and Forster, eds, *King record*, IV, 12, 8, 54; WLMK to Violet Markham, 5 Jan., 14 Aug. 1949.

Chronology

William Lyon Mackenzie King had a long and active life. The following list provides only a few of the key dates in that life, as well as some of the appointments referred to in this study, and is designed only to give the reader some points of reference. Detail is given only for the early, less familiar years of his career.

1874–1900

1874	Born 17 December at Berlin, Ontario
1891–5	Attended University College, University of Toronto (BA 1895, LL B 1896)
1895–6	Studied law and worked as journalist for Toronto *News* and Toronto *Globe*
1896–7	Attended University of Chicago
1897–1900	Attended Harvard University (MA 1898, PH D 1909)

1900–19

1900	Editor of *Labour Gazette* and deputy minister, Department of Labour, 1900–8
1901	Death of Bert Harper
1903	Bought property at Kingsmere (property added to in 1928)
1908	Elected member of parliament
1909	Joined cabinet as minister of labour
1911	Defeated in general election
1913	Editor, *Canadian Liberal Monthly*, 1913–14
	President, General Reform Association (Ontario), 1913–14
1914	Worked for Rockefeller Foundation, 1914–17
1915	Death of sister Bella, 4 April
1916	Death of father, 30 August

1917	Unsuccessfully contested the federal election
	Death of mother, 18 December
	Freelance industrial relations work in u.s., 1917–19
1918	*Industry and humanity* published

1919–50

1919	Elected leader of Liberal party of Canada, August
1919	Elected member of parliament, October
1921	Prime minister of Canada, December 1921 to June 1926
1922	Death of brother, 18 March
1926	King-Byng crisis, June
	Leader of opposition, June to September
	Prime minister, September 1926 to July 1930
1930	Leader of opposition, July 1930 to October 1935
1935	Prime minister, October 1935 to November 1948
1937	Visited Hitler
1948	Resigned as prime minister, November
1950	Died 22 July at Kingsmere, Quebec

Index

Aberdeen and Temair, Ishbel Maria, Marchioness of 164
Aberdeen and Temair, John Campbell Hamilton Gordon, 1st Marquess of 164
Allport, G. 102
Amery, L.S. 206
appeasement 191, 202, 209, 214
Arthurian legends 51, 161
Ashley, Professor W.J. 111
Atkinson, J.E. 66
Austria 212

Baker, Dr 97
Baldwin, Stanley 210
Balfour Declaration (1926) 207
Barrie (Ont.) 33
Beauharnois scandal 174
Bennett, R.B. 147; and appointment of governor general 166–7; 'new deal' legislation 195; and O.D. Skelton 183
Berlin (Germany) 210, 211
Berlin (Ontario) 26, 37, 102, 110, 210, 212
Bessborough, V.B. Ponsonby, 9th Earl of 167
Bickersteth, J. Burgon 178–9
Bishop Strachan School 25, 26
Boer War 63, 191, 200
Borden, Sir Robert 181, 202

Boston 37, 49
Bowman, Dave 31
British Empire/Commonwealth: compared to family 206–7; French Canadian view of 204; imperial defence 202; imperial federalism 203–4; self-government within 201, 202
Brown, George 141
Buchan, John, 1st Baron Tweedsmuir 159, 213, 214, 230; appointment as governor general 165–7; and appointment of Bickersteth 179; *Augustus* 169; death 172; as governor general 168–9; relationship with WLMK 164, 167–72
Buchan, Susan Charlotte, *née* Grosvener 165
Bunyan, John 213
Byng, J.H.G., Viscount Byng 158, 164, 170, 230

California 77
Cambridge (Eng.) 37
Cameron, Mina 27
Canadian Club (Ottawa) 182
Carnegie Corporation 123
Carnegie family 86, 87
Carnegie Foundation 82
Carruthers, Violet, *see* Markham

Cascadden, Miss 26
Chamberlain, Neville 201, 207, 211, 213, 214
Chanak incident 204–6
Chicago: WLMK living in 32, 34, 35, 37, 39, 45, 59; visit to 49
Christianity: evangelical writings 8; importance for WLMK 101–4, 105–7, 108; and peace 201; and sanctification of action 107
Christie, Loring C. 181–2, 183
Churchill, Sir Winston 218
Colorado: WLMK visits Max 82; WLMK visit postponed 121
Colorado Fuel and Iron Company strike 81, 105, 109
Colorado Plan, see Rockefeller Plan of Industrial Representation
Commission on Industrial Relations (U.S.) 76, 109n, 142
Canadian Forum 143
communism 146
conscription crisis 6, 218
Conservative party, Britain 109
Conservative party, federal 109; in 1919 148; after 1925 election 158; WLMK's view of 142, 143, 191–2, 202
Cooper, Nurse 26
Co-operative Commonwealth Federation (CCF) 151, 194
Crerar, T.A. 153, 154–5
Curzon, G.N., 1st Marquis Curzon 205, 206, 209
customs scandal (1926) 158

Dafoe, J.W. 147, 155; and coalition of Farmers and Liberals 156; and WLMK 153; on Liberal leadership 151; on Liberal party 149–50; on success in politics 153
Dawson, R. MacGregor 59, 60, 200
Denver, Colorado 82
Devonshire, V.C.W. Cavendish, 9th Duke of 164, 230

diary: interpretation of 7, 8; keeping of 126
disallowance: Alberta legislation 189
Dominion Office 206
Douglas, Billy 23, 29
Downie, Josie 46
Drury, E.C. 185

elections: cooperation between Liberals and Farmers 155; corruption 144; (1911) 64, 144, 157; (1917) 88, 157; (1921) 148, 156, 157; (1925) 144, 157–8; (1930) 159; (1949) 215
Elliot, Lady Ruby 53
England: WLMK visits 66, 67, 68, 71, 193, 209
Erikson, Erik H. 4, 5
Europe: WLMK on 1909 war enthusiasm 202; WLMK on 1936 situation 210–11; WLMK visits 139
External Affairs, Department of: and Loring Christie 181, 182; and O.D. Skelton 182–3

Family Compact 143
Farmers' movement 148, 150; and W.S. Fielding 153; 1921 election 157; WLMK attempts to woo 151–2, 154–6; see also Progressive party
federal-provincial relations 189, 194–5
Fielding, William Stevens 136, 153
Fisher, Sydney 137, 173–4
Forke, Robert 159
Fosdick, Raymond B. 77
Fowler, Miss 53

Gardiner, James 188
Gatineau Hills 168
George VI, King of England 162; visits Canada 171–2
George, Lloyd 214
Germany 211
Gilbert, Martin 214
Gladstone, William Ewart 138, 141
Globe (Toronto) 111

Goering, Hermann 211, 212
Gouin, Sir Lomer: attitude to WLMK
152; Quebec wing 153; relationship
with WLMK 185, 187–8
Government House 71
Graham, George P. 64, 130, 136
Grand Canyon 77
Grange Rd (Toronto) 82
Greenstein, F.I. 4
Grey, Albert Henry George Grey, 4th
Earl 71, 201, 230; patronage of
WLMK 164; relationship with
WLMK 72, 165
Grossert, Mathilde 53, 56; WLMK's
view of 47, 48; relationship with
WLMK 45–51
Guelph 31
Gunther, John 212

Halifax 63
Hall, H. Duncan 205
Hankey, Sir Maurice 178–9
Hanson, R.B. 132
Hardy, Arthur: WLMK on 174; and
Liberal party finances 173, 177
Harper, Henry Albert (Bert) 33, 53,
100, 168; on WLMK 44; relationship
with WLMK 59–63, 71, 73, 75, 178;
death of 62, 63; WLMK feels
presence of 127
Harvard University: WLMK student at
20, 40, 46n, 51, 111; WLMK accepts
scholarship to 37; WLMK talks of
returning to 41
Haydon, Andrew 174
Heine, Heinrich v, 72
Heeney, Canon W.B. 180
Heeney, Arnold 62, 183; appointed
secretary 179–80; on WLMK 170
Henry, H.R.L. 183
Herridge, Marjorie: relationship with
WLMK 53–7
Herridge, Dr W.T. 54, 56
Hitler, Adolf 162, 191, 192, 207;
WLMK's visit to 6, 210–13

House of Commons: cooperation of
Liberals and Progressives in 154,
156; Lapointe supports WLMK in
189; speeches by WLMK in 139–40,
146, 184, 192, 194; see also Parliament
Howe, C.D. 188
Hutchinson, Bruce 132
Hull House (Chicago) 26, 35, 36
Hunter, Miss 26

Idylls of the King v, 57
Ilsley, J.L. 188
immigration 42
Imperial Conference: (1923) 205–6;
(1926) 182; (1937) 208; Gouin a
delegate to 187
Industrial Disputes Investigation Act
195, 199
industrial relations 70, 76; WLMK
advises Rockefeller on 77; WLMK
on 102, 191, 200–1; see also Labour
relations
Industry and humanity 79, 84, 199, 200,
214
international relations 120, 200–1,
209

Jacksonian liberalism 141
Japan 214
Joan of Arc 212
Jones, Thomas 178
Judicial Committee of the Privy
Council 194

Kelley, R.I. 142
King family: dysfunctional elements
13, 19; distortion of structure 16;
after death of Isabel 95; interrela-
tionship of 41
King, Isabel (Bella) 113, 118; companion of WLMK 25; education 13; and
ideal of Christian service 14; illness
and death 80–2
King, Isabel Grace, née Mackenzie
80, 81, 95, 96, 113; attitude towards

_ WLMK 14, 19, 39–40; attitude to WLMK's possible marriage 35–6; attitude to WLMK's profession 33–4; character of 12–13, 18, 42; compared to Joan Patteson 100; early years 11–12; and financial security 110; illness and death of 66–7, 83–5, 89, 90; effect of death on WLMK 97, 127; communication after death 130–1; WLMK's view of 91; and relationship with WLMK 117; role in family 12, 16, 21, 197; view of world 103; will 115, 123

King, Janet (Jennie) (Mrs H.M. Lay) 81, 83–4, 95; attitude to WLMK 14–15; companion to Mulocks 13; looks after parents 82; looks after mother during 1917 election 88–90; and parents' estates 115–23

King, John 33, 34, 79, 119, 126, 139; character 13; death of 83–4, 113; effect of inadequacies 14; financial state of 41, 110; and financial arrangements with WLMK 37, 115–16; illness 66–7, 80; and Liberal party 13, 141n; as model 12, 21; and Sir William Mulock 60; and pamphlet on Mackenzie 24; and Woodside 11; view of world 103

King, Lyon 96

King, Max 63; career 13; illness 80–1; expenses of illness 110; death 95; WLMK advises 15, 194; WLMK visits in Colorado 82–3; loans from WLMK 113; and parents' estates 115–23

King, William Lyon Mackenzie: ambitions 64, 163; and annual accounting 125–6; and belief in personal contact 6, 120, 209–10; and conscience 22; and career opportunities 66; and concept of the enemy 108–10, 142–4; as compromiser 191; as conciliator 198–9, 213; desire for close

friendships 22–3; diary 7–8, 126; and effect of distance on intimacy 55, 61, 73, 78; and defence mechanisms 95, 109–10, 115, 121, 123–4, 132, 180–1; and dog 128; and health of 48, 50, 51, 56, 67, 117, 175, 217; and identity confusion 3, 6, 21, 64–6, 68, 70, 77, 135, 138; and *Industry and humanity* 79, 121; and influence of W.L. Mackenzie on 15, 24–5, 125, 164; and memoirs 216, 221; and need for love 39, 161–3; and nickname 21n; and obsession with record 126, 131; philosophy of 141–2; and peace 196–7, 201; and perception of time 193, 199; and piety 8; and purity 46–7, 51; and reaction to criticism 104, 121–2; and reaction to conflict 194, 198–9; as a reformer 59, 185; and relations with staff 5–6, 62, 162–3, 177–8; and ritual 123–5, 128; and sacrifice 105–6; secretiveness of 115, 119; and *The secret of heroism* 63; and self-control 124, 129; and sexuality 3, 30–2, 46–7, 65, 96–9 passim, 101; and spiritualism 95, 126–32, 159; and trust 116, 117, 121, 156; and visions 129–30; and will 221; and work habits 125; and work identity 3, 58–9, 63, 65, 73, 109, 135; and war 200–1, 215–17
– attitudes to: appeasement 191, 201–2; big business 75–6, 142; Conservative party 142–5; British connection 102, 109, 171, 178, 202–7; employment 111; French Canadians 117; monarchy 171; partnership 197; prominent people 162; significant dates 125; socialism and social welfare 145–7; status symbols 103
– education: under-graduate life 20–2; 1895 student strike 24; study of law 33–4; post-graduate work 33–

4, 37; study habits 124; thesis 55
- family: ideal of 19–20, 95; treatment in 15–16; attitude towards father 16–18, 119; financial agreements with father 111–12, 114–16; attitude towards mother 17–18, 36–7, 85–91; and family ill health 66–7, 82–3; attitude to Jennie 83–4; attitude to Max 15; and autonomy from 34–5, 80–1; and career 13; relationship with 33–4, 36, 38–9, 43, 79–91, 95–6, 113; relationship with nephews 96; dispute with Max and Jennie over estates 115–23
- Liberal party: leadership 90, 147, 172, 192; attitude to party 102, 109–10, 192–3; attitude to Quebec wing 155; and rebuilding of party 148–58; concept of Liberalism 150–1
- personal finances: attitude to capital 194; and debt 111; and savings 110–14, 195; and personal fortune 65, 112, 114, 123, 219–20
- political life: as politician 3, 63; attitude to politics 70, 103–5, 108, 216–17; and cabinet selection 184–90; and campaigning 175–6; and Chanak incident 205–6; and constitutional crises 158–9, 166–7, 171–2; and 1917 election 88–90; and 1921 election 156–7; and 1925 election 157–8; and 1930 election 159, 217; and 1935 election 217; in opposition 129; on Meighen government 150; organization of prime minister's office 177–9, 181; and policy making and implementation 113, 194–5; and policy of non-involvement 207–9; and relationship between politics and money 119; and retirement 69–70, 217–21; and role of governor general 163–72; and personal role in party politics 180; and tariff issue 195–6; and third-party movement 149, 151–6
- religion 8, 30, 128; and ideal of Christian service 26–7, 61, 102–3, 106, 108; and importance of 101–10; Presbyterianism 142, 169; religious behaviour 125–6; religious beliefs 72, 82, 129; relationship to politics 142
- women: adolescent relations with women 25–6; ideal of womanhood 45–6, 48, 52; attitude to marriage 51–3, 74, 91, 95, 97–9; and prostitutes 26–32; romantic approach to women 43–4; relationships with eligible and ineligible women 52–3; and use of term love 30

King St (Toronto) 27, 28
Kingsmere 42, 55, 56, 83, 100, 126, 168, 170, 180, 197
Kingston, Courtney 23
'Knights of the Holy Spirit' v, 72
Korean crisis 218

Labour, Department of 43, 100
Labour Gazette 58, 59, 60
Labour party 148, 150
labour relations: WLMK's interest in 60, 63, 72, 120; WLMK's approach to 109; WLMK's view of 198; *see also* Colorado Fuel and Iron Company strike; Rossland, B.C., strike; Valleyfield, Que., strike
Lapointe, Ernest 187; Quebec lieutenant 188; relationship with WLMK 189–90
Larkin, Peter 206, 221
Laurier, Sir Wilfrid 24n, 69, 130, 209; death of 135; guides WLMK 112, 141n; and WLMK's ambitions 64, 136, 147; WLMK's defence of 202; and Liberal party 150; and Charles Murphy 185, 186; model for WLMK 138, 139; relationship with WLMK

143, 164, 205; and tariff issue 194,
195; tells WLMK to contest 1917
election 88, 89
Laurier House 179
Lay, Arthur 96
Lay, Jean 90
Lay, Jennie, *see* King
Lay, John 90
Lay, Harry M. 89, 118
League of Nations 187, 218
Lemieux, Rodolphe 187, 204
Liberal party, Britain 72, 141
Liberal party, federal 7, 148, 201, 205;
defeat (1911) 64; condition (1919)
148–9; contenders for leadership
after Laurier 136–7; leadership
convention (1919) 137–8, 153, 185,
192, 195, 203; under WLMK 140–1;
and Niagara memorial 219;
organization 149–58, 173–4, 218;
policy
– towards empire and
commonwealth 202–4
– influence of on government
192–3
– WLMK's view of 114
– platform (1919) 194
– provincial rights 146–7
– on tariffs 195, 196
philosophy of 142; returned to
office 129; view of Conservative
party 145
Liberal party, Ontario 141n; WLMK
offered leadership 66; and Presbyterian base 142
Liberal philosophy: Gladstonian 141,
143; and social democracy 145–6
Liberal Unionists: election of 1921
157; *see also* Liberal party
Lindsey, Charles 18, 24
London 59, 191
'Ludlow massacre' 76
Lynch, Mrs 58
Lynch, Florence 57–8

McClelland, David 126
Macdonald, Mr (member of WLMK's
staff) 183
Macdonald, Angus 188
Macdonald, Edith 29
Macdonald, Florence 29
MacDonald, Ramsay 209
McGregor, F.A.: WLMK's secretary
173, 174; on WLMK 78, 201; rela-
tionship with WLMK 178
Mackenzie, Alexander 141
Mackenzie, William Lyon 11; atti-
tude of Isabel King towards 15;
and liberalism 141; influence on
WLMK 15, 199; as masculine model
24–5, 136, 138
Mackintosh, Eliza 18
Macphail, Agnes 185
Mallory, J.R. 166, 167
Mansergh, Nicholas 209, 213
Marcus, Steven 30n, 31, 48n
Markham, Violet 66, 68, 230; advises
WLMK 69, 70; and appointment of
Buchan 164–6, 168; letter to
Buchan 170; criticizes WLMK 104;
on election of 1919 138; engage-
ment of 75; gives financial assist-
ance to WLMK 112–13, 220; on
WLMK in 1930 160; on WLMK's visit
to Hitler 214; and letters from
WLMK 76, 79, 82, 90, 106, 108, 125,
127, 144, 152, 154, 155, 156, 159,
174, 178, 179, 193, 208, 209, 221;
relationship with WLMK 71–5, 100–
1; visits North America 71n, 219
Mason, Mrs 25
Massey, Alice 130, 174, 175
Massey, Vincent 130; and National
Liberal Federation 174; Canadian
high commissioner 177; relationship with WLMK 174–7
Meighen, Arthur 148, 158, 181; and
appointment of governor general
166; government of 150; on WLMK

140, 156, 192; and leadership of
Conservative party 145
Mercer's Reformatory 27
Mimico Asylum 28
Minto, G.J. Elliot, 4th Earl of 162, 230
Mitchell, Walter 187
Montreal 49
Moses 107
Morley, John, 1st Viscount Morley
141
Morton, W.L. 148
Moulton College 26
Mount Pleasant Cemetery 117
Mulock family 13
Mulock, Sir William 41, 180; advises
WLMK 112; relationship with
WLMK 59–60, 75–6, 205
Munich 207, 213
Munro, John 182
Murphy, Charles 152; as cabinet
material 185; relationship with
WLMK 186–7, 188
Muskoka 44
Mussolini, Benito 162; WLMK has in-
terview with 209

National Liberal Advisory
Committee 193
National Liberal Federation:
establishment 174; organizational
work 175
national unity 193, 202, 209
Nazi party 212
Neatby, H. Blair 102, 141
Newmarket, Ont. 87
New York 86, 87, 91, 219
Niagara: excursions to 29
Niagara Falls Bridge Commission
218
North York (riding) 88, 91, 136, 137

oedipal issue 16–17, 40, 84, 91
Ontario Reform Association 66
Oxford University 37

Ottawa: WLMK's residence in 40–3
passim, 53, 57, 62, 80, 81, 84, 110,
186; WLMK moves mother to 85, 87,
89, 90

parliament: and constitutional
change 203; and imperial or for-
eign involvement 208; strain of on
WLMK 196; see also House of Com-
mons
Passmore Edwards (London) 26
Patteson, Godfroy 100
Patteson, Joan 189, 212; relationship
with WLMK 99–101; ignorance of
WLMK's financial affairs 220–1
Paul, St 107
Pearson, Lester B. 182
personality: and political behaviour 6
Pickering, E.A. 181, 183
Port Burwell, Ont. 43
Port Hope Conference 130, 175
Power, C.G. 188
prairie radicalism 150; see also Far-
mers' movement, Progressive
party
Presbyterian Ladies College 26
Progressive party 185, 193; see also
Farmers' movement

Quebec: and external relations 204
Quebec City: royal visit 171
Quebec East (riding) 136
Queen's Park 83

Ralston, J.L. 188
rebellion of 1837 11–12
reciprocity, see tariff
Reik, Theodore 58, 69
Ribbentrop, Joachim von 212
Rideau Club (Ottawa) 90
Riordan, Kitty 44
Rockefeller, John D., Jr 98; and
financial dealings with WLMK 95;
offers WLMK job 86, 159; on WLMK

77, 78; WLMK criticizes 105; WLMK visits 219; relationship with WLMK 75–9, 100, 101
Rockefeller Foundation 52, 75, 80, 81; offers WLMK position 70; WLMK ends association 104–5; WLMK's work for 88, 109
Rockefeller Plan of Industrial Representation (Colorado Plan) 79
Rogers, Norman McLeod 179, 188
Rokeach, Milton 109
Roosevelt, Franklin D. 162, 210, 219
Roosevelt, Theodore 42
Rosedale (Toronto) 26
Rossland, B.C.: strike at 62, 109
Round Table 202
Russell County 150

St Andrew's Presbyterian Church (Ottawa) 169
St Laurent, Louis 221
Seagram, Joseph 144
The secret of heroism 63
Sick Children's Hospital 26, 27
Sifton, Sir Clifford 149, 152, 156
Skelton, O.D. 62; and Department of External Affairs 182; relationship with WLMK 182–4; on visit to Hitler 210
social democracy 145–6
socialism 145–7
social welfare 195; see also Social democracy
social work: interest of WLMK in 59n, 72; see also Hull House
South Africa 63
South Oxford (riding) 176
Spender, John Alfred (?) 167
spiritualism 212; and WLMK
– attempts to contact loved ones 99
– dependence on 95
– meaning for 126–32
– participation with Joan Patteson 101

Stacey, C.P. 27–8, 30, 56, 182
Standard Oil 76
Stanhope, J.R. Stanhope, 7th Earl 202, 206
Star (Toronto): WLMK offered position on 66
Statute of Westminster 207
Stevenson, J.A. 182

tariff issue 153, 191; Gouin vs WLMK on 187; and WLMK
– approach to 195–6
– importance 6
– 1924 speech on reform 143
Teilhard de Chardin, Pierre 107
Tennyson, Alfred Lord v
Thistle, Dr 81
Thomas à Kempis 57
Thornton, A.P. 206
Toronto: King family moves to 32; King family residence 43, 49, 80, 82, 83, 89; WLMK spends summer in 55
Toynbee, Arnold 59, 109
Tweedsmuir, Baron, see Buchan

unionism 198; see also Labour relations
Unionists 148
United Kingdom: Canada's relations with 191; and imperial policy 204–6; local parliaments 203; 1937 trade agreement with Canada 196; and World War II 217
United Nations 218
United States 11, 38; Canada's economic relations with 195, 196
University College 20, 60; see also University of Toronto
University of Chicago 20, 33, 34, 111
University of Pennsylvania 37
University of Toronto 24, 34, 37; see also University College

Valleyfield, Que.: strike at 198
Vancouver 147
Victorian attitude to sex 31, 48n
Walkerton, Ont. 115
Washington 42
White, Miss 29
Willingdon, F. Freeman-Thomas, 1st
  Earl of 166

'Woodside' 11, 12, 126
Woodsworth, J.S. 185
World War I 201, 217
World War II 6, 214–15, 216
Worthy, Miss 29

Young Men's Christian Association
  (YMCA) 25, 27